LARRY GOLDSTEIN

COLLEGE AND UNIVERSITY BUDGETING
A GUIDE FOR ACADEMICS AND OTHER STAKEHOLDERS

FIFTH EDITION

Library of Congress Cataloging-in-Publication Data

Goldstein, Larry, 1- author. | Goldstein, Larry, College & University Budgeting.

College and University Budgeting : A Guide For Academics and Other Stakeholders / by Larry Goldstein.

Fifth Edition. | Washington, DC : National Association of College and University Business Officers, [2019] | Previous edition: 2012.| Includes bibliographical references and index.

LCCN 2019008907 (print) | LCCN 2019010934 (ebook) | ISBN 9781569720257 ()

Universities and colleges--United States--Finance. | Universities and colleges--United States--Business management.

LCC LB2342 (ebook) | LCC LB2342 .M43 2019 (print) | DDC 378.1/06--dc23

LC record available at https://lccn.loc.gov/2019008907

TABLE OF CONTENTS

NACUBO

FOREWORD

It was all laid out for me 25 or so years ago, during a long conversation with the vice president for finance of a midsized independent university ... and I was overwhelmed.

As he explained, he was responsible for managing a pretty big business. That business had multiple units, pricing paradigms, locations, and delivery mechanisms; it was reliant on volatile investment returns and sometimes fickle gift-giving; and it required considerable ongoing investment in both people and plant.

This business operated in a constantly changing environment. Changes to brand value, demographics, competition, and technology created opportunities and risks. In any given month, the economy or capital markets could conspire to significantly impact resources, even while a growing list of environmental, health-related, or social events/trends threatened business as usual.

Additionally, this business was responsive to a long list of stakeholder groups. These included the board of trustees and its several committees, the president, the provost and other senior officers, faculty, staff, students, alumni, rating agencies, accreditation boards, and the local community, to name a few. These stakeholders sometimes shared, but often did not share, a common vision of the importance of any given aspect of the business, how it should be managed, or how it should move forward (if at all).

This shape-shifting business needed to be constantly analyzed and understood in consideration of realized and projected outcomes. The vice president had to keep track of where the business was and where it was going, even as the ground moved beneath his feet.

Then, he explained, that was just the half of it.

Besides running this big business in an ever-changing landscape, he also had to field; evaluate; and sometimes implement, let's call them, ideas—and there was no shortage of them. Sometimes, the ideas were presented as one-offs or expedients, designed to fix a particular problem or capture a particular benefit. However, in the best of circumstances, these ideas were offered as a rationalized (strategic, capital, or operational) plan, with a long list of bulleted initiatives and projects designed to better position the enterprise to mitigate looming risks or take advantage of, or even create, opportunities. In any case, the initiatives and projects, whether operational in nature or requiring capital investment, each had alternative versions, with different timing, cost, and funding options.

The vice president was responsible for wrangling and evaluating these ideas and plans. He had to analyze their incremental and integrated impacts. In short, he had to develop a business plan for each bullet point on the list, fold those business plans into and atop the organic business model, and understand each in context of the full portfolio of possibilities. He had to communicate his analysis (sometimes differently) to the various stakeholders and use it to drive decision-making.

Since that conversation more than two decades ago, I have come to understand that this multipronged, complex effort is, in whole or part, the responsibility of essentially every college and university business officer. I have served as a financial advisor for the better part of 25 years. My company provides financial and investment advice to colleges and universities, big and small, throughout the country and even abroad. As financial advisors, we touch on many of the issues described above, especially as subsumed into the debt issuance and credit-rating processes. As investment managers, we sit at the nexus of our clients' investment portfolios and the capital markets. Over the past 15 years, I have particularly focused on helping higher education institutions manage their institutional complexity by utilizing financial forecasting software as the basis of decision-making and stakeholder communication.

Based on this experience, I have come to believe that business officers need an inclusive, consistent, transparent, and comprehensive process to understand and manage this complexity—resulting in a well-designed plan supported by a budget, supplemented by a forecasting regime, to allocate scarce resources to competing priorities in support of the institution's mission.

However, I have further come to realize that as important as budgeting and forecasting are as management constructs, that mechanistic view is only half of the story. Perhaps more (or at least equally) importantly, the budget and forecast are reflections of the institution's values, culture, goals, and strategy.

Since an institution's goals and strategy are intimately dependent on what is practically possible and financially achievable, the budget and forecast become decision-making tools for pursuing priorities and developing strategy. At the same time, the budget and forecast help draw a road map to achieve the institution's plans, assess their viability, and establish accountability. They are the curbs that keep the institution pointed in the direction that it plans to go.

Additionally, budgets and forecasts are often wireframes used to organize, make sense of, and communicate what is sometimes a very long list of strategic and tactical possibilities. They inform what plans are possible and help ensure that those plans are efficiently implemented—a virtuous feedback loop.

With all this said, I was very happy to have this opportunity to partner with NACUBO and Larry Goldstein on the latest edition of this book—*College and University Budgeting: A Guide for Academics and Other Stakeholders*. This book offers an introduction to the key aspects of higher education budgets, forecasts, and their processes—the mechanistic view. However, it also makes sense of these more abstract notions and, in this regard, is a great introduction.

For those new to this sector, it provides a primer on planning, budgeting, and forecasting basics—the types of plans and budgets; the key components thereof; best practices in establishing (or improving) processes; and understanding and preparing for the realities of exogenous impacts, among other important topics. For those with more experience, it offers some nuanced insights into ways to understand and utilize the planning, budgeting, and forecasting processes.

For everyone, this book offers a chance to understand planning, budgeting, and forecasting as practical management tools, but it also explains plans, budgets, and forecasts as manifestations of the institution's entire raison d'être. Any reader will be well served.

Brett Matteo
President
Whitebirch
(whitebirchsoftware.com)

Managing Director
The PFM Group
(pfm.com)

March 11, 2019

PREFACE

The budget is an essential management tool for colleges and universities. Planning sets the route for the trip, but it's the budget that puts the gas in the tank. There are too many clichés related to budgeting, so let's say it plainly. The budget deals with the most critical issue related to institutional success—resources. Money isn't everything—and should rarely be the prime factor in decision-making—but the most elegant plans will achieve nothing if the institution cannot resource them. This book is about resources, primarily how to manage them for the best outcomes.

Nothing in the book will create additional resources for an institution. But adhering to the principles presented herein can help institutions get the maximum value from the resources they have available. A deeper understanding of higher education budgeting will help institutions—the people working in them and the people governing them—make wiser decisions about the deployment of resources to support priorities established through an effective planning process.

Resources will always be scarce or at least insufficient to achieve everything institutions seek to accomplish. Even when the political climate or demographic shifts are not adversely affecting institutions' abilities to carry out their missions, there never will be a time when it can be said that there are enough resources. Not only are there additional things that institutions would like to tackle, there is a never-ending quest for improved quality.

Things had changed pretty radically for higher education between 1994, when the second edition of this book was published, and 2005, when the third edition was released. Since then, the environment in which higher education operates has shifted even more dramatically. Apart from issues related to pedagogy, we see new technology, increased expectations from students and their parents, and possibly of greatest concern—higher education's reputation has taken a serious hit. Yes, it has happened before. Anyone who lived through the Vietnam era, when unrest on campuses peaked, recognizes that. What feels different this time is how long the adverse environment has continued.

There are attacks on the academy because of views that are unpopular with one political movement or another, too-frequent athletics scandals, tuition increases that exceed the rate of inflation, etc. Some people now are even questioning the value of an education. And they don't let facts or data get in their way. Despite all the evidence of the increased economic returns over a lifetime that correlate nicely with increased levels of education, some believe that the money needed to obtain a degree could be put to better uses. Yes, too many students leave college with excessive debt, but—with relatively few exceptions—the debt is repaid from their enhanced earning power. Given the criticisms and the competition from other sectors for scarce resources, it is crucial that every dollar expended provide maximum value.

The intended audience for this primer remains the same as for the previous edition, which expanded beyond new academic administrators and faculty interested in better understanding the resource allocation process. A conscious decision was made to try to better serve the needs of these two groups and also to expand coverage that would appeal to board members, senior administrators, and others interested in the resource allocation process. This edition should prove especially valuable to individuals who recently have accepted positions in higher education institutions after working in other industries—especially those from the for-profit sector. Its particular value to the latter group is its focus on the collegial decision-making processes prevalent in higher education.

Readers of this book should gain a better understanding of the budget process at their institutions. They will learn that the most effective budget processes are driven by plans—in particular, plans developed using open and inclusive processes. And they will realize that resource allocation decisions in higher education rarely mean a choice between good and bad options but rather between good and better options.

A BRIEF OVERVIEW

This book will enable readers to ask meaningful questions about the budget process on their campuses. Although it does not aim to address every possible budgeting variation one might encounter, it identifies the most important elements of the budgeting process and provides information about the ways in which internal and external factors influence the budget.

More specifically, Chapter 1 explains why budgeting is an important element of policy making. This introductory chapter describes the type of budgets used in higher education and demonstrates how they go beyond mere numbers to communicate what an institution is all about.

The broader political and regulatory contexts affecting higher education are the focus of Chapter 2, and they include the extensive range of federal rules and regulations that affect campuses and, in the process, impact resources. New coverage in this edition addresses the challenges created in the aftermath of the 2016 national election. In addition, the chapter briefly explores the impact of inflation on higher education's costs and the problems this creates for those seeking to suppress tuition prices.

The shift from politics to the national economic climate occurs in Chapter 3. It discusses the changes affecting for-profit institutions within higher education and other major trends such as sustainability, competition, technology, and changing student demographics.

Chapters 4 through 6 address different sides of the same coin. They focus on the acquisition and utilization of resources and provide insights about the relative importance of specific categories. Chapter 4 tackles revenues and resources typically available to higher education institutions, while Chapter 6 examines expenses and costs. Both chapters are organized by sector based on the institutions' structure and governance. Specific sections are devoted to public, independent, and for-profit institutions. This is partially driven by the differing rules applicable to financial reporting by public versus independent institutions, but also because of the relative reliance on various revenue sources.

New for this edition is Chapter 5 addressing the many facets of enrollment management. Its focus is the critical issues of attracting, retaining, and serving higher education's most vital stakeholders—the students.

The chapter bridges the revenue and expense chapters because of the significance that tuition represents as a revenue source to the vast majority of institutions and the reality that attracting students depends heavily on institutional financial aid. Accounting rules dictate that all but a small portion of student financial aid is reported as an offset to tuition revenue rather than as expense, but institutional aid represents a consumption of resources not unlike more typical expenses. The majority of institutions address the setting of tuition rates in concert with decisions about institutional financial aid, and both of these exert significant impact on the budget.

Chapter 7 addresses the many forms of planning that are needed on college campuses and stresses the importance of integrating them with each other. The discussion identifies and describes strategic, infrastructural, and operational planning—highlighting that the latter needs to be adopted more broadly. It also highlights the value from aligning planning with budgeting and assessment. Critical to all of these processes are transparency and broad-based participation.

The material in the next chapter, Chapter 8, represents updated thinking and a new structure from the previous edition. It addresses the budget process and combines content that previously was included with the planning chapter with considerations related to structuring the budget process for maximum effectiveness. Topics addressed include the factors that commonly influence the budget process such as institutional character, decision-making authority, transparency (including clarity), and communication. Beyond that are topics related to participation and the roles that different stakeholders perform, including the board, faculty, and students (for those institutions that involve students in the budget process). The chapter closes with information about monitoring the budget throughout the fiscal year.

Chapter 9 describes the key elements of the most common comprehensive budget models—formula, incremental, responsibility center, and zero-based budgeting—as well as two special-purpose budget models: initiative-based budgeting and performance-based budgeting. In addition to providing details about the various models, the chapter highlights the reality that few institutions adopt a "pure" budget model. Instead, most approach the available models as they would a buffet and create a hybrid model by selecting characteristics from several of the models.

In-depth coverage of the elements of the operating and capital budget cycles is provided in Chapter 10, along with the key considerations related to the budget calendar. Coverage of the capital budget cycle, for example, includes a discussion of deferred maintenance and its implications for both operating and capital budgets.

The attention then shifts to budget management. Chapter 11 addresses how to achieve maximum budget flexibility to accommodate fluctuations in enrollment, revenues, and expenses. It also addresses the reality that there may be emergencies that impose impacts on the ability of an institution to stay within its budget. There also may be opportunities that should be pursued, and the budget must accommodate all of these possibilities. Also related to flexibility is the impact that institutional policies exert on the budget. Chapter 12 dives into this area and explores how institutional policy decisions can impact the budget.

Chapter 13 tackles what probably is the most sensitive area of budgeting. What to do when extraordinary circumstances present themselves. It discusses the difficult decisions that arise when an institution faces severe economic challenges—whether driven by broad-based economic catastrophes, natural disasters, or simply poor management—and offers both short- and long-term responses to difficult financial times. This chapter also suggests planning approaches that can help the institution avoid retrenchment—or address it if it becomes necessary.

The final chapter, Chapter 14, highlights key points and offers advice for readers who seek to apply the principles presented in this book on their campuses.

Two appendices are included in this edition. The first, Appendix A, addresses several accounting issues relevant to budgeting, including noncash expenses (and the related issue of funding depreciation), financial aid (and the importance of avoiding double counting the revenues and expenses), and the impact of differing accounting standards. It also previews new standards that will take affect soon for independent institutions as well as standards that would affect public institutions and are in the preliminary stages of consideration by the relevant standards setter.

This book is intended to serve readers interested in both U.S. and Canadian higher education. However, portions of some chapters may be less relevant to Canadian readers. Appendix B is included to highlight areas of particular importance to Canadian readers as well as identify those that may not be as relevant.

A UNIQUE APPROACH

Every campus has an institutional character, culture, and operating style that dictates how its budget is developed. The same factors also influence which individuals—by title, role, responsibility, or personality—have the greatest influence over the final product. In some organizations—small independent institutions, for example—faculty voices may be heard loud and clear throughout the budget process. In other institutions—especially large community colleges and some research institutions—the faculty may not be as actively involved in the budget process. Traditions are important when dealing with something as sensitive as a budget process and everything it represents, but they should not be used as an excuse to justify "doing what we've always done."

Effective budgeting, appropriately linked to planning and assessment, provides a wonderful and recurring opportunity to review options and reprioritize an institution's agenda. Understanding the process for developing a budget, as well as the role an individual can play in that process, can significantly affect the future success of a campus.

That said, there is nothing magical about budget work. It's hard work because the stakes are high and the choices are difficult. Nevertheless, those who are willing to invest the time to participate in the related processes of planning and budgeting can reap significant rewards. The more knowledgeable and informed they are, the greater those rewards will be.

ACKNOWLEDGMENTS

Special thanks go to Richard J. Meisinger Jr., coauthor of the first edition and sole author of the second edition of this book. I hope he would be pleased to know that so many of his original words and concepts have survived into a fifth edition.

Much gratitude is due to Tadu Yimam, National Association of College and University Business Officers (NACUBO) senior director of online learning and publications. She has been a wonderful colleague over the last many years and provided invaluable support and encouragement throughout the writing process. Another person who contributed significantly to this project is Rosalie A. Lacorazza, who served as editor and improved the final product significantly with her incredible skills.

The crew at Carel Creative, led by their founder Brisa Baron, were wonderful to work with and demonstrated great flexibility in responding to many requests for format and layout changes.

With the ever-increasing complexity of higher education and the desire to cover as many topics as possible, I was the beneficiary of significant assistance from experts in a variety of areas. Numerous individuals weighed in to help me, including NACUBO staff Liz Clark (political and regulatory environment), Sally Grans-Korsh (sustainability), and Ken Redd (endowments). Amir Mohammadi (Slippery Rock University) was very generous with his time in helping me understand the many ways that sustainability considerations are affecting colleges and universities. Both Mary Nucciarone (University of Notre Dame) and Steve Kimata (University of Virginia) were incredibly helpful with financial aid coverage. Finally, Jessica Shedd (Tulane University) significantly expanded my knowledge of assessment and accreditation.

With the decision to tackle Canadian higher education in this edition, it became crucial to have access to excellent resources. Serving in this capacity were Brett Fairbairn and Matt Milovick (Thompson Rivers University) as well as Nathalie Laporte (Canadian Association of University Business Officers [CAUBO]). The three of them provided a wealth of information about Canadian higher education, and this gave me the confidence to develop the material in Appendix B directed toward readers who would be most interested in this aspect of the book.

Also appreciated is Brett Matteo, president of Whitebirch, for enhancing the book by writing its Foreword. Brett has been a longtime leader in terms of providing the tools and services related to financial forecasting in higher education. I greatly appreciate his interest in the project and his support for it.

The next group deserving special recognition includes the members of the advisory committee assembled by Tadu and Sue Menditto, NACUBO's director of accounting policy. They provided invaluable guidance and suggestions to enhance the final product. In addition to Tadu and Sue, they include Craig Becker (Lafayette College), aforementioned Brett Fairbairn, Nicole Ferretti (University of Virginia), Linda Kroll (University of Notre Dame), Brett Powell (Henderson State University), aforementioned Jessica Shedd, and Jessica Davenport Williams (formerly of Columbia College Chicago).

I wish to express appreciation to several individuals who have contributed significantly to my professional development. Pat Sanaghan of The Sanaghan Group has been a longtime colleague and thought partner. He taught me a great deal about planning, including the need to engage the masses in an open, participative process. Along the same lines, special thanks go to Bob Dickeson, president emeritus of Northern Colorado University—the creator of the prioritization process described in these pages. Working with Bob has been a wonderful experience, and it has afforded me the opportunity to benefit from his years of experience in higher education. Finally, Ron Salluzzo and Phil Tahey, former KPMG partners and coauthors of the publications presenting the Composite Financial Index, have been friends and colleagues for more than 20 years. They are wonderful thought partners who have contributed significantly to my understanding of higher education finance. Last, but certainly not least, is NACUBO's Maryann Terrana. Maryann and I began working together more than 20 years ago, and she has remained a good friend an invaluable resource for all matters related to higher education.

One other group must be acknowledged and thanked, although it is not possible to list these individuals by name. I want to express appreciation to my current and former colleagues in higher education financial management—those on campuses as well as those working in the association community and the commercial sector providing services to higher education. I'm richer for having known you, and this is a better product because of the lessons I've learned from you.

Last, and most important on a personal level, I want to thank my wife, Sue, for encouraging me throughout the effort to finalize this fifth edition. As in the past, she had to take care of many of my home responsibilities while I focused on client engagements and writing. Hopefully, we can spend more time together again and with our children and grandchildren.

Larry Goldstein

Crimora, Virginia
March 2019

CHAPTER 1: AN INTRODUCTION TO BUDGETING

Resource allocation is one of the more challenging issues faced by organizations—especially higher education institutions. There is no shortage of good ideas, but every institution—even the wealthiest—faces the challenge of spreading limited resources across the institution's operations to achieve maximum outcomes.

Organizations require many different types of resources, and five are particularly important to programmatic success in colleges and universities: people, money, space, technology, and equipment. Almost without exception, everything accomplished on a campus requires the consumption of each of these to one degree or another. Technology can sometimes supplant space—e.g., for telecommuting employees or distance education—but for the most part, each activity requires faculty or staff, dedicated or at least available space, and access to various forms of technology. Equipment may be less important to some activities, but when it's budgeted centrally, as is the case at many smaller institutions, it becomes just as important as the others. This is especially true for those units and activities that rely heavily on different items of equipment.

There are other forms of resources. Information and leadership attention are two examples. The difference between these resources and the five mentioned earlier is that they are not as easy to manage or allocate. Except in particularly secretive institutions, everyone can find out how people, money, space, technology, and equipment are deployed throughout the organization. This cannot always be said of information. As such, it is not a resource that can be directed in the same way as staffing or access to technology.

Historically, especially in what now is referred to as the nonprofit sector, most activities were managed on a cash basis. Activities and service levels varied based on the presence or absence of adequate resources. By the late 1800s, public administration had evolved to the point revenues were being anticipated. This information was then used to develop expenditure plans.

Budgets provided a mechanism for dealing with both known and anticipated financial challenges in an organized manner. Even before adopting full accrual accounting—which measures revenues when earned (rather than when cash is collected) and expenses when incurred (rather than when paid)—budgets proved valuable in reducing the uncertainty that comes with pure cash accounting. Given that needs always exceeded resources, the relatively recent advent of planning and budgeting helped organizations set priorities and direct resources toward those priorities.

WHY BOTHER WITH BUDGETING?

Even more than the vast majority of nonprofit organizations, colleges and universities have a complex operating environment. The variety of revenue sources, the compliance requirements to which they are subject, and the nature of the restrictions attached to many of their resources make both planning and budget development challenging propositions. Still, without an effective budget process, managing a college or university from a financial perspective would be nothing less than chaos.

Effective budgeting starts with effective planning. When an institution becomes intentional about trying to drive outcomes, it starts by developing realistic plans. Plans establish priorities and provide signals to an organization about where it is going and how it anticipates getting there. Truly effective organizations use planning as a way to direct resource distributions. As such, the budgets that support established plans should show significant changes from year to year. If an institution is serious about achieving outcomes, it will periodically add new activities, drop some that no longer contribute to success, and transform others to achieve improved results. Each action of this type should result in a change to the existing budget.

An effective planning process leading to a clearly articulated budget provides a means of tracking revenues and expenses so that resources can be used most effectively to meet the institution's goals while still complying with external constraints. The more effective institutions build on the planning and budgeting activities by adding ongoing assessment to help confirm the appropriateness and success of institutional activities.

Collectively, the alignment and coordination of planning, budgeting (or resource management), and assessment represent three critical processes necessary for intentional institutional effectiveness.

Budgeting also enables an institution to highlight the costs of particular activities and their respective claims on resources. This exercise is especially valuable for activities supported with unrestricted resources—those without external stipulations regarding their use. Typically, there isn't a direct link between the unrestricted sources of revenue allocated to an activity and the expenses incurred by the activity. There are different considerations when managing restricted resources because of the specific requirements regarding the resources' use. When revenues restricted for a particular purpose are reduced or eliminated, it generally is apparent that the activity will experience operational cutbacks or be terminated.

On the other hand, when unrestricted resources are expected to increase, the institution has an opportunity to increase the resources allocated to particular activities, undertake new activities, or simply increase amounts reserved for future use. These decisions become more evident when articulated through the budget. And as suggested above, they become easier to make and implement if they are guided by an effective planning process.

In short, a budget is a map that guides an institution on its journey to carry out its mission. The budget should be the result of a series of decisions undertaken during a planning process. The budget is not the plan. It's the financial manifestation of the plan. Failure to engage in planning results in the budget being the de facto plan. A major problem with this situation is that it almost guarantees that there will be excessive reliance on perpetuating the activities that occurred during the previous period—irrespective of their relative success.

For nearly every educational institution, the mission includes multiple elements such as instruction, research, and public service. Some institutions have an additional mission element—patient care. Regardless of the specific elements of an institution's mission, an effective budget will address them all.

You can learn a great deal about an institution merely by reviewing the budget—especially if prior-year budget information is available for comparison. Comparing the projected revenues and anticipated expenses provides clues about the institution's priorities. Even a cursory review will suggest the relative importance of the mission components and detail what revenues are anticipated and how they will be deployed in carrying out the mission.

THE BUDGET'S ROLES

Budgets take many forms but usually include at least two components: quantitative and narrative information. The quantitative component details the numbers that indicate the expected revenue—by category and by amount. It also provides the basic information about how funds will be expended. Some quantitative formats are highly aggregated, showing just the major categories of revenues (for example, tuition or governmental appropriations) and expenses (for example, instruction and public service or compensation and utilities). Others are more detailed, showing individual expense categories aligned with the institution's organizational structure.

The narrative component provides additional information about the numbers that appear in the quantitative budget. Depending on the approach taken, the narrative may highlight the specific priorities addressed, the assumptions used in developing the budget, and the constraints that affect the numbers in the budget. It also may refer to specific goals and objectives for the institution as well as its individual units.

Budgets serve many purposes and perform various roles. Specifically, the budget is: **the financial manifestation of the institution's various plans—whether strategic, infrastructural, or operational (as discussed further in Chapter 7)**. It is developed through iterative processes and, once completed, presents the results of a multitude of individual resource allocation decisions. These decisions are not made in a vacuum. They reflect the results of past assessment activities, advice and guidance from the board, discussions among senior managers, and—in the most effective settings—dialogues involving the institution's various stakeholders.

Unless driven by the institution's plans, the budget will not achieve the ultimate purpose of intentionally moving the institution toward enhanced service and improved quality. Some people mistakenly believe that the budget *is the plan*. But if that's the case, the budget process represents constrained thinking because it is overly influenced by the previous budget. Beginning the budget process after engaging in effective planning that identifies institutional priorities in light of current resource realities is one step toward ensuring that resources are deployed most effectively.

A contract between management and the operating units charged with carrying out the plans. The budget indicates what resources the institution will provide to the units and, in broad terms, what the units will accomplish by utilizing those resources. Like many contracts, however, it does not represent a guarantee. Effective budgets include provisions for contingencies. They possess specific lines within expense categories for unknown circumstances that may consume resources. Even with this practice, circumstances could be worse than anticipated and prevent the institution from providing all the resources identified in the budget. Despite these potential challenges, both management and the units should view the budget as a shared commitment. Absent catastrophic events or large, unforeseeable revenue shortfalls, units have the right to expect to receive the resources presented in the budget. Intentionally developing and approving a budget that will not result in resources being deployed as presented represents a leadership failure at best or unethical behavior at worst. And unlike for-profit enterprises' need to closely guard internal financial information, higher education budgets should be transparent and readily available within the community. When linked with narrative information explaining the intentions reflected in the budget, they should be easily understood by the vast majority of community members.

A forecast of the institution's financial picture at a future time. Assuming that a budget covers an annual operating cycle that coincides with the institution's fiscal year, the institution can prepare pro forma financial statements that assume all revenues and expenses will materialize as predicted. These pro forma statements depict the institution's expected financial condition at the end of the cycle. If reasonably accurate in its predictions, the institution will know what to expect. This effort also can influence the development of the budget. Performing a "what if" analysis can help avoid excessive spending that would adversely affect the institution's financial health.

Financial ratio analysis (see Chapter 7) can be used to measure the financial health of an institution. By projecting the results of the budgeted operating and capital activity—and making assumptions about investment performance—the institution can project its financial health at the end of the cycle. Most likely, the actual results will vary because of unforeseen factors and the unpredictability of financial markets. Nevertheless, operational results typically have the greatest impact on an institution's financial health. Therefore, preparing pro forma financial statements based on anticipated or approved budgets can be beneficial to an institution that has established a goal of achieving certain financial objectives, along with its programmatic objectives.

An indicator of risk tolerance. Assumptions and predictions made throughout the planning and budget development processes cover items as critical as the number of expected entering freshmen and transfer students and as mundane as the expected increase in elevator maintenance fees. Some decisions are imposed on the institution, such as increased utilities or snow removal costs, while others—such as faculty salary increases—are imposed *by* the institution. The specific decisions and their impact on the institution's financial health indicate the level of risk it can tolerate.

The greater the risk tolerance, the smaller the contingency built into the budget. Institutions with a relatively higher tolerance for risk usually budget revenues more aggressively and allocate most resources for expenses (including appropriate additions to reserves for future use). On the other hand, institutions that are less comfortable with risk are more likely to budget revenues conservatively and include contingency amounts to address revenue shortfalls, expense overruns, or take advantage of opportunities that may materialize.

Regardless of the institution's tolerance for risk, it should allocate a portion of the budget to address contingencies. This can be a mix of recurring and one-time reserves that can be used in response to unanticipated opportunities or challenges.

A political instrument. To create the budget, administrators from various units strike bargains and make trade-offs. Throughout the process, many people seek to exert their leadership to influence the ultimate distribution of resources. The final outcome reflects a series of negotiations and compromises about which activities should be funded and at what levels.

Often, multiple budget cycles overlap, making it common for negotiations in one cycle to influence other cycles. Although these negotiations rarely result in complete satisfaction for the parties involved, the process is worthwhile. The negotiations provide the opportunity to communicate needs for services and the resources required to provide them. This process can lead to a better understanding of other activities competing for the same scarce resources. Care is needed though because negotiations can be counterproductive if not properly managed. It is important that the process afford each perspective the opportunity to be heard and to receive feedback about the rationale for final decisions in a transparent manner.

PRELUDE TO A BUDGET

As mentioned earlier, in a well-managed institution, the budget is the financial manifestation of the institution's plans and reflects the relative priorities assigned to different activities. It also takes into consideration all stakeholders' needs and interests. Because planning should precede budget development, many key decisions already will have been made before the budget development begins.

Planning in higher education is not about choosing between good and bad ideas. It's about choosing between good and better ideas. Both the planning and budget processes should have the same ultimate objective—driving institutional success. This is accomplished by effectively deploying what typically are limited resources in support of the institution's established priorities, thus leading to the realization of its vision while fulfilling its mission and honoring its values.

That's why an institution should decide its priorities before beginning the budget process in earnest. Some priorities are large in scale and established through a strategic planning process, while others are more immediate.

And still others—for instance, infrastructural plans—though not necessarily reflected in the strategic plan, have implications for budgets over multiple periods. Individual resource allocation decisions should grow from the decisions made throughout the various planning processes. Unfortunately, too few higher education institutions use effective planning mechanisms. And many of those that engage in planning do not use it to intentionally guide the resource allocation process.

In extreme situations, rather than engage in effective planning, some institutions begin with the prior year's base budget and make minor tweaks. Typically, this happens when the bulk of the budget is adjusted incrementally or decrementally. Some institutions rely excessively on incremental budgeting—adjusting the vast majority of the prior year's budget by a fixed percentage to address changes in available resources. While reasonable for addressing portions of the budget, this approach is often used to excess, resulting in the institution perpetuating nearly all past activities into the future—even those activities that no longer contribute to institutional success. While still employing incremental budgeting for subsets of the budget, a willingness to use other approaches driven by plans and assessment results will produce better institutional outcomes. This blending of approaches enables the institution to underwrite new initiatives, achieve enhanced results on continuing efforts, build on areas of identified strength, and successfully move toward its vision.

The lack of planning that sometimes accompanies excessive reliance on incremental budgeting creates two embedded flaws in the resulting resource distribution. First, there is an assumption that the way resources are deployed currently is the optimal distribution for the institution and, second, that all units have approximately equal needs for additional resources. Moreover, it assumes that maintaining the status quo is in the institution's best interests. Excessive reliance on incremental budgeting does not lead to enhanced outcomes because it is highly unlikely that the current budget—the starting point—is allocated in the optimal manner. Activities that might flourish with disproportionately increased resources likely will remain underfunded, while others that may have outlived their usefulness or value to the institution continue to consume resources (or too many resources compared to their needs).

Two factors may help explain the continued popularity of excessive reliance on incremental approaches—despite the fact that regional accreditation agencies identify the explicit linkage of resource allocation to planning as evidence of institutional effectiveness. First, a system relying primarily on incremental budgeting is deemed to be fair: All units receive the same relative percentage of increased resources (or reductions in times of contraction). Second, it is efficient because it provides a starting point and a fixed percentage for adjustments.

The presumed fairness and efficiency, however, come at the expense of effectiveness. A system that blindly perpetuates embedded inequities cannot be deemed fair. Instead, a sizable portion of resources should be available to reward high-performing units with increased resources, and these units should be spared from cuts if they become necessary. Similarly, activities with the greatest potential to contribute to or enhance the institution's effectiveness should receive relatively more resources than units that no longer contribute to institutional success or otherwise underperform relative to others within the institution.

The bottom line is that incremental budgeting may be highly efficient but, if used to excess, is simply ineffective. When utilized in this manner, it ignores the results of planning, which—when done properly—identifies priority areas. Without question, the most successful approach to budgeting starts with a realistic plan—one developed with extensive input from all institutional stakeholders—and develops the budget based on the decisions reflected in the plan.

TYPES OF BUDGETS

At the highest level, budgets focus on the resources higher education needs for programmatic success. As mentioned earlier, these include people, money, space, technology, and equipment. Most budgets focus on money because it is the easiest resource to measure and monitor. But budgets also reflect resource allocation decisions made with respect to positions, space, technology, and equipment. For example, the number of faculty positions (or lines) assigned to a given unit translates into salaries and benefits—represented by dollars—for those positions. In turn, space, technology, and equipment will be affected by decisions involving positions.

Higher education institutions use different budgets for a variety of purposes. The most common types of budgets are operating and capital. These are used by almost every institution, and there are many others as well. Some budgets focus just on compensation, others on travel, and still others on subsets of the institution such as a department or division. A budget can address any aspect of an institution that is deemed to be worth considering. Care must be taken, however, not to distort reality when assembling budgets. It's one thing to focus exclusively on the compensation budget—that is, salaries, wages, and benefits—but it would be inappropriate to imply that this is a comprehensive budget. Special-purpose budgets must be clearly labeled and explained to avoid confusion about what they represent. The labeling should specify the subject of the budget, the organization (or organizational unit) it addresses, and the time period covered. This is particularly important for budgets that show both continuing and one-time funding. A budget for a unit may show all available resources for a given period. Yet some of those resources may be available only for the current period, and once it ends, the new budget will not reflect the resources that were made available on a one-time basis.

As its name suggests, the operating budget identifies the investments being made to carry out the various recurring activities in the form of expenses and the revenues and resources available to support those activities. This includes revenues resulting from service efforts (for example, tuition and patient charges) and those derived from other sources (for example, appropriations and gifts). It addresses the various elements of the institution's mission (e.g., instruction and research) and also focuses on support and ancillary activities such as libraries and intercollegiate athletics.

Operating revenues either finance current expenses, repay debt, or contribute to institutional reserves—a form of savings. The vast majority of revenues received during a given period will be expended on operations and related activities during that period. After covering the costs of operations and providing for any debt repayments that come due, any remaining unexpended resources will be added to reserves—resources set aside for specific purposes, typically for use in the future. In some cases, however, reserves merely serve as a cushion against future financial challenges.

In addition to revenues and reserves, operating budgets present the day-to-day expenses incurred by the institution as it carries out its mission. Colleges and universities incur a wide variety of expenses. Some, such as salaries and wages, make up a significant percentage of the budget. Others may be relatively small and vary significantly based on the character of the institution. For instance, maintenance costs for residence halls typically do not represent a significant expense for most community colleges.

Expenses in an operating budget may be displayed in either of two broad categories: *natural* classification and *functional* classification (sometimes called programmatic classification). Natural classification refers to expenses identified by type rather than purpose and includes things like salaries, benefits, travel, and supplies. Though valuable for many purposes, a budget prepared using the natural classification approach provides little information about the activities being conducted. For instance, the natural classification budget for a healthcare organization might look very similar to one prepared for a research institution because both entities require a substantial property investment and are labor-intensive. A functional expense budget would be more valuable as an aid to understanding what is taking place.

Functional classification organizes expenses by the nature of the activity the expense supports. Examples of functional categories for a college or university include instruction, public service, and academic support. Instructional expenses include various natural-class expenses such as salaries, employee benefits, supplies, and travel. Similar expenses would be incurred in the other functional categories.

A matrix displaying natural-class expenses in functional categories is a useful representation of an operating budget's expense side. It indicates the relative investments by functional category and the proportional amount of types of expenses incurred to achieve the multiple programmatic objectives.

Table 1-1

Operating Expenses Matrix Illustrating Expenses by Natural and Functional Classification (amounts in millions)						
	Natural Classification Expenses					
Functional Classification Expenses	Compensation	Services & Supplies	Utilities	Depreciation	Scholarships & Fellowships	Total
Instruction	$ 90.77	$ 14.90	$ 0.79	$ 1.91	$ 0.28	$ 108.66
Research	51.72	22.18	1.00	1.44	0.24	76.57
Public service	27.53	12.40	0.89	1.33	0.01	42.17
Academic support	22.23	5.85	0.80	1.85		30.73
Student services	10.46	5.17	0.19	0.49	0.01	16.31
Institutional support	13.48	4.45	0.18	0.28		18.39
Operation and maintenance of plant	11.56	9.37	3.74	6.31		30.97
Student financial aid	0.00	0.11			4.02	4.13
Auxiliary services	17.96	25.01	3.45	6.46		52.88
Total	$245.71	$99.43	$ 11.04	$20.07	$4.55	$380.81

Capital budgets map out the finances for construction or other acquisition plans related to the built environment (i.e., physical facilities and campus infrastructure). It also details the sources and uses of funds for renovating or updating existing facilities. As with the operating budget, a capital budget addresses inflows and outflows—either expenses or additions to asset balances. The revenues can come from various sources, including tuition and fees, governmental appropriations, and gifts.

In addition to revenues, financing for facilities comes from *reserves* and *borrowing*. Reserves are funds that have accumulated through savings or have been set aside as part of the operating budget. Institutions often set aside a certain portion of the annual operating budget to cover costs that will be incurred in a future period. This practice is typical for auxiliary enterprise units such as residence halls, bookstores, and parking systems (all of which should be self-supporting). For example, residence hall systems typically rely on borrowed funds to finance new construction. It is a fairly standard requirement of bond covenants that a certain portion of annual system revenues be set aside for facilities maintenance, such as carpet replacement, painting, and roof repairs. These funds are maintained in a reserve and invested until they are needed.

Borrowed funds are either short-term construction loans or long-term bonds that finance the acquisition or construction costs for new facilities, major equipment, or infrastructure upgrades or additions. The long-term debt serves the same purpose as a home mortgage for an individual. Colleges and universities frequently issue tax-exempt bonds to fund capital expansion. For some public institutions, the state issues the bonds or provides the resources needed to repay the bonds as they come due.

Many institutions that issue their own debt have established complex financing arrangements to support their capital expansion programs. These usually are supported by board-approved debt plans. Variable-rate debt is a staple among many financing choices to obtain resources needed for longer periods. A number of institutions have relied on various forms of short-term debt to finance construction projects until the institution is ready to convert the obligation to long-term debt.

Internal banking arrangements have become popular over time. With an internal bank, the institution issues long-term debt and redistributes the proceeds, as needed, throughout the institution. The various units receiving the proceeds are then assessed principal and interest charges to generate the resources needed to compensate and repay the bondholders who purchased the institution's long-term debt.

Expenditures appearing in a capital budget include construction costs that will be capitalized as well as other costs that must be recognized as expenses during the year they are incurred due to accounting rules. (Capitalized costs establish an asset that will provide benefits beyond one year.) As an example, consider the cost of painting a residence hall at a smaller institution. Given the infrequency of this and the magnitude of the expense, it may be too large to include in the institution's operating budget, so it would be included in the capital budget. However, painting a building is a maintenance activity and, therefore, would not be capitalized.

Both operating and capital budgets can be developed for the institution as a whole or for subsets of the institution. For instance, a capital budget might apply to an individual project, such as construction of a particular building, or it can address all currently approved capital projects for a given period. Similarly, operating budgets can address the complete range of activities for the institution, or they can simply cover activities within a department or a single programmatic area such as instruction or student affairs.

Special-purpose budgets address specific situations. For instance, some institutions prepare special budgets focused only on restricted funds. Restricted budgets indicate resources provided by external parties that carry stipulations about how they must be expended. Examples include gifts provided to acquire library books and income from an endowment established to fund scholarships for undergraduate students from a particular locale. Another example is a grant from a governmental entity that must be expended for specific types of research.

SUBJECT TO REVISION

These are among the most challenging times ever experienced in higher education. There is genuine uncertainty about what the future holds for many institutions. Whether it's concerns about enrollment, retention, workforce demographic changes, the willingness of state or provincial governments to support their institutions, or many other issues, those working in higher education face uncertainty. This doesn't reduce the need for a budget, but it means that the budget, as prepared, may be less likely to unfold as originally developed. As such, there is greater pressure to devote increased energy to monitoring external factors to try to anticipate their impact. It has become more about scenario planning than predicting. Nevertheless, even the most effective planning processes simply cannot anticipate some events and developments. Therefore, all budgets are subject to revision. In fact, the ink on the latest budget document probably will not be dry before circumstances dictate that adjustments be made.

In most cases, the budget for a given cycle begins with the most recent plans and the budget from the current or most recently completed cycle. Presumably, the starting point reflects the cumulative impact of all revisions to the previous budget other than temporary (or one-time) situations. Even so, the budget will continue to change over time. That's why the budget process and the budget itself must be flexible enough to respond to these changes (see Chapter 11).

Apart from the unpredictability of some expense categories, revenues can vary widely from one year to the next. All institutions have uncertainty regarding the amount of revenue that some sources will generate (for example, investment income). Enrollment unpredictability can be an even greater concern for many institutions, particularly those described as enrollment dependent. Enrollment-dependent institutions are those in which 85 percent or more of the revenue comes from enrollment-driven revenues such as tuition, required fees, operating appropriations (when tied to enrollment), and auxiliary sales and services.

For an enrollment-dependent institution, a relatively small decrease in enrollment can substantially affect the pool of available resources. And this can happen without materially altering the level of expenses that will be incurred. For example, when the freshman class entering a small high-priced institution falls a few dozen students short of the number budgeted, the impact on revenues can approach a half-million dollars. Yet those students may be spread throughout the institution's programs in such a way that the same number of faculty will be needed. In this scenario, the reduced enrollment may not bring any cost savings. This is one factor that encourages institutions to diversify their revenue stream and establish contingency funds.

Different institutions address the unpredictability of revenues in different ways. For institutions that have budgeted revenues conservatively, positive net financial results may lead to increased allocations of resources for use in the current period. Similarly, institutions that include expense contingencies in the budget periodically will make adjustments to reallocate available resources from the contingency line to the expense category or unit that has experienced the cost overrun. This enables the institution to properly reflect its utilization of resources. In contrast, charging expenses directly to the contingency budget will understate the expense category or unit that experienced the overrun. Moreover, if the situation is likely to continue, the starting point for the subsequent budget will not provide a true picture of resource needs.

The number of budget adjustments tends to be lower for conservative institutions compared to those that budget more aggressively. Aggressive budgeters often need to make more adjustments because they are more likely to experience revenue shortfalls and expense overruns in specific categories. With luck, the net impact of the shortfalls and overruns will not create an overall deficit situation, but it is an increased possibility for institutions that rely on aggressive budget assumptions.

One thing to keep in mind is that the budget, once approved, becomes an official institutional document. In rare instances, it even can be designated as a legal document. Irrespective of its status as a legal document, midyear changes to a budget may require approval by a level of authority other than management. It's a typical requirement for an institution's board or the system office to approve the budget that is intended to be relied upon. Therefore, changes to that budget may require notification to, or approval by, the original approving entity.

As suggested earlier, however, budgets are continually changing throughout the year. It would be incredibly burdensome to report and/or gain approval for each such change. Instead, the most common practice is to make the necessary changes in the background and only seek approval if the projected bottom line—net surplus or deficit—changes. In other words, if revenues or expenses shift among types without modifying the total, there is no need to inform the board. If changes occur such that both projected revenues and expenses are adjusted in a way that the bottom line doesn't change, again, there is no need to present this information to the board. If, however, the changes cause the budgeted surplus or deficit to be larger or smaller than originally projected—and the budget was subject to external approval—it would be prudent to seek approval for the change. Similarly, in some situations, the board seeks to be informed whenever contingency funds are utilized irrespective of whether they affect the bottom line.

KEY POINTS

▶ A budget can have many roles. At its core, it is a map—expressed in financial terms—guiding an institution on a journey as it carries out its mission. A budget is *not* a plan; it is a product of the planning processes.

▶ Budgeting is a form of resource allocation. Effective institutions align resource allocation with planning and assessment. Plans determine what will be done, while budgets dictate the level of resources to be deployed in executing the plans. Budgets must be flexible to respond to changing needs and circumstances.

▶ Expenses can be displayed in either of two classification categories: functional (e.g., instruction, academic support) or natural (e.g., salaries, supplies).

▶ Operating budgets provide details on anticipated revenues and on investments needed to carry out the institution's day-to-day activities. A capital budget provides financial details on the institution's near-term and long-term plans related to the built environment. Many other budgets, referred to as special-purpose budgets, address specific issues such as compensation, restricted funds, etc.

CHAPTER 2: THE POLITICAL AND REGULATORY ENVIRONMENT

Various economic, political, and regulatory developments influence an institution's budget. Most are beyond the control of individual institutions or even the national higher education community. Accordingly, budgeters must not only respond to existing conditions, they have to be forward looking and consider what may be coming at them. They must anticipate changes in economic and political conditions that could affect the amount of revenues available and, of equal importance, the expenses the institution may have to bear. Unless an institution's budget can withstand the pressures created by external forces, the institution's survival may be in jeopardy.

Institutional closures are not tracked officially by any organization. Anecdotal evidence suggests that closures and mergers have accelerated in recent years, especially since the Great Recession.*

The problems are most significant for small independent institutions. Of the independent institutions that have closed or been absorbed by larger, more financially stable institutions in recent years, nearly all of them qualify as small colleges and universities. This is not an epidemic by any means, but the numbers far outpace what has happened historically.

Various organizations, as well as some pundits, suggest that the day of reckoning is upon us or will be very soon. Standard & Poor's termed the 2018 outlook for higher education bleak due to various factors, including the new excise tax on endowments and the disconnect between parent and student expectations versus their willingness to pay the costs of education.[1] Moody's terminology was different, choosing grim versus bleak, and expressed concerns about revenue streams, especially tuition. Other factors supporting the negative outlook included the rate of growth in expenses.[2]

Alarm bells about higher education's future have been sounded in the past, and for the most part, the industry has avoided the predicted doom and gloom. Whether higher education will again demonstrate its resiliency is a matter for debate. What is not debatable is that these are trying times

---

*The Great Recession is the term applied to the severe global economic downturn that followed the collapse of the U. S. real estate market and the related subprime mortgage crisis of 2007 through 2009.

for institutions—both from a political perspective and a regulatory one. And though this discussion focuses primarily on independent institutions, the impacts are being felt by public institutions as well.

The current period of uncertainty and difficulty actually began as long ago as the late 1990s and is not expected to end anytime soon. Economic challenges have significantly affected higher education institutions, and this led to a sea change in the nation's support for, and confidence in, the sector. In a recent survey by the Pew Research Center,[3] 61 percent of survey participants believe higher education is heading in the wrong direction and chose the following reasons for their belief:

▶ Eighty-four percent opted for high tuition, and nearly two-thirds indicated that students are leaving college without the skills needed to succeed in the workplace.

▶ Fifty-four percent attribute higher education's problems to institutions being too concerned with protecting students from views they might find offensive.

▶ Finally, 50 percent selected institutions' excessive concern about faculty who bring their political and socials views into the classroom.

The most alarming aspect of the results may be the deep divide indicated based on political party affiliation—especially with respect to the latter two factors. The gap on protecting against offensive views is 44 points, with 75 percent of Republicans (and those leaning Republican) and 31 percent of Democrats (and those leaning Democrat) believing this. The gap for the impact of professors' political and social views entering the classroom is even larger at 62 points, with Republicans at 79 percent and Democrats at 17 percent.[4]

Higher education faces significant challenges to its previously high ranking on national, state, and local societal agendas. Other sectors now capture resources previously reserved for higher education, especially public sector resources. Whether the focus has shifted to public safety, K–12 education, healthcare, or general social service programs, higher education no longer is viewed as a top priority for funding. Part of this shift stems from a change in perception. Higher education no longer is universally recognized as a public good. Instead, it now is perceived to be a private benefit by many—especially some in highly influential positions. Moreover, some even question the value of a degree, despite numerous studies demonstrating the financial return from investments in education at all levels. Finally, there are signs that the rest of the world is catching up to the United States in terms of educational quality. Undoubtedly, the United States still has the top institutions in the world, but the gap between our best and the rest of the world is shrinking.

In today's environment, higher education must defend itself continuously against criticism from numerous quarters. In years past, it was enough to highlight the economic value of a college education or point to the discoveries growing out of campus-based research. Such arguments no longer sway a nation that focuses less on one's ability to pay and, instead, on the cost of a degree. For many, the issue has shifted from concern about the *ability* to pay to one of individuals' and families' *willingness* to pay. As college prices have escalated—at rates greater than the Consumer Price Index (CPI) in most years—both the federal government and the general population have questioned whether higher education is being managed effectively.

To some degree, higher education has rebounded from the Great Recession—but it took a long time, and the bounce has not been nearly as high as hoped. Inflation continues to be held in check, but campuses still are experiencing significant cost increases in critical areas. At the same time, various revenue sources are depressed with nothing to suggest that things will turn around in the short run. In fact, even some prestigious institutions have suspended programs, eliminated positions, or resorted to other cost-cutting measures that have dramatically affected program delivery. A climate like this requires careful examination of external factors.

THE POLITICAL CLIMATE

Higher education leaders have plenty of issues to keep them awake at night, with the U.S. Congress often providing the impetus. In recent years, congressional (or federal agency) initiatives have focused on higher education issues as diverse as college costs and affordability, the size of higher education endowments and annual endowment spending, and institutional responses to sexual abuse complaints.

As the country's political winds shift due to party changes in the White House and Congress, different issues likely will receive favor—e.g., taxing endowments—while others may take a backseat—for instance, concerns about accreditation of for-profit institutions. What is certain, however, is that we have not seen the last of federal government efforts focused on improving higher education's effectiveness or challenging it to become more efficient.

For instance, the U.S. Department of Education set a goal of bringing tuition price increases down, and it appears to have succeeded. The most recent comprehensive reauthorization of the Higher Education Act was in 2008—more than 10 years ago. One of the key issues addressed was what were believed to be excessive price hikes. As reported by the College Board, the fiscal year 2018–19 average tuition increase was 2.5 percent for in-state students at public four-year institutions and 2.4 percent for their out-of-state counterparts.[5] The comparable numbers for students at four-year independent institutions was 3.3 percent.[6] For in-district public two-year institutions, the increase was 2.8 percent.[7] Unlike the period leading up to the act's reauthorization, the price increases compare favorably with inflation, as measured by the Consumer Price Index for All Urban Consumers (CPI-U), which fell to 2.9 percent during the year that tuition prices were being set for 2018–19.[8]

Tracking Cost Increases

Costs incurred in higher education do not mirror costs used to track inflation in the general economy. That's why many in higher education rely on alternative indices rather than the traditional ones provided by the Bureau of Labor Statistics. For instance, the Commonfund Higher Education Price Index (HEPI) is an alternative to the more popular CPI and is favored by many. The CPI is deemed too general and not representative of the types of purchases typically made by higher education institutions. The HEPI cost components include faculty salaries, administrative salaries, clerical salaries, service employee salaries, fringe benefits, miscellaneous services, supplies and materials, and utilities.[9]

The HEPI has attracted critics, however, and may no longer represent the accepted standard for higher education price changes. One reason the HEPI has not enjoyed universal acceptance stems from the fact that it was initially developed in the private sector. Also, some questions have arisen about the validity of the method used to calculate the index. However, it now is maintained and managed by Commonfund Institute, which may help mitigate some of the concerns previously expressed about the HEPI.

Another commonly used index is the CPI-U—a variation of the CPI based on goods and services purchased by the typical urban consumer. Some argue that because the HEPI and the CPI-U have not differed dramatically for some brief periods, the CPI-U is a reasonable choice. Others contend that significant variances can occur over time. As a result, efforts continue to identify a reliable index for use by higher education.

The State Higher Education Executive Officers (SHEEO) organization has attempted to bridge the gap between the HEPI and the CPI-U by offering the Higher Education Cost Adjustment (HECA). The HECA is developed by weighting and combining two federally developed and maintained indices. The Employment Cost Index, managed by the Bureau of Labor Statistics in the U.S. Department of Labor, provides 75 percent of the weight. The Gross Domestic Product Implicit Price Deflator, part of the Bureau of Economic Statistics in the U.S. Department of Commerce, provides the remaining 25 percent.[10]

The growth in endowments to prerecession levels raises a legitimate question: How much endowment is enough? Various quarters have increased their calls for institutions to spend down endowments to moderate or eliminate tuition price hikes. But for the most part, this has not happened. Some substantial increased endowment spending occurred during the period following the recession, but this was not sustained. Spending rates returned to previous levels soon afterward. Many institutions sought to hold tuition increases to a minimum, but endowments still remained an attractive target to various critics of higher education's financial structure. The continuing improvement in the financial markets during 2017, with the resulting growth in endowment market values, led to resumption of demands to tax endowments. And this time they met with success.

The Tax Cuts and Jobs Act signed by President Trump in December 2017 enacts a 1.4 percent excise tax on net investment income. However, it affects only independent institutions with enrollments of at least 500 students and net assets of $500,000 per student. Estimates at the time suggested that the number of institutions affected may be less than 40. The regulations needed to enact the legislation are not yet finalized, so it's unclear of the actual impact and the numbers affected.

The endowment tax is but one example of the act's impact on the tax-exempt community, which includes higher education. Others include an excise tax on the five highest paid individuals earning $1 million or more annually and the designation of employee parking benefits and costs related to on-campus gym usage by employees as unrelated business income. Also problematic is the removal of the provision allowing organizations to offset unrelated business income with unrelated business losses—a routine feature available to almost all other taxpayers. An additional potential impact is the increase in the standard deduction, which could discourage some taxpayers from making contributions to colleges and universities because they no longer will benefit from the charitable tax deduction.

Despite its potential significance for many institutions that will be affected, the tax act is far from the most significant impact higher education is feeling as a result of the election. A state of confusion has been created because of the cancellation of existing regulations before replacements are available. Examples of issues affected include Deferred Action for Childhood Arrivals (DACA), sexual assault under Title IX, and borrower defense repayment rules in situations involving for-profit educational institutions that cease operations.

There is a general state of uncertainty across campuses because of pervasive concerns about the federal regulatory environment. This has led to difficulty for institutions seeking to comply because of a lack of clarity about which regulations to follow, especially in areas where courts have struck down or stayed enforcement/implementation. Moreover, resolution of the problem seems stalled due to the polarization between Republicans and Democrats and their respective agendas.

Effective planning and cost management can accommodate steadily increasing prices, but most institutional budgets cannot withstand major fluctuations within short periods of time. Furthermore, exceptional cost increases in any category can wreak havoc on even a well-managed budget. For instance, colleges and universities continually face the prospect of replacing expensive instructional and research equipment as it becomes obsolete. Unless institutions have funded depreciation and maintained reserves for this purpose (see Appendix A), the impact from these purchases will be a significant charge on the current budget and may have significant cash-flow impacts as well. Some exceptional situations may even force a college or university into a serious financial crisis.

IMPACT OF FEDERAL REGULATION AND SOCIAL PROGRAMS[*]

Some costs of doing business in any industry can be attributed to informal social pressures and government mandates in various areas. For instance, personal security and safety, participation and due process, public information, and environmental protection are issues of concern to higher education. In addition to these universal pressures, colleges and universities experience additional costs unique to their specific missions, which include protection of students' privacy and federal financial aid programs.

---

[*] This section is based largely on: Howard Bowen, *The Costs of Higher Education: How Much Do Colleges and Universities Spend per Student and How Much Should They Spend?* (San Francisco: Jossey-Bass, 1980).

At What Cost?

Federal regulations and mandated social programs touch all aspects of institutional operations, from athletics to the care of laboratory animals. It has proven difficult, if not impossible, to isolate the true cost of externally imposed regulations and guidelines. A primary reason is that compliance with the mandates often cannot be separated from the routine operations of the institution. Another reason is that colleges and universities frequently support the objectives of imposed regulations and programs and would initiate similar actions on their own even without the requirements.

Consider the following factors when assessing the impact of federal regulations and social pressures:

- ► The adoption of programs can increase or decrease costs. For example, a mandated staff training program may lead to greater employee morale and improved productivity, thereby reducing operating costs.
- ► Socially imposed programs have two types of costs: the cost of program operations and the cost associated with compliance (for example, reporting). In many cases, the concern about program cost is focused on the compliance aspects rather than the substance of the program.
- ► How costs are counted and when they must be incurred introduce another set of issues. The overall cost of a program may not be significant when measured over time. Too often, however, the mandate requires significant up-front investments that become a burden on a single year's budget.
- ► The implementation of some programs may not increase aggregate expenses but may force a shift in priorities. For instance, resources once earmarked for library acquisitions may be diverted to cover safety and security mandates.

Overall, commercial entities have an advantage in dealing with socially imposed costs. First, many regulations do not apply to commercial entities because they do not typically receive federal funding. In addition, when they are subject to external mandates that increase operating costs, commercial entities can pass these costs along to their customers. While independent institutions have control of their tuition, this is not always the case for public institutions. Frequently, a state agency or the legislature has the authority to set tuition at public institutions. When institutions are unable to generate sufficient tuition or other revenues to offset the costs of mandated programs, the only option is to cut back in other areas—either in the primary programs of instruction, research, and public service or in a support activity.

To illustrate the range of issues campuses must address, here are some of the mandates and requirements applicable to higher education today:

Personal security and safety. The Social Security Act of 1935, as amended, addresses retirement pensions, survivors' benefits, disability insurance, unemployment compensation, and health insurance. The Occupational Safety and Health Act of 1970 (OSHA) establishes employee safety and working condition standards. The Employee Retirement Income Security Act of 1974 (ERISA) provides safeguards for employees participating in pensions offered by independent institutions. There are many other federal laws in this arena targeted specifically to higher education. One example is the legislation addressing radiation safety and the protection of human and animal subjects used in research and teaching. Also significant to higher education is the Clery Act of 1990—establishing the Campus Sexual Assault Victims Bill of Rights and the Campus Sex Crimes Prevention Act—and Title IX of the Education Amendments Act of 1972. Although Title IX historically focused on the prohibition of sexual discrimination in education, especially in the area of intercollegiate athletics, its applicability recently has been extended to include sexual assault and sexual harassment.

Labor relations. One of the major laws in this area—affecting all colleges and universities—is the Fair Labor Standards Act of 1938, which establishes minimum wage levels, maximum work hours, and overtime compensation rules. Of less significance because it affects only those institutions with unions is the National Labor Relations Act of 1935, establishing the rules applicable to collective bargaining and employee organizing. Finally, there is the Equal Pay Act of 1963, mandating that employees doing similar tasks receive equal pay regardless of sex.

Personal opportunity. Various courts have reduced protections in some areas related to affirmative action, but guidelines remain in force through federal regulations and laws. There are a multitude of laws in this general area. Executive Order 11246 of 1965, as amended in 1967, prohibits discrimination on the basis of sex, while age discrimination is prohibited by the Employment Act of 1967. Title VII of the Civil Rights Act of 1964, as amended by the Equal Employment Opportunity Act of 1972, prohibits discrimination on the basis of sex, race, creed, or national origin. The aforementioned Title IX prohibits discrimination on the basis of sex in educational policies, facilities, programs, and employment practices. Federal student financial aid program rules impose significant administrative burdens and, in some instances, require institutional contributions. Internal Revenue Service (IRS) regulations prohibit discrimination in favor of highly compensated individuals in benefits programs.

Participation, openness, due process, and privacy. The guiding legislation in this area includes the First Amendment to the Constitution, and various laws have been passed to amplify its requirements. The National Labor Relations Act of 1935 protects employees covered by collectively bargained agreements, and the Family Educational Rights and Privacy Act of 1974 (FERPA, or the Buckley Amendment) protects students against the improper release of personal information. (Terrorist actions and threats have somewhat clouded privacy issues, with campuses occasionally caught in the middle in terms of complying with FERPA while responding to requests for information from federal agencies.) The Gramm-Leach-Bliley Act of 1999, primarily aimed at financial institutions but also applicable to colleges and universities, imposes requirements to protect the privacy of consumers engaging in financial transactions. Regulations commonly known as the Red Flags Rule require institutions to maintain a protection program designed to detect warning signs (or "red flags") of identity theft in their daily operations.

Public information. Requests for information primarily relate to consumer protection, fundraising, enforcement of government programs, general statistical needs of society, national security, and the general public's demands for accountability. The Office of Management and Budget (OMB) must clear all surveys funded under federal grants. OMB also promulgates rules for calculating indirect or facilities and administrative (F&A) cost rates applicable to federally sponsored activities. Federally funded student financial aid participation requires verification and audit reports, along with participation in the U.S. Department of Education's National Center for Education Statistics Integrated Postsecondary Education Data System (IPEDS), which collects data from institutions annually. The Student and Exchange Visitor Information System (SEVIS), which grew out of the events of September 11, 2001, requires all colleges and universities to provide information on international students, scholars, and other visitors.

Environmental protection. Increasingly, pollution control requirements, restrictions on research involving hazardous materials and recombinant DNA, and vandalism and the problems of neighborhood deterioration call for action by colleges and universities. The Environmental Protection Agency (EPA), for instance, assesses fines under the Resource Conservation and Recovery Act, which also mandates specific safety steps related to the treatment of hazardous waste. The Toxic Substances Control Act, also administered by the EPA, mandates storage and usage procedures for industrial chemicals.

Disabilities. The Americans with Disabilities Act of 1990 (ADA) specifies how to make programs and facilities accessible to people with disabilities and requires employers to make those accommodations in the areas of employment, education, and commercial activities. This alone has had staggering implications for campuses, which have invested in technology and facilities for students and employees with special needs. As an example, supporting just one hearing-impaired, full-time student can equal the cost of a full-time employee.

Audit standards and mandated management practices. Institutions receiving federal support in the form of student financial aid or sponsored grants and contracts are subject to rules promulgated by the sponsoring federal agencies as well as OMB. These are typically referred to as the Uniform Guidance. The relevant OMB rules are provided in the Electronic Code of Federal Regulations. Specifically, Part 200 governs the broad categories of administrative requirements, cost principles, and audit requirements for federal awards. Subpart A addresses acronyms and definitions; Subpart

B addresses general provisions; Subparts C and D address preaward and postaward requirements, respectively; Subpart E, discussed below, addresses cost principles; and Subpart F addresses audit requirements. In addition to the items specified here, Appendix XI of Part 200 contains an annual compliance supplement with guidance to auditors conducting the audits required by the Uniform Guidance. Components of the supplement address both agency-specific and more general requirements.

Most colleges and universities should undergo only one federal financial audit annually. All federal agencies are supposed to rely on that audit to ensure proper management of their resources. In practice, however, many federal agencies go beyond the single-audit requirements of Subpart F and conduct their own audits. When this occurs, the audit process is governed by the agencies' individual policies and practices. One area of relief provided to large research universities is to reduce the frequency of the required in-depth federal audit.

Shared costs in federal grants and contracts. Institutions are expected to absorb some costs associated with conducting research that is sponsored through federal grants and contracts. Cost sharing may involve matching on individual grants and contracts. Especially frustrating to campuses is the federal government's complex approach to the reimbursement of F&A costs related to sponsored programs, as outlined in Subpart E of OMB's guidance for federal awards. In theory, the mandated calculation should support a negotiation designed to ensure the government and the institution each pay a fair share of the direct and indirect costs of federally sponsored projects. The federal government, however, has unilaterally disallowed some cost categories and imposed seemingly arbitrary caps on others. These actions force campuses to bear an increasingly larger share of the F&A costs of conducting research.

At the same time, the government has imposed additional requirements that increase the amount of unreimbursed costs by incorporating provisions of the Cost Accounting Standards Board (CASB) in OMB Circular A-21, Subpart E's predecessor. Many of the CASB standards, initially designed to address issues in the for-profit defense contracting industry, do not recognize the nonprofit approach taken by colleges and universities. One particularly burdensome requirement applies to institutions that receive the largest amount of federally sponsored support. These institutions must prepare and submit a comprehensive filing with the federal government—the DS-2 Disclosure Statement—describing their accounting practices in significant detail. If they subsequently change anything addressed in the disclosure statement, they must justify the change to the government.

Although accountability for the use of taxpayer funds is appropriate and necessary, some requirements are excessive and impose significant additional costs on institutions. For instance, the receipt of grant and contract funds comes with strict accounting requirements, affecting both direct project expenses and the institution's method for claiming project-related indirect costs. Cumbersome processes, collectively referred to as effort reporting, require faculty, staff, and graduate students to document the effort they devote to sponsored projects. The institution must have a methodology to ensure that each project is charged only the appropriate salary for the amount of effort invested by those working on the project.

Equally daunting are regulations related to federal student financial aid programs that provide scholarship, loan, or work-study funds to students. The rules specify how and when funds may be disbursed, the methodology for returning funds to federal programs when students withdraw before a term ends, and the collection procedures that must be used to recover amounts loaned. These complex regulations change regularly, making it difficult to remain in compliance. As is the case with sponsored programs funding, however, the benefits of federal financial aid funds far outweigh the costs of compliance and the negative impact on institutional flexibility. In fact, few institutions could survive if their students did not participate in the federal student aid programs.

Special costs of teaching hospitals and clinics. Although primarily targeted to hospitals and physicians serving the general public, the Health Insurance Portability and Accountability Act of 1996 (HIPAA) imposes significant burdens on higher education student health and counseling clinics, which must ensure the privacy and security of patient information.

In addition, institutions with teaching hospitals and clinics are subject to a wide range of restrictions and guidelines. Topics addressed include review of patient care, patient privacy, accreditation and licensure, accounting procedures, control and care of drugs and blood, use of radiation, and use of human and animal subjects for research purposes.

Higher education is unlikely to receive relief from these regulatory mandates any time soon. As much as the Trump White House had touted regulatory relief, most of the attention has been directed toward manufacturing and industry. As long as the federal government continues investing significant amounts in postsecondary education, it will seek ways to ensure that institutions operate effectively and efficiently—and not always in that order.

ISSUES UNIQUE TO PUBLIC INSTITUTIONS

In addition to the federal regulations affecting all higher education institutions, public institutions must comply with regulations imposed by state agencies and departments. The following represent just some of the areas in which states have promulgated regulations affecting public colleges and universities. (It should be noted that many of the same issues have impacts on independent institutions. The main difference is that these institutions have chosen to adopt rules that affect their operations. For public institutions, the choice was not theirs alone.)

Formula allocation procedures. In general, budget formulas guide institutions in developing their funding requests. Formulas are intended to simplify what otherwise would be a complex process for determining the level of support required to operate an institution. The formulas, however, do not represent how campuses actually operate. In fact, they are nothing more than a form of shorthand to ease the difficult process of allocating scarce resources. It is almost never the case that the formulas are used to make allocation decisions *within* the institution.

The restrictiveness of formula allocation procedures stems not from their use as a means to generate budget requests, but from the perception of formulas as an implicit or explicit commitment of how funds will be used. The more that state-level decision-makers perceive the formula as an instrument of accountability—as opposed to a tool for allocating resources—the more complex it becomes to manage the variety of activities taking place on campus. In this way, formulas can lead to a more restrictive budgetary environment.

Enrollment ceilings. To control institutional demand for financial support, some states have imposed enrollment ceilings on colleges and universities. The state usually agrees to support instructional and other costs up to the level required to serve the target enrollment. That leaves institutions to absorb the excess costs of educating students at levels beyond the target—or simply decide not to admit those students. A backlash to this approach has led many states to replace enrollment ceilings with appropriation formulas, which are adjusted to manage the state's financial commitment. The burden still falls on the campus to find resources to finance its operations, but the state does not become the target of an unhappy population.

Some states employ enrollment thresholds when making their appropriations. The state establishes a bandwidth for enrollment projections of, for example, plus or minus 2 percent of a specified target. If actual enrollments fall within the 5 percent range, the appropriation remains unchanged. If enrollments exceed the projection by more than 2 percent, the state provides additional funds to accommodate the increased enrollment. Similarly, if enrollment is lower than the floor of the bandwidth, the institution receives less funding. In this example, the institution would cover any funding deficiency caused by enrollments exceeding the projection by 2 percent or less and retain the full appropriation if enrollments fall short but within 2 percent of the projection.

Performance funding. One of the major shifts taking place in some states is in the area of performance-based funding. A number of states have shifted away from funding via enrollment-based formulas toward funding on the basis of achieving specified outcomes. The challenge with this approach is the lack of agreement on measurable outcomes to guide appropriation distributions. Moreover, in some cases, the outcomes being identified actually represent outputs (e.g., graduation rate) that can lead to unintended consequences. Although graduating students is critically important, undue emphasis on it can create incentives for suboptimal approaches. For instance, public high schools are awarding diplomas to students who may not have mastered the academic content the diploma represents. There is the same potential in higher education if the wrong outcomes are identified.

Appropriations bill language. The contents of the state appropriations bill may restrict an institution's flexibility. Some states include all institutional resources in the appropriation—even resources that do not come from taxpayers. Other states appropriate only the resources provided directly by the state. In general, the fewer items addressed in the appropriations bill, the more control the institution has over its resources.

Many states use the appropriations bill to regulate activity within colleges and universities. This approach can be troublesome because, unlike the more typical process for establishing state regulations—which usually involves department and agency staff—appropriation bills tend to be developed by legislators and their staff. Without the expertise of staff from departments and agencies, it is possible—if not probable—that the bill will have impacts beyond what the legislature anticipated. Items that might be addressed in this manner include faculty productivity, student-faculty ratios, travel, intercollegiate athletics, campus security, technology standards, and distance education. Serious problems may arise with this oversight mechanism because states usually don't have provisions to waive legislation.

State agency staff. Many state agencies and departments directly influence daily operations on public college and university campuses. State agencies, for example, often draft statewide plans for higher education, review new and existing academic programs, weigh in on budget requests, and usually have a say on proposed capital projects. In addition, staff members in various state legislative and executive offices influence the development of policies affecting campuses and, in some states, wield tremendous power over financial matters affecting higher education.

Position control. States commonly control the number of authorized employee positions at public institutions. Some grant campuses a great deal of latitude to determine the mix of employees, setting an overall maximum number of positions and leaving the detailed decision-making to the institutions. Provided they don't exceed the maximum at any point during the year, the institutions can hire as needed. Other states attempt to control only full-time employment and leave institutions with the flexibility to rely on part-time employees or independent contractors for some services.

Still other states prescribe the number and types of employees a campus may employ in a given period. This approach limits the way in which salaries and wages are spent and may prevent the institution from optimally deploying staff and faculty resources in response to changing needs.

Year-end balances. It is not unusual for colleges and universities to spend a disproportionate amount of their annual budgets in the latter part of the fiscal year. In many states, this flurry of activity is driven by a requirement to revert unexpended funds to the state treasury at year-end. Unfortunately, such "budget balance sweeping activity" may lead to purchasing unneeded materials and supplies to avoid returning funds. It's usually based on the thinking that unexpended funds may lead to future budget reductions because legislators will believe the budget was too generous.

The overall goal should be to expend resources for those things that are necessary in time for them to be available when they are needed. A more rational policy allows unspent funds to be carried forward from one fiscal year to the next. This policy reflects the reality that the timing of an expenditure may be as critical as the expense itself. When carryover is allowed, institutions and their departments no longer feel obliged to spend every dollar just to avoid the appearance of having more resources than needed.

Some institutions operating in states that allow carryforward of funds don't extend the same flexibility to their own units. In doing this, the institution essentially encourages units to spend unwisely to avoid losing funds in future budgets. Admittedly, managing the budgets to allow carryforward is difficult and time-consuming, but it usually leads to improved effectiveness. Institutions that invest the effort to manage the carryforward process will achieve better operating results and more effective resource utilization.

In general, states rely on controls rather than incentives or accountability to ensure that funds are expended appropriately. A common method for distributing appropriated resources is the allotment process. Essentially, this rationing process makes appropriated funds available to institutions on an established schedule, such as monthly or quarterly. The more frequent the allotments, the greater flexibility institutions enjoy. Because purchasing commitments usually require having the funds on hand, receiving less frequent allotments may force a campus to postpone some purchases.

Salary savings targets. A few states rely on a management device intended to force the early return of a portion of an institution's appropriation. Such programs are known by various names, including salary savings, budgetary savings, turnover savings, vacancy savings, and forced savings. State agencies, including public colleges and universities, are expected to return a specified portion of their total appropriations, usually expressed as a percentage of salaries and wages. The practice is most prevalent in states that do not allow carryover of unspent funds as well as in states that budget personnel costs using a line-item approach.

States created these programs when they began focusing on unspent amounts at year-end related to position vacancies at agencies and institutions. This approach can be problematic for colleges and universities because it often takes a long time to recruit faculty, especially at senior levels. By specifying savings targets and requiring the return of the funds throughout the year, rather than at year-end, some states can increase appropriations in a given year and accelerate the distribution of those funds. In other cases, however, states use such programs to reduce the level of support provided to higher education.

Salary savings programs do not generate new resources but shift existing resources. They merely recognize that not all compensation can be spent in a given period. Rather than allow state agencies and institutions to make judgments about how best to use the savings, the states capture the savings and then use them to fund specific initiatives or increase contingency reserves.

In most cases, a higher education institution meets the specified target by either holding back enough resources from the appropriation or passing the savings target on, pro rata, to all campus units receiving state funding. The first approach ensures the institution will meet its savings target, but it shields the units most likely to generate salary savings through turnover. It also enables units to retain the savings from position vacancies and use them for internal activities that may not reflect the highest institutional priorities. The second approach ensures that individual units do not benefit from savings at the expense of other institutional priorities. On the other hand, distributing the target among all units can place a large burden on the smaller ones, which may not experience the turnover needed to generate the required savings.

A third approach combines the first two. Rather than meet the target completely from central resources or distribute it to all units pro rata, the administration assigns the majority of the target to the major budget units and allows them to determine how their departments will meet the target. Some administrators assign variable targets to their departments, thereby shielding the highest-priority areas, while others distribute the target pro rata to all departments within the major budget unit. Shortfalls arising when departments are unable to meet the target due to a lack of turnover are addressed on a case-by-case basis.

Topics of Discussion

Issues of greatest importance will vary by institution and by state. Here's just a sample of what state-level officials and campus representatives might discuss during their interactions:

- ▶ Acceptance by four-year institutions of credits for courses taken at public two-year institutions
- ▶ Auxiliary enterprise policies, especially as they relate to competition with the private sector
- ▶ Budget review practices
- ▶ Continuing education, evening programs, and summer programs
- ▶ Debt policies
- ▶ Deferred maintenance
- ▶ Distance education
- ▶ Economic development
- ▶ Faculty workload standards
- ▶ Financial aid policies
- ▶ Funding formulas
- ▶ Fundraising activities and the role of foundations
- ▶ Investment policies
- ▶ New facilities needs and infrastructure renewal
- ▶ Procurement policies
- ▶ Relative importance of athletics and whether it can be subsidized by revenues from other areas
- ▶ Research policies and funding
- ▶ State appropriations—both operating and capital
- ▶ Sustainability
- ▶ Technology transfer
- ▶ Time to degree
- ▶ Travel policies
- ▶ Tuition and fee policies, especially as they relate to access and affordability

In addition to the above issues affecting all colleges and universities, institutions receiving state support are affected by an additional set of laws, regulations, and policies. They vary from state to state but address issues as diverse as enrollment ceilings, staffing levels, and reversion or carryforward of year-end budget balances.

Relationship between state policy makers and higher education institutions. The operating environment in public higher education varies tremendously from state to state. Some states rely on a central system office to oversee all public institutions. In other states, individual campuses are freestanding entities and not part of a state system. Still others use a combination: Some campuses are part of a system, while others operate as freestanding entities with their own governing boards. As another option, states may rely on the use of a coordinating body in place of a central system office. The coordinating agency serves as an interface between the executive and legislative branches and the individual campuses.

Regardless of the organizational model, public institutions must ensure that key decision-makers in their state have an in-depth understanding of the issues colleges and universities confront. Even when a state system or coordinating agency advocates on their behalf, campus officials must leverage opportunities to interact directly with state executive and legislative staff as well as with staff from state agencies that influence higher education.

Formal opportunities for interaction occur on a semiregular basis—for example, at legislative budget hearings or capital project review hearings. Although important, such formal interactions may carry less overall significance than the informal contact that occurs from time to time—for example, at college athletic events. The informal exchanges between campus representatives and state-level decision-makers at sporting events provide the opportunity to share information and advocate for specific decisions that will provide the maximum benefit to the institution.

MINORITY-SERVING INSTITUTIONS (MSIS)

Before leaving this area, there is one more major issue to consider in terms of the political and regulatory environment—MSIs. This term has specific meaning in U.S. higher education and refers to three different sets of institutions. The most well-known include historically black colleges and universities (HBCUs). These institutions—established prior to the Civil Rights Act of 1964—enroll and serve primarily, but not exclusively, African American students. There are both public and private colleges and universities among the approximately 100 HBCUs in the United States, all of which are eligible for federal funding under Title III of the Higher Education Act.

Also eligible for federal grants are Hispanic-serving institutions (HSIs). There are nearly five times more HSIs than HBCUs because the designation is available to any accredited degree-granting institution with Hispanic or Latino students comprising 25 percent or more of its undergraduate population.

The final, and smallest, category of MSIs is tribal colleges and universities (TCUs). There are approximately 30 such U.S. institutions, and their essential characteristic—in addition to serving Native American students (both American Indians and Alaska Natives)—is that they each are controlled and operated by an American Indian tribe or Alaska Native village.

KEY POINTS

▶ The current federal regulatory climate for higher education is in a state of flux as a result of the termination of some regulations prior to the availability of their replacements.

▶ Higher education institutions are subject to a wide array of external mandates affecting how they conduct their operating and capital activities.

▶ The federal government is responsible for the vast majority of rules and regulations to which higher education institutions are subject. Although their total resources provided pale in comparison with the resources provided by state governments, the impacts of the federal requirements far outweigh those of the states.

▶ The Higher Education Act is the comprehensive legislation affecting American higher education, and it has not been reauthorized in more than 10 years.

CHAPTER 3: THE ECONOMIC ENVIRONMENT

The financial health of all institutions is linked with the national economy, which is increasingly connected to the world economy.

The U.S. economy suffered serious damage with the Great Recession. The annual deficit peaked at $1.4 trillion in 2009,[11] and the total national debt grew to $14 trillion in 2010.[12] This represented the largest one-year debt increase ever at $1.7 trillion. The situation had improved significantly by 2017 with the deficit dropping to $665 billion[13] and the national debt falling to $20.5 trillion,[14] an increase of only $516 billion over the previous year. Though somewhat volatile, the Dow Jones Industrial Average has achieved record highs multiple times since 2017, and unemployment rates equaled modern lows during 2018. From a macro perspective, there are many reasons to be optimistic about the economic future of the United States.

The big question facing colleges and universities—particularly publics—is when will their resourcing return to the funding levels enjoyed prior to the recession? Although state support increased during 2017 in absolute dollars, on an inflation-adjusted basis, institutions continue to lag prerecession levels. Moreover, nothing has been done to restore the ground lost during and after the recession. In other words, institutions have not been made whole for the support they didn't receive between 2009 and 2012.

Delivering high-quality education is an expensive endeavor. As of 2016, the United States had just under 4,600 degree-granting institutions, including public, independent, and for-profit institutions. In fiscal year 2015-16 (the most recent year for which data are available), there were total expenses of $355 billion in public institutions,[15] $189 billion in independent institutions,[16] and $16 billion in for-profit institutions[17] for a combined total of $560 billion. This represents slightly more than 3 percent of the average U.S. Gross Domestic Product for 2015-16 of $18,372 billion.[18] These funds were expended in support of 20 million full- and part-time students[19] enrolled in 4,583 degree-granting institutions.[20]

The same economic and political pressures that affect major social programs across the country are experienced by colleges and universities.

Exacerbating the impact of these pressures is the increased demand for resources from higher education's competitors. The remainder of this chapter focuses on the major economic and related issues having the greatest impact on higher education—their implications and various ways in which colleges and universities are responding. Many of the topics are also covered in terms of their financial relevance in Chapters 4 and 6 addressing revenues and expenses, respectively.

SUSTAINABILITY

When sustainability entered the higher education lexicon, it was focused primarily on ecology and related issues. Significant attention was paid to matters as routine as the recycling of plastic, paper, and aluminum cans. Eventually, attention became focused on the ways in which the built environment affects the planet. This coincided with the establishment of the U.S. Green Building Council and its LEED program—Leadership in Energy Efficiency and Design. An early mark of sustainability distinction for many colleges and universities was completing the first campus building to achieve LEED status.

From these early days, sustainability has taken on much broader significance. Like many industries, higher education continues to face pressures related to going "green." And while other industries occasionally hear from special interest groups, few of them have higher education's built-in, vocal constituency. Students, who often have a formal voice in the way activities are conducted on their campuses, champion sustainability— through environmental, social, and economic means—as a way to protect their future and preserve the planet.

Economic sustainability has grown to include the full range of activities that either provide financial resources or consume them. A primary emphasis for all institutions is managing resources to ensure they are used wisely and contribute to the long-term financial viability of the institution.

Social sustainability refers to the way an institution coexists or interacts with its community and neighbors. An institution, for example, may invest in the local economy for housing, transportation, or neighborhood beautification, and the ways in which these are carried out impact the lives and livelihood of others.

Environmental sustainability may be the broadest application of the concept because it encompasses all of the effects an institution has on the planet through energy consumption, impacts on natural resource, the generation of waste through everyday operations, etc.

Numerous higher education associations, including APPA: Leadership in Educational Facilities, NACUBO, and the Society for College and University Planning for instance, tackle various issues related to sustainability. Several of the associations cosponsor the CampusERC, the environmental resource center for education. However, the Association for the Advancement of Sustainability in Higher Education (AASHE) serves as the umbrella organization focused on providing resources and educating the higher education community about sustainability issues. It has established a framework that institutions can use to measure their sustainability performance. STARS—the sustainability tracking, assessment, and rating system—is a self-reporting framework through which institutions can measure and monitor their sustainability efforts. AASHE has established a very broad definition of sustainability "encompassing human and ecological health, social justice, secure livelihoods, and a better world for all generations."[21] The goal of STARS is to allow institutions to establish measurable objectives for sustainability at the campus level in the areas of environmental, social, and economic performance.[22]

Whereas the early emphasis for sustainability on campuses may have been recycling, it now encompasses every facet of college and university operations and activities. Included are a wide range of topics addressing a diverse spectrum of issues. They include the way in which curriculum and research address sustainability as a topic for study and investigation, the implications of sustainability for procurement practices, and living wages for both institutional employees and those of contractors serving the institution.

AASHE organizes sustainability issues in four broad categories: academics, engagement, operations, and governance. Curriculum and research obviously comprise the academic focus, while engagement refers to both interactions and impacts on campus and with the public. Governance encompasses issues such as coordination and planning, diversity and affordability, investment and finance, and well-being and work. Operations is the largest category and includes air and climate, buildings, energy, food and dining, grounds, purchasing, transportation, waste, and water.

There is a large body of knowledge around sustainability in each of these areas and that creates new opportunities for campuses. On the other hand, it also creates pressures on colleges and universities to do more. There is a broad spectrum of actions that can be taken by institutions: Whether it's establishing standards related to waste in food-service contracts, building according to LEED standards, or capturing rain water for reuse in groundskeeping, opportunities exist. Some require a financial investment, while others actually result in either resource conversation or revenue generation. For instance, performance contracting in the area of utilities can reduce energy consumption while at the same time saving money—which is then shared with the firm that provided capital and expertise for energy-conservation projects.

In summary, campuses need to recognize the actions they can take to enhance their sustainability effectiveness in all forms. One place to start is AASHE's STARS program because of its comprehensiveness and educational value. Another source of valuable information for campuses results from the joint effort by APPA and NACUBO to undertake the Key Facilities Metrics survey. Participation in the survey provides access to data to help institutions gain a deeper understanding of their built environment and how well it's being managed. Additionally, they should pursue operational strategies that help reduce adverse effects on the environment in any of several ways. For instance, through shifts from fossil fuels to renewable energy sources, construction practices that rely on recycled materials when possible, or campus transportation systems that incorporate energy-efficient people movers and bicycles. Similarly, opportunities exist to incorporate sustainability awareness in campus governance by educating senior leaders and boards to ensure that sustainability issues are considered whenever relevant topics are being discussed. This can be in the area of cultural considerations for campus minorities, living wage standards both for employees and contractors, and town-gown relations. Finally, economic sustainability must be considered in all aspects of resource management.

The Numbers for For-Profits

Between 2005 and 2014, the number of for-profit educational institutions grew from 879 to 1,424—the largest number in history.[56] At that time, for-profit colleges and universities accounted for 30 percent of all degree-granting institutions. This 62 percent expansion was staggering compared with the 6 percent growth in independent institutions and the 4 percent shrinkage among public institutions.[57] Things turned around dramatically during the next two years. While there was a net loss in total institutions from 4,724 to 4,583—representing a 3 percent contraction—by 2016, more than 11 percent of for-profit institutions ceased operations.[58] The number of for-profit institutions now stands at 1,262.[59] Over the same period, five of 1,625 public institutions were merged with other institutions and the number of independent institutions grew by 26.[60]

Enrollment data, available through fall 2014, show that the for-profit sector enrolled 1.6 million students, or 7.8 percent of the total enrollment of 20.2 million students.[61] Five years previously, for-profits enrolled more than 2 million students, representing 9.6 percent of the total enrollment of 21 million students.[62] There are a variety of factors that have affected for-profit institutions, and the most significant is the increased attention they received during the latter years of the Obama administration. Due to a number of large-scale issues—particularly the gainful employment standards—more scrutiny has been directed toward this sector, and it has led to some institutions shuttering and others being sold.

Figure 3-1

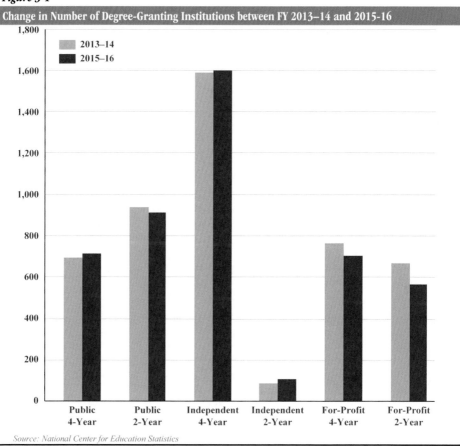

Change in Number of Degree-Granting Institutions between FY 2013–14 and 2015-16

Legend:
- 2013–14
- 2015–16

Categories (x-axis): Public 4-Year, Public 2-Year, Independent 4-Year, Independent 2-Year, For-Profit 4-Year, For-Profit 2-Year

Source: National Center for Education Statistics

COMPETITION

Higher education competes for both students and faculty. Attracting students may lead to tuition discounting—using institutional resources to award scholarships that encourage students to enroll. Essentially, the institution sets tuition at a higher level to generate revenues, which can fund scholarships for students who possess particular academic, athletic, or artistic talents deemed desirable by the institution in terms of the student body's diversity. Students may also receive aid simply because the amount they pay, over and above the aid received, represents a revenue contribution. (See

Chapter 5 for a detailed discussion of tuition and financial aid, including both aid funded from institutional resources and from public support.)

One hidden cost of higher education is the amount of foregone revenue represented by institutional financial aid provided through tuition discounting. Managing tuition discounting—both through pricing and institutional aid—is somewhat of an art. The goal is to recruit the most desirable student body while maximizing net tuition revenue.

Competition for faculty also has intensified. Historically, this issue was limited to research institutions, but it has expanded to other institutional categories as well. The investment required to attract a highly successful researcher—or a leading practitioner—can reach millions of dollars in terms of one-time and continuing investments.

The one-time investments tend to focus on facilities and related costs. Eminent researchers, for example, require significant amounts of space to accommodate the staff and equipment needed to support their research. This translates into significant facilities renovations and equipment investments when those faculty accept an offer.

Then there are the ongoing costs related to staffing. When a high-profile researcher leaves an institution, he or she usually brings research staff and graduate students to the new institution, which then must provide salaries and benefits. The prestige gained by having a high caliber of faculty on campus makes this effort a good investment. Still, the costs can stress an already constrained budget.

There are many other forms of competition as well. Competition for sponsored programs support from all sources—federal, state, corporate— is of significant concern to many campuses and is discussed later in the chapter. Competition for philanthropic support never ends. Although it's not a zero-sum game, it often feels that way on campuses. Furthermore, the competition isn't always between institutions and other charitable organizations. Sometimes, it's competition for donors among units within the institution. There is great consternation on the part of faculty over the amount of private support received by athletics because it represents giving that is not coming to academic areas. And within academic areas, there is a concern about gifts that are received by the library instead of by a school or college. Suffice it to say that competition is a fact of modern existence in the academy.

LABOR

Higher education institutions employed 3.9 million individuals during fall 2015,[23] just under two-thirds of whom were full time. Of the total employment, the largest single category is faculty, amounting to 1.6 million employees.[24] The next largest category consists of 441,000 staff providing office and administrative support.[25] Other large employment categories include graduate assistants (370,000); management personnel (257,000); various service occupations (244,000); computer, engineering, and science staff (232,000); business and financial operations staff (204,000); student and academic affairs staff (172,000); and myriad other specializations.[26]

In this labor-intensive industry, compensation—encompassing salaries, wages, and benefits—represents the largest single expense category. Current staffing models result in some campuses spending as much as 70 percent of their total budgets on compensation. What's more, the educational model does not lend itself to dramatic gains in productivity, which higher education defines as increases in the value of services without corresponding increases in costs.

Some service industries—particularly financial services—have employed technology to achieve significant gains in productivity without raising overall costs. In contrast, technology provides only marginal improvement in productivity within higher education. Certainly, instructional technology can dramatically increase the number of students taught by a single faculty member, via either large lectures enhanced by technology or web-based instruction. But for the most part, low student-faculty ratios are still believed to produce the most effective outcomes. A true gain in productivity requires the quality of the service to remain high while output levels increase. Thus, larger classes will increase a faculty member's productivity only if quality of instruction can be maintained.

With such a large proportion of costs being personnel related, achieving significant economies depends upon controlling salaries or benefits. When revenues remain flat or decline, average compensation or the number of employees must decline—or deficits may develop. Institutions that anticipate financial difficulties and plan accordingly will have more options than institutions that do not manage their finances effectively. Planning for possible personnel actions before a financial crisis erupts enables the institution to make informed decisions without the heightened pressure of the moment. (See Chapter 13 on responding to extraordinary financial circumstances.)

One of the common practices in other industries that has yet to arrive in meaningful ways in higher education is succession planning—especially at senior levels. It's not uncommon for line managers to have invested time to identify and groom successors, but it's not a pervasive practice. Moreover, it's nearly unheard of for senior leaders in an institution to be replaced by a subordinate. Instead, there appears to be a general bias in favor of external candidates. There is a huge cost to this practice both in dollars and institutional impact. Invariably, outside hires command higher salaries and more perks. Beyond that, however, is the common practice for senior leaders brought in from the outside to want to build their own team rather than rely on existing talent. The combination of these practices leads to significantly higher compensation levels for administrative positions. Apart from the fact that this alters the cost structure of the institution and places greater demand on revenues, it provides ammunition to various stakeholders who are concerned about the increased amount of resources devoted to areas other than instruction.

Baby boomer retirements have begun in earnest, and higher education is not exempt from this phenomenon. The workforce on many campus areas has aged in place and now is departing through retirements. This can represent a significant loss of institutional memory in the absence of an intentional plan to transfer knowledge to those who remain behind.

Even when plans have been developed in advance, serious financial difficulties may call for staffing reductions. These may be accomplished through normal attrition (for example, retirements and resignations), enabling an institution to avoid involuntary terminations when relatively small savings are needed. If large-scale savings are needed, however, involuntary personnel actions are inevitable. Be aware that cutting faculty and staff positions will dramatically affect morale—especially if done over a short time period. Moreover, rapid workforce reductions are difficult to accomplish in higher education because of tenure and contracts.

Some benefit programs provide current protection for employees or their families. These include workers' compensation; health, life, and disability insurance; and unemployment compensation. Other benefits provide protection for the employee once he or she retires. This category includes Social Security, pensions, and postemployment benefits such as retiree health insurance. The cumulative investment in these benefits is substantial and continues to grow dramatically.

Some institutions, particularly independent ones, used to cover the full cost of most benefits—even family healthcare coverage, but employees now commonly share the cost of health insurance premiums today. In some institutions, the proportion of the cost borne by the employee has risen dramatically. Similarly, many institutions have converted their pension plans from defined-benefit—under which the institution was obligated to contribute enough funds to guarantee a specified level of retirement benefits based on age and service—to defined-contribution. The latter approach specifies the amount of current contribution required of the employer but does not guarantee a specific level of benefit.

These changes, coupled with the increasing popularity of retirement savings options for individuals, has resulted in many employees participating to the maximum extent possible in individual retirement accounts, 401(k) (income deferral) plans, and 403(b) (tax-sheltered annuity) plans. Yet other employees, especially hourly and younger workers, care less about benefits and are seeking higher current wages. This can be challenging for institutions because it is not possible to suspend benefits for classes of workers—especially workers who are relatively lower paid.

BUILT ENVIRONMENT

Most institutions invested heavily in facilities and infrastructure to accommodate increased enrollments and an expanding research enterprise during the 1960s, 1970s, and 1980s. The situation had stabilized somewhat during the 1990s, with expansion slowing down as the industry adjusted to various financial ups and downs, along with student demographic changes. However, leading up to the Great Recession, higher education had returned to an expansion mode in terms of new and upgraded facilities. Competition for students was fierce, and it was thought that the built environment could be a deciding factor in attracting prospective students to campuses. That changed significantly with the economic downtown, but there recently has been a return to more traditional behavior. As this edition is being written, there has been a slight uptick in interest rates that had plummeted during the economic recovery of the mid-2010s. Debt remains affordable for those institutions that are upgrading, renewing, or adding facilities, although some are beginning to pay more attention to the cost of borrowing as the Federal Reserve begins increasing interest rates.

There has been an ongoing state of concern within higher education as it relates to the buildings constructed during the second half of the 20th century. Many are nearing the end of their useful lives, and others—though still in service—have far surpassed their life expectancy. These buildings require disproportionately high investments in repairs and maintenance. Even relatively newer construction, if not maintained properly, can lead to increased operating costs.

This situation is particularly acute because many campuses routinely postpone needed maintenance to meet their budget numbers. Because the average person can't see many facets of facilities maintenance, senior administrators often elect to postpone needed investments. The problems then compound. A built environment not being properly maintained today costs more to operate tomorrow and deteriorates more rapidly. In addition, research demonstrates facilities that have fallen into disrepair can adversely affect student recruitment and retention.*

---

*For further information, see: Gary L. Reynolds & David Cain, *Final Report on the Impact of Facilities on the Recruitment and Retention of Students* (Alexandria, Virginia: APPA: The Association of Higher Education Facilities Officers, 2006).

While some institutions make no formal provisions for maintaining facilities, others have established policies that prohibit the addition of new facilities unless adequate resources are available to maintain them. This approach will help address future maintenance needs, but it does nothing to address the current backlog. There are no established standards for investing in ongoing facilities maintenance, although institutions that annually spend 1.5 to 2 percent of the built environment's replacement value on routine repair and maintenance should be well positioned to avoid serious problems.

Facilities may require upgrading to accommodate new technologies or pedagogy. With the ubiquity of technology throughout an institution's operations, nearly every campus facility must be connected to the internet through hard wiring or wireless technology. And every learning space must accommodate technology used in support of instructional activities. Adding technological capabilities represents a significant cost but, without these investments, institutions will have trouble meeting the demands of faculty and students.

Ancillary costs—utilities, in particular—account for another substantial expense for institutions. Many institutions incur facilities costs around the clock, as they provide services through auxiliary units that serve students 24 hours per day. Given the significance of these expenses, it behooves institutions to optimize systems to save energy while still providing a comfortable environment.

Performance contracting offers one means of potentially reducing utilities costs. It involves partnering with energy conservation firms, which are compensated based on savings they achieve through reduced energy costs. Another tactic is using long-term debt to finance energy conservation investments. With relatively low interest rates, an institution with sufficient debt capacity and access to the requisite expertise in energy conservation can achieve significant ongoing savings with a relatively small initial investment.

A number of campuses have established various types of revolving funds that can finance energy-savings initiatives. In some cases, the institution undertakes energy (or other utility) projects that, over time, will result in lower operating costs. However, the amounts previously budgeted remain at the same levels, and the net savings are used as a revolving fund to undertake future projects that will reduce overall utility costs.

Another major opportunity available to institutions is public-private partnerships (P3). Under these arrangements, a third-party developer constructs a project on or near campus after executing an agreement with the institution. The agreements specify the financial terms and any related responsibilities of the parties. For instance, with a student housing project, it's typical that the institution commits to assigning students to the project to help ensure high occupancy rates. It's also possible that the developer arranges to accommodate residence life staff who operate under the direction of the institution's residence life management.

Other P3 arrangements are possible. For instance, one institution entered a 50-year agreement that transfers control of its entire inventory of parking to a third-party investment firm in exchange for a substantial lump-sum payment. Another form of P3 affects bookstore or dining operations. In these arrangements, one of the major bookstore or dining vendors executes a contract with the institution to provide the relevant services in a net-revenue-sharing arrangement. In addition to the traditional business terms for these arrangements, it's not uncommon for the company to invest significant sums to upgrade the physical character of the bookstore or dining venues. Though not usually referred to as P3, the principles of the arrangements are very similar to more common P3 projects.

TECHNOLOGY

As society depends more on technology, institutions must keep pace to meet their own needs and to teach the most current technologies to their students. To boost their efficiency, institutions have invested heavily in administrative software and technologies that bring increased capabilities. In fact, technology is the second fastest-growing expense category in higher education. To maintain and gain maximum benefit from the technology, institutions often must increase their investment in personnel as well.

Obtaining reliable data for technology expenditures proves difficult because much of the investment comes from decentralized budgets. It is believed that approximately 5 to 8 percent of total campus spending is devoted to various forms of information technology. Academic computing—comprised primarily of instructional technology and research—consumes approximately one-third of the total technology investment. Whether considered in terms of the costs of implementing administrative applications, such as an enterprise resource planning system (ERP) that can cost tens of millions of dollars or the introduction of technology into the classroom, technology is expensive.

Since 2000, EDUCAUSE—the higher education association focused on technology and related issues—has conducted an annual survey of its members to identify the most challenging technology issues they face. Throughout the 20-year history of the survey, there is only one year (2018)[27] when information technology funding did not appear on the list. It has ranked as high as first and as low as seventh, and on average, it has ranked third.[28] That ranking isn't surprising because technology represents a moving target. No sooner had institutions wired all of their facilities than wireless access became the standard. And as soon as campuses invested in wireless access, they had to start exploring ways to employ mobile technology in and outside of the classroom.

Technology has multiple facets with varying cost patterns. Hardware costs, for example, have declined significantly over time. Almost any item—whether a laptop computer, tablet, or cell phone—costs less today than it did a year or two ago. Yet when a computer wears out or becomes obsolete, users seek a faster and more powerful model with increased functionality—which leads to a higher-cost purchase. Similarly, new software has more features but also a higher price tag.

When the previous edition was being developed, the newest innovation was widely available open source software. It has been employed for some applications, but it has not taken off as predicted when originally introduced. One of the latest innovations is cloud-based technology. Though not necessarily new, its popularity has grown tremendously, and many campus administrative and instructional support applications now reside in the cloud. This introduces obvious security concerns, which have become pervasive across all forms of technology, but the benefits are believed to far outweigh the risks. And with the ability of the provider to apply upgrades and improve performance across platforms, institutional technology costs have decreased.

Another change introduced with cloud-based technology is the tendency to shift away from packaged solutions with multiple components to "best of breed" solutions. One of the benefits gained from the advent of ERPs is the reliance on packaged solutions that integrate seamlessly with the various modules and applications provided by a single vendor. With cloud-based software as a service, there is a growing trend of acquiring add-ons to supplement the ERP's capability. Various functionality is being acquired in this way to address customer relationship management, e-commerce, e-procurement, data mining to support business intelligence, and a plethora of other special-purpose applications that typically are not part of an ERP.

One benefit of this approach is that it creates the opportunity to examine current processes to abandon inefficiencies in favor of more sophisticated approaches. Moreover, these applications frequently provide an enhanced approach to responding to regulatory burdens. Rather than devote in-house staff to applying changes to maintain compliance with regulations, the providers assume this responsibility as part of their ongoing upgrade process for the applications.

The power of today's information technology infrastructure, applications, and tools means that institutions need more sophisticated staff in information technology operations, including network administrators, systems analysts, helpdesk support personnel, database administrators, and curriculum designers. Beyond staff working directly in information technology units, staff in other areas (for example, accounting, human resources, and facilities management) must possess as much technology knowledge as functional area expertise. An accountant, for instance, must be able to understand the principles of cost analysis as well as manipulate data using sophisticated analytical tools. An architect must be capable of employing computer-aided design techniques when developing the layout for space renewal as part of a building renovation. Whether for the accounting office or facilities management, staff must have more sophisticated—and, therefore, more expensive—skill sets than before.

Technology for academic purposes is likely to increase dramatically, especially in the area of web-enabled distance education. Based on 2015 data, more than 6 million students report taking at least one online course.[29] This represents 29.7 percent of all students.[30] Students participating exclusively via distance courses has reached 14.3 percent, and students participating in a combination of distance and nondistance courses is 15.4 percent of total enrollment.[31] Of these students, just under 5 million (83 percent) are studying at the undergraduate level.[32]

STUDENT PREPARATION

One difficult-to-measure impact relates to the students who arrive at college unprepared to do the work required to earn a degree. Students lacking the core skills necessary to perform at a college level, as well as those who do not have sufficient command of the English language, translate into extra learning labs, increased office hours for faculty, and tutoring services on campuses.

No matter how an institution addresses this problem, the impacts are significant. After assessing students' preparedness for college, some institutions slot them into remedial classes. In other situations, especially at public four-year institutions, state policy precludes offering remedial classes. Problems may also arise with student financial aid because some courses do not count toward participation requirements established for federal student aid programs.

There is a flip side to the issue of underprepared and unprepared students that can affect four-year institutions. Dual enrollment refers to the practice of high school students earning college credits before graduation. In extreme cases, there are students who arrive at their four-year institution having earned the equivalent of an associate degree. Similarly, some high school students take advanced placement courses that are more rigorous than traditional classes. Students successfully passing the related exams may receive college credit for the courses and/or be able to skip introductory courses when they begin their college studies.

CHANGING DEMOGRAPHICS

Historically, higher education primarily served a traditional college-age population of 18- to 24-year-olds. Nontraditional students, however, now represent a sizable percentage of enrollments—not just for two-year institutions, where they have always been a significant factor, but for four-year institutions as well.

During the 50 years (for which data are available) since passage of the first Higher Education Act in 1965, there have been only 10 years that saw enrollment decline from the previous year. Three of those years occurred between 2011 and 2014.[33] Enrollments had risen steadily from 1995 through 2010, and many assumed that this would be the case going forward. Even with up-and-down changes in the U.S. population growth rate, there was a high level of confidence that a U.S. education would be attractive to international students.

The projections regarding traditional students are based upon current enrollments in elementary and secondary schools, so they are considered reasonably accurate. The population of nontraditional students, however, holds significant potential for positive fluctuations for two reasons. First, the size of the potential nontraditional student population is substantially larger as a percentage of the total population. Second, and possibly more important, employers increasingly view advanced education as a requirement for meaningful employment. Although not all nontraditional students pursue degrees, more of them will seek advanced training and education.

An alternative way to examine these data is by sector. Degree-granting institutions enrolled 20.2 million students during fall 2014.[34] Of this number, 14.7 million students attended public institutions,[35] 4 million students attended independent institutions,[36] and 1.6 million students attended for-profit institutions.[37]

The United States is experiencing dramatic shifts in high school graduation numbers, and this trend is projected to continue for the foreseeable future. The total number of expected high school graduates in the United States in 2019–20 is 3.41 million.[38] This number is projected to fluctuate over the next dozen years, peaking at 3.56 million in 2024–25, before falling back to 3.3 million in 2031–32.[39] The net reduction in graduates from 2019–20 to 2031–32 is projected to be 109,000.[40]

Changing demographics will affect different regions and types of institutions in different ways. The majority of institutions recruit on a regional basis. Therefore, trends among high school graduates often point to what may happen at the college level. A range of factors has caused the number of annual high school graduates to vary by region. Of greatest significance is the general population migration from the North and Midwest to the South and West. The South continues to have the largest number of high school graduates annually, followed by the West. The Midwest and Northeast not only lag the South in terms of the number of graduates per year but, along with the West, they will see the gaps grow larger by 2032.[41]

The South—with projected 2019–20 graduates of 1.27 million—is expected to reach peak graduation of 1.35 million by 2024–25 before dropping back to 1.27 million in 2031–32.[42] It is the only region that is projected to have a net gain in high school graduates (1,800) during the period under review.

The West's projected graduates during 2019–20 of 819,000 are projected to top off at 862,000 in 2023–24 before dropping to 789,000 by 2031–32[43]—a net loss of 30,000 graduates during the period. The biggest projected drop will occur in the Midwest, which is expected to fall from 721,000 graduates in 2019–20 to 673,000 graduates in 2031–32[44]—a net loss of 48,000 graduates. There is significant fluctuation during the period with projected graduations peaking at 733,000 in 2024–25 and falling steadily until 2031–32.[45]

Similar to the Midwest, the Northeast is expected to see fluctuation during the period with three different years projected to show increased numbers of graduates over the preceding year. However, the overall change is expected to be negative to the tune of 34,000 fewer graduates in 2031–32 as compared with 2019–20. The number of graduates in 2019–20 is projected to be 597,000 with 563,000 expected in 2031–32.[46] In the regions with decreasing graduation projections, institutions that are tuition dependent and attract one type of student—such as traditional day students or students interested in just a few areas of study—may face an enrollment challenge.

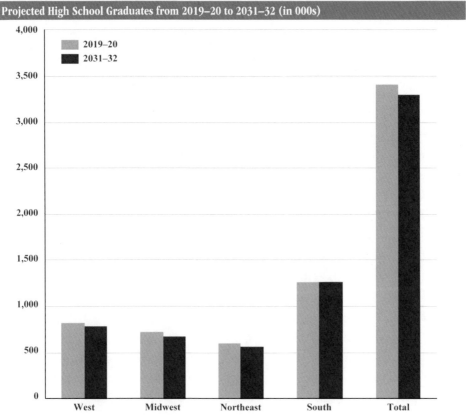

Figure 3-2

Projected High School Graduates from 2019–20 to 2031–32 (in 000s)

Source: *National Center for Education Statistics*

The International Scene

Although they still represent a relatively small percentage of the total student population in the United States, international students make a difference—especially for some institutions. During the most recent 10-year period, total international student participation in for-credit education demonstrated sustained growth with numbers increasing each year. Starting in 2007–08, when 567,000 international students were enrolled, participation grew to 891,000 by 2017–18.[63] An additional 203,000 visitors on F-1 visas were engaged in Optional Practical Training (OPT) related to their studies.[64] This brought total international participation to 1.1 million in 2017–18.[65] As a percentage of total enrollment, international participants (including OPT) grew from 3.5 percent to 5.5 percent during the 10 years ended in 2017–18.

China and India remain the largest exporters of students to the United States by a very substantial margin. Together, they provided just more than half of all international students studying in the United States, with 363,000 and 196,000 students, respectively, during 2017–18.[66] The majority of international students enroll in traditional degree programs with 75 percent enrolled at the undergraduate and graduate level, 6 percent in nondegree programs, and 19 percent in OPT.[67]

The United States is a net importer of students, but there are a significant number of U.S. students participating in various forms of international study. Based on data for 2016–17, there were 333,000 U.S. students engaged in credit-based study-abroad programs.[68] And only a small minority of them emulate international students studying in the United States by being overseas for an extended period. Just over 2 percent of U.S. students studying abroad spend an entire year overseas.[69] The largest number, 63 percent, will travel only for summer, or a term of eight weeks or shorter.[70] The balance, slightly more than a third, will pursue a program of one semester or two quarters. In addition to students engaged in credit-based instructional programming, an additional 37,000 students—representing 10 percent of all U.S. students participating in study abroad—pursued noncredit coursework, internships, or educationally related volunteer opportunities.[71]

The International Scene

Another aspect of international education is the practice of U.S. institutions partnering, primarily with European and Asian universities, to create opportunities to extend the American institution's reach and reputation while also bringing international faculty and students to the United States. Some arrangements also create natural opportunities for U.S. students to study abroad at partner institutions via a more streamlined enrollment approach.

There are various forms for these arrangements. In some cases, there is a formal partnership agreement that details the rights and responsibilities of each party and establishes enrollment minimums and maximums. In other cases, U.S. institutions have purchased or leased real estate oversees to establish an international branch campus. Finally, in still other arrangements, a foreign government has contracted directly with one or more U.S.-based institutions to establish overseas campuses to supplement the educational opportunities in the foreign country. One of the primary objectives for the latter arrangements is access to high-quality education for the government's citizens.

Given these changing demographics, colleges and universities will continue to engage in intense competition for students—especially within regions with declining school-age populations. Even institutions not seeking to increase enrollments will attempt to improve the overall quality of their student bodies by aggressively pursuing transfer students, shifting to web delivery for many programs and courses, and offering classes at times more convenient to students. They're also likely to increase the amounts invested in institutional student aid.

SHIFTS IN FEDERAL FUNDING

The manner in which the federal government funds social programs in general, and higher education in particular, will greatly affect institutional revenues for the foreseeable future. On a relative basis, the U.S. government will direct fewer dollars toward higher education in the future because of several factors. Serious questions are being asked about the value of education, especially compared to its cost. Additionally, there are significant changes in funding philosophy and growing competition from other public sectors. In addition to the increased demands on Social Security and Medicare caused by the baby boomer generation's retirements, the federal budget must accommodate increased defense spending and interest obligations due to the burgeoning national debt.

Federal funds for higher education are divided between student financial aid and support of research through grants and contracts. Student financial aid represents a slightly larger share of the total. During federal fiscal year 2017, direct support to postsecondary education from the federal government totaled $121 billion.[47] Of this amount, $36 billion (26 percent) supported research conducted by colleges and universities.[48] The remainder, $101 billion (74 percent), was for various student financial aid programs.[49] (These figures do not include tax credits related to the Hope Scholarship or Lifetime Learning Credits Programs. Programs like these represent indirect federal support of higher education because the amounts are provided in the form of tax deductions or credits rather than direct funding. An additional $94 billion was provided through "off-budget" program support. Off-budget support refers to programs that are not subject to traditional appropriations through the federal legislative process. Examples include the Direct Loan Program, Supplemental Educational Opportunity Grants, and Federal Work Study.)

It is important to note that federal support for higher education does not favor either public, independent, or for-profit institutions. The federal government has pointedly avoided favoring one sector over the other; however, it has established special requirements for different sectors. For instance, independent institutions are subject to financial responsibility standards established by the U.S. Department of Education. These standards are designed to ensure institutional financial stability and to protect students participating in federal financial aid programs. Another example is the 90/10 rule applicable to for-profit colleges and universities. Under this rule, for-profit institutions must be able to demonstrate that at least 10 percent of their revenues are derived from sources other than federal financial aid.

Originally, the philosophy guiding federal support of higher education focused on enhancing access through student aid. Over time, the concept of access broadened to include not just low-income individuals but also the middle class. For many years, higher education was viewed as the primary driver of social mobility. As a result, federal support in the form of student assistance helped achieve societal goals by providing enhanced access to education.

As noted above, the U.S. student population has changed to include more part-time and adult students, including online learners, who seek college training while supporting families and maintaining jobs. Many of these students prefer a community college, where they can pursue education without sacrificing full-time employment. In addition, an increasing number of individuals are returning to college for recertification, to upgrade their professional skills, or to pursue training for an entirely new career.

For these and other budgetary reasons, the relationship between the federal government and higher education continues to evolve. The federal government now bears less of the overall burden of supporting students in pursuit of advanced education, with states and individual consumers of higher education (and their families) expected to bear a greater share of the costs. One example of this is the striking shift in financial aid from grants to loans. Another is the attention given to community service as a way for students to be relieved of the responsibility to repay federal loans.

STATE AND LOCAL FACTORS

Not too long ago, state and local government represented the largest single contributor of revenues to higher education. Then, as a result of the Great Recession, a major shift occurred. Although state and local government support continues to exceed higher education revenues from federal sources by a small margin, they have been overtaken by tuition and fees.

Of the $562 billion of revenue received by all public, independent, and for-profit degree-granting institutions during fiscal year 2015-16, tuition and fees represented $164 billion (29.1 percent). The next largest source was state and local government providing appropriations, grants, and contracts amounting to $88.5 billion (15.7 percent). Coming in third was the federal government, with appropriations, grants, contracts, and independent operations support totaling $74 billion (13.1 percent). The remainder came from various sources, including sales and services of auxiliary enterprises and hospitals, investment income, gifts, and miscellaneous sources.

Generally, the stronger the competition for resources in a state, the smaller the share allocated to any one social service. When states struggle financially, higher education's priority for state funding typically declines. There is nothing to suggest that this situation will change. In fact, other programs will likely place greater demands on limited state resources, resulting in further cuts to higher education support. Moreover, as the federal government increasingly shifts the burden for various social services to the states, relatively lower-priority services—including higher education—will receive smaller shares of state and local resources.

Another determinant of appropriations is the nature of a state's higher education structure. A system comprising many community colleges is considerably less expensive to operate than one with a comparable number of four-year institutions. Similarly, a system with multiple research institutions will have higher operating costs than one with only one research institution and several comprehensive institutions. Some states, particularly those in the Northeast, traditionally have a strong independent sector and depend on those institutions to enroll large numbers of students who otherwise would attend public institutions. A few states, such as New Jersey, experience a considerable outmigration of potential students and allocate relatively fewer resources to higher education. Some states, such as Maryland, base their contributions to the independent sector on the level of support for public colleges and universities.

Other state and local economic and political factors influence the financial fortunes of individual institutions. For example, the cost of energy and labor generally is lower in the Sunbelt than in the Northeast. Housing typically costs more in metropolitan areas than in rural areas, which factors into the salary structure for faculty and staff as well as the housing rates charged to students. State and local regulations, which often mirror federal programs, can increase an institution's costs in areas such as workers' compensation, safety codes, public health standards, occupational health and safety programs, unemployment compensation, and state retirement programs.

Another significant factor affecting many public institutions across the country is mandated tuition remission for active-duty military, first responders, spouses and dependents of deceased individuals in these categories, and others. Some states have created an unfunded mandate by requiring institutions to provide the educational opportunities with no form of support from the state. Other states have implemented a mechanism to provide at least limited support to institutions based on the number of such students enrolled at the institutions.

PHILANTHROPY

American higher education has relied on private financial support since John Harvard provided the 1636 gift to establish what has grown to become Harvard University. Many of today's colleges and universities, including several that now are part of state systems, were established through gifts from private individuals and/or religious institutions. In some cases, the gifts took the form of real estate, but there also were substantial amounts of cash given to establish or sustain colleges and universities.

Reliance on philanthropic support increased significantly in 1917 when the deduction for charitable contributions was added to the tax laws. It grew even more during World War II when the percentage of the employed U.S. population subject to income taxes rose to 75 percent. This reliance—if not dependence—continues today, although there are some concerns about the potential impact of the Tax Cuts and Jobs Act of 2017 because it increases the standard deduction. This could cause some donors to reduce their contributions due to the elimination of the tax benefit for contributions by individuals using the standard deduction.

One of the major challenges facing higher education is the competition for philanthropic support. More and more 501(c)(3) charities—those eligible to receive tax-deductible contributions—are established each year. Every one of them is a potential competitor for support that might otherwise be provided to colleges and universities. Coupled with this is the fact that donors are becoming more and more sophisticated. Unrestricted gifts are becoming rarer, and restrictions are becoming even more specific. Additionally, new gift approaches have developed that complicate things for the institutions.

Donor-advised funds (DAFs) represent one of the latest innovations. Although it is not a new vehicle, it's becoming more popular in higher education. Through these arrangements, a donor establishes a charitable vehicle to receive assets that produce a charitable tax deduction for the donor. The fund, which can be managed by the donor or others appointed by the donor, can identify a college or university (or one of its foundations) as a beneficiary, and the resources sit in the DAF until the donor recommends their distribution. Under these arrangements, the institution or foundation ends up negotiating with the donor for support.

Long before now, giving to colleges and universities has relied on complex arrangements. Traditional forms of gifts such as cash, marketable securities, real estate, etc. are being employed to fund various types of split-interest gifts. A split-interest gift is one in which the donor (or beneficiary identified by the donor) shares in benefits with the charity receiving the gift; hence the term "split-interest."

There are many forms of split-interest gifts, and each type has unique characteristics. However, all split-interest arrangements require the transfer of assets to a trust, charity (i.e., college or university), or a related foundation with stipulations about the treatment of earnings and the disposition of principal after some period of time. The vast majority of split-interest agreements have restrictions directing how the earnings or remaining gift will be used by the institution.

Under a charitable lead annuity trust, the assets are invested and a specified annual amount is made available to the institution or its foundation. At the end of the specified period, the remaining assets revert to the donor or are transferred to a specified beneficiary. A variation of this arrangement is a charitable-lead unitrust in which the specified amount is stated as a percentage of the trust's market value.

A charitable-remainder annuity trust is an agreement that requires the transfer of assets as above, but the periodic amount is paid to a designated beneficiary rather than the institution or its foundation. At the end of the specified period, the remaining assets become the property of the institution and must be used for the restricted purpose established by the donor. If no restrictions were established, resources may be used for any purpose. As above, there is a variation for this arrangement—a charitable remainder unitrust—which requires the payment of a specified percentage of the market value to the beneficiary rather than a specified amount.

Another variation is the charitable gift agreement. It operates in a manner similar to a charitable-remainder annuity trust but without a formal trust. The institution holds the resources and makes payments to a designated beneficiary for a specific period of time or until the beneficiary's death. Because no trust is involved, the assets transferred are immediately available to the institution and the obligation to the beneficiary becomes an institutional liability.

The increasing complexity of gift arrangements does not create a deterrent to pursuing or accepting gifts, but it does make things difficult for the development officers and others engaged in fundraising. Colleges and universities will continue to employ full-time fundraisers who work either in central development offices or in various decentralized operations serving colleges and schools, other academic units, and even athletics. Beyond these full-time staff, nearly all higher education executives and senior leaders have some responsibility for engaging in fundraising or supporting those that do.

During the fiscal year ended June 30, 2018, donors provided $46.7 billion of private support to higher education, representing a 7.2 percent increase over the prior-year level.[50] The support comes from four major sources: foundations, alumni, nonalumni individuals, and corporations. Foundations accounted for $14 billion of total support (30 percent),[51] alumni provided $12.2 billion (26 percent),[52] nonalumni pitched in with $8.6 billion (18.3 percent),[53] corporations provided $6.7 billion (14.4 percent),[54] and the balance of $5.3 billion (11.3 percent) came from other organizations.[55]

Finally, one of the most important factors in terms of philanthropic support for higher education is the condition of the national economy and, in particular, financial markets. There is a strong correlation between private giving to charities, including colleges and universities, and the performance of the stock market. The stronger the economy, the more private giving institutions receive. And beyond that, the better their endowments perform.

KEY POINTS

▶ Higher education is subject to the same economic forces as businesses and private individuals—and even more (e.g., competition for philanthropic support). The Great Recession took a major toll on all institutions, leaving a changed landscape. Reduced public support for higher education characterizes the "new normal."

▶ Higher education is a major industry, whether considered in terms of the number of institutions, the financial magnitude of operations, or the number of employees.

▶ The most significant economic issues facing colleges and universities are sustainability in all its forms, competition for students and staff, the built environment, technology, and funding.

▶ For-profit institutions had become a significant segment, once growing by leaps and bounds, but now has contracted to approximately 1,250 institutions serving 1.6 million students (down to less than 8 percent of all students attending degree-granting institutions).

CHAPTER 4: REVENUES AND RESOURCES

Institutions in the three sectors of higher education—public, independent, and for-profit—rely on a variety of sources for financial support. Although the sources are similar across the sectors, the relative reliance on a particular source depends on the institution's mission and character. Independent and for-profit institutions, for example, count more on student tuition and fees than do public institutions, which receive state appropriations to help defray the cost of attendance for in-state students. Large research-oriented universities receive a greater percentage of revenues from sponsors than would a comprehensive or two-year institution. Unlike for-profit institutions and colleges with smaller intercollegiate athletic programs, institutions with National Collegiate Athletic Association (NCAA) Division I athletics programs receive significant revenue from ticket sales.

A DIVERSE POOL

Clearly, higher education has a varied pool of resources with which to fund its operations. The key for institutional success is having a diverse mix of revenues, with reduced reliance on any one source. Table 4-1 presents each of the various sources and types of revenue received by colleges and universities as well as the nature of the transaction that generates the revenue. All institutions rely on nearly every source, although significant variances exist in the degree of reliance on the source across the sectors.

Table 4-1

Institutional Resources by Source and Type		
Source	**Type of Revenue**	**Received Through**
Students	Tuition and fees	Customer charges
	Interest income	Loans
Government		
Federal	Appropriations	Subsidy
	Grants and contracts	
	–Direct costs	Exchange for services
	–Indirect costs	Reimbursement for services
State and local	Appropriations	Subsidy
	Grants and contracts	
	–Direct costs	Exchange for services
	–Indirect costs	Reimbursement for services
	On-behalf payments [1]	Subsidy
Private		
Individuals	Contributions	Gifts
	Contributed services [2]	Subsidy
Corporations and foundations	Contributions	Gifts
	Grants and contracts	
	–Direct costs	Exchange for services
	–Indirect costs	Reimbursement for services
	Contributed services [2]	Subsidy
Investments	Endowment income	Investment of long-term pooled funds
	Investment income	Investment of idle cash balances
Sales and services	Educational activities	Customer charges
	Auxiliary enterprises	Customer charges
	Hospitals and clinics	Customer charges
Licenses	Royalties	Contractual payments
Notes:		

1. *It's common for some state governments to pay insurance, fringe benefits, or debt service for public colleges and universities. Such payments are recognized as both revenues and expenses.*
2. *Contributed services meeting specified criteria are recognized as revenues by independent institutions but not by public institutions. The value of such services is recognized as both a revenue and an expense.*

Every institution participating in Title IV federal student financial aid programs must participate in a series of annual surveys that collect their revenues, expenses, staffing levels, and various factors related to tuition and financial aid. The data presented below are for fiscal year 2015-16 (the latest available) and draw from the database housing the information collected annually. The database is housed in IPEDS. The IPEDS data are presented based on the classification structure for the respective sector's financial reporting model and in the order presented in IPEDS reports. Because of the reporting variances, along with recognition and measurement differences, direct comparison of revenues between the sectors is not possible.

Source	Public	Independent	For-Profit	Total	Percent
Total Higher Education Institution Revenues, Fiscal Year 2015-16 (amounts in billions)					
Tuition and fees	$ 76.593	$ 72.117	$ 15.348	$ 164.058	29.1%
Federal appropriations, grants, and contracts	49.835	23.457	0.713	74.005	13.1%
State appropriations, grants, and contracts	86.313	2.162	0.047	88.522	15.7%
Private gifts, grants, and local contracts	38.939	28.623	0.016	67.578	12.0%
Sales and services of educational activities		7.044	0.329	7.373	1.3%
Sales and services of auxiliary enterprises	27.581	17.593	0.312	45.486	8.1%
Sales and services of hospitals	45.956	24.107		70.063	12.4%
Investment return	3.938	-2.737	0.027	1.228	0.2%
Independent operations	1.538			1.538	0.3%
Other	33.698	10.209	0.267	44.174	7.8%
Total Revenues	**$364.391**	**$182.575**	**$17.059**	**$564.025**	**100%**
	64.6%	32.4%	3.0%	100.0%	

Source: National Center for Education Statistics

PUBLIC INSTITUTIONS

The IPEDS revenue data for public institutions are divided into three broad categories: operating, nonoperating, and other revenues and additions. There are subcomponents in each of these categories that match the public institution financial reporting model. Table 4-2 details the total revenues by source for each sector. The discussion below is accompanied by tables that disaggregate the sector revenue between four-year and two-year institutions.

Table 4-3

Public Higher Education Institution Revenues, Fiscal Year 2015-16 (amounts in billions)			
Source	4-Year	2-Year	Total
Operating Revenues			
Tuition and fees	$ 67.536	$ 9.056	$ 76.592
Federal grants and contracts	26.107	1.574	27.681
State grants and contracts	6.006	1.782	7.788
Local and private grants and contracts	12.470	0.507	12.977
Sales and services of auxiliary enterprises	25.984	1.598	27.582
Sales and services of hospitals	45.956		45.956
Independent operations	1.538		1.538
Other	19.994	0.870	20.864
Nonoperating Revenues			
Federal appropriations	1.618	0.049	1.667
State appropriations	53.088	14.114	67.202
Local appropriations	1.052	11.162	12.214
Federal nonoperating grants	11.524	8.964	20.488
State nonoperating grants	3.009	1.848	4.857
Local nonoperating grants	0.171	0.212	0.383
Gifts available to support operations	8.208	0.283	8.491
Investment return	3.783	0.155	3.938
Other	4.723	0.750	5.473
Other Revenues and Additions			
Capital appropriations	4.741	1.723	6.464
Capital grants and gifts	3.457	0.299	3.756
Additions to permanent endowments	1.106	0.013	1.119
Other	6.793	0.568	7.361
Total Revenues	**$ 308.864**	**$ 55.527**	**$ 364.391**

Source: National Center for Education Statistics

Figure 4-1

Public Higher Education Institution Revenues, Fiscal Year 2015-2016

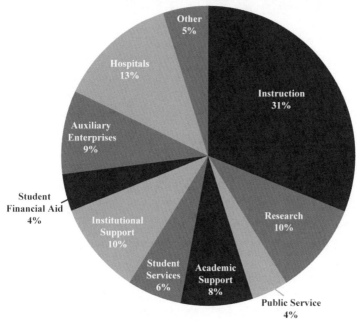

Source: National Center for Education Statistics

OPERATING REVENUES

Operating revenues are generated from the day-to-day recurring activities taking place within colleges and universities. In broad terms, they represent the ongoing teaching, research, and service activities, along with the activities needed for their support. Operating revenues provide resources for the multitude of operational activities taking place daily on college and university campuses.

TUITION AND FEES

Chapter 5 presents a more thorough discussion of tuition and fees and their importance to colleges and universities. The key point to understand is that the tuition and fees reported in IPEDS reflect the net amount after being reduced by the financial aid recognized as revenue elsewhere in the institutions' financial statements. This avoids double counting the revenues. Independent and for-profit institutions account for tuition and fees using the same approach.

Public four-year institutions' tuition and fee revenues amounted to $67.5 billion, which represented 21.9 percent of total revenues.[72] The comparable amounts for two-year institutions were $9.1 billion and 16.3 percent.[73]

FEDERAL GRANTS AND CONTRACTS

Federal grants and contracts are the revenues provided to support research, training, and various other sponsored activities. They are a significant revenue source, especially for research universities. Grants are awarded on a competitive basis, and the federal government does not differentiate by sector or type of institution when making awards.

The largest portion of funding comes from the following agencies and departments: the U.S. Department of Agriculture (USDA), U.S. Department of Defense (DOD), U.S. Department of Energy (DOE), National Institutes of Health (NIH) in the U.S. Department of Health & Human Services (HHS), National Aeronautics and Space Administration (NASA), and National Science Foundation (NSF).

Most grants include funds for direct and indirect costs or F&A. Direct costs represent the expenses incurred by the institution in undertaking the activities being supported by the grant or contract. These funds must be used exclusively for the purposes specified in the award. Typical direct costs include the salary and benefits for the principal investigator, graduate assistants, and technicians assigned to the project. Additional direct costs would include supplies, travel, and any other operating expenses authorized under the award.

The portion of the award related to indirect or F&A costs typically is calculated as a percentage of direct costs. It is intended to reimburse the institution for expenses not directly related to the specific project, but that provide necessary support to the project's activities. Examples include utilities, operating expenses of various units that support the project's business aspects (such as the accounting and payroll offices), and the cost of maintaining the space in which the project is conducted.

The applicable percentage is determined through a periodic negotiation with either of two federal cognizant agencies—HHS or the Office of Naval Research. Each institution develops a proposal using one of two formats and presents it to the relevant agency. The more common format, the long form, is used by research universities. A simplified method is available for institutions with a modest amount of federal support for research or other sponsored activities. The long-form proposal takes months to prepare and is the result of an extensive series of calculations that frequently rely on specialized cost studies related to administrative support costs as well as facilities-related costs (e.g., repair and maintenance, depreciation). Once agreed upon, the rate typically is in force for three to five years. (An adjunct to this negotiation is an extensive study related to fringe benefits. The same federal agency will approve rates to enable the institution to recover the costs of fringe benefits for various categories of employees such as faculty, staff, and others.)

Federal grants and contracts in public four-year institutions contributed $26.1 billion of revenues, which represented 8.5 percent of their total revenues.[74] Much less research is conducted at public two-year institutions, and their revenues from federal grants and contracts were only $1.6 billion and 2.8 percent of total revenues.[75]

STATE GRANTS AND CONTRACTS

State grants and contracts are similar to federal grants and contracts in terms of what they support but do not represent as large a revenue source. As a percentage of total revenues, they are significantly more important to public two-year institutions than public four-year institutions.

Public two-year institutions received $1.8 billion of state grants and contracts, which represented 3.2 percent of their total revenues.[76] The comparable numbers for public four-year institutions were $6 billion and 1.9 percent of total revenues.[77]

LOCAL AND PRIVATE GRANTS AND CONTRACTS

It is unfortunate that local grants and contracts are combined with private grants and contracts in IPEDS because this hides the significance of sponsored support from private sources such as foundations and industrial sponsors. Comparatively speaking, local grants and contracts represent a minor source of support for public higher education institutions.

Corporate- and industrial-sponsored program support is important to selected disciplines—particularly engineering and medicine. Corporate sponsors typically are more willing to pay both direct and indirect costs but not necessarily at the same levels as the federal government. This is especially true of the pharmaceutical industry, which provides significant resources for clinical drug trials. In most of these arrangements, the corporate sponsors have established an arbitrary cap on overhead. Because the dollars are so substantial, institutions have accepted this practice and receive reduced reimbursement as compared with most federal sponsors. Foundations also tend to pay either little or nothing for F&A costs, instead directing the vast majority of their support to direct costs. However, many foundations have more flexible guidelines about what can be reimbursed as a direct cost.

Public four-year institutions received combined local and private grants and contracts of $12.5 billion, which represented 4 percent of total revenues.[78] Public two-year institutions' support from local and private grants and contracts was only $507 million, which represented just less than 1 percent.[79]

SALES AND SERVICES OF AUXILIARY ENTERPRISES

Auxiliary enterprises constitute the various business-like operations of colleges and universities. These are self-supporting activities providing services and goods to students, faculty, staff, and—to a more limited extent—the general public. Operations include bookstores, dining, residence halls, parking, and various other activities provided as a convenience for campus stakeholders. At most NCAA Division I institutions competing in football, athletics revenues are reported as auxiliary enterprises. This would include ticket sales, sponsorships, licensing of brand apparel, etc.

As with tuition and fees, auxiliary enterprises revenues are reported net of any financial aid applied to the payment of fees for housing, dining, books, etc. Those receipts would be reported as revenues for the respective services to avoid double counting the revenues.

Public four-year institutions received $26 billion of revenues via auxiliary enterprises, which was 8.4 percent of their total revenues.[80] The comparable amounts for public two-year institutions were $1.6 billion and 2.9 percent.[81]

SALES AND SERVICES OF HOSPITALS

Hospitals are essential to the teaching of medical students. The United States has approximately 150 accredited medical schools that are served by more than 400 accredited teaching hospitals and health systems. Institutions with medical schools either own and operate hospitals directly or contract with local hospitals to provide a venue for hands-on training of aspiring physicians and other healthcare professionals. Accounting standards require that their financial results be reported separately from other sales and services operations, and this results in a separate presentation in IPEDS.

Hospital and medical clinic revenues are relevant only for public four-year institutions. No two-year institutions report revenue from hospitals despite the need for hands-on experience for their healthcare professions students. The experience is gained through affiliation agreements between the two-year institutions and the healthcare operations in their communities. Public four-year institutions generated $46 billion of hospital revenues, which amounted to 14.9 percent of their total revenues.[82]

INDEPENDENT OPERATIONS

Independent operations is the category used to report activities within major federal research laboratories financed on a contract basis with the government. Examples include the Lawrence Livermore National Laboratory (LLNL) affiliated with the University of California, Berkeley. Because of the magnitude and unique nature of its operations, LLNL is not considered core academic operations and is presented in a separate category within the university's audited financial statements.

Similar to the situation with hospitals, only public four-year institutions manage these federal laboratories. The revenues they generate amounted to $1.5 billion and less than 1 percent of total revenues.[83]

OTHER OPERATING REVENUES

Colleges and universities are complex organizations with a wide range of activities. The standard categories specified for the reporting of revenues do not always align with the unique operations carried out in public colleges and universities. Therefore, a catchall category is required and labeled other operating revenues.

Public four-year institutions realized $20 billion of revenues from miscellaneous sources, which amounted to 6.5 percent of their total revenues.[84] Public two-year institutions realized $870 million of other operating revenues, which represented 1.6 percent of their total revenues.[85]

NONOPERATING REVENUES

Nonoperating revenues fall into two broad categories for public institutions. The first includes resources that are generated via reoccurring subsidies from various sources such as governments and donors. The other category of nonoperating revenues includes resources that are not received regularly or are precluded from being reported as operating revenues. Accounting standards relevant to public colleges and universities require that both types of revenues be segregated from operating revenues.

FEDERAL APPROPRIATIONS

A relatively small number of public institutions are supported by federal appropriations, which are awarded through a legislative process. This process is different from federal grants and contracts because such funds are competitively awarded and support individual projects, while the appropriations provide targeted resources for large-scale operations in a specific programmatic area. Federal appropriations are directed primarily to support four-year institutions designated as land-grant institutions (Land-grant institutions eligible to receive benefits under the Morrill Acts of 1862, 1890, and 1994). A very small number of two-year institutions share in appropriated revenues from federal sources.

Federal appropriations provided $1.6 billion and less than 1 percent of revenues at public four-year institutions.[86] The comparable numbers were $49 million and less than 1 percent at public two-year institutions.[87]

STATE OPERATING APPROPRIATIONS

Second only to tuition and fees, state appropriations are the largest revenue source for public institutions—both four-year and two-year. These resources generally come with few strings attached. They are available to support ongoing operations and generally can be used for any legal purpose consistent with the institution's mission. A state government occasionally may attach specific conditions applicable to the use of appropriated dollars, but this is the exception rather than the rule. Although the public four-year institutions receive significantly more state operating appropriations, these revenues represent a much greater share of total revenues for public two-year institutions.

Public two-year institutions received $14.1 billion of revenue from state operating appropriations, which amounted to 25.4 percent of their total revenues.[88] Public four-year institutions realized state operating appropriations of $53.1 billion, which represented 17.2 percent of total revenues.[89]

LOCAL OPERATING APPROPRIATIONS

While there are relatively few locally supported public four-year institutions, there are a significant number of public two-year institutions that receive appropriations from municipal or county sources. Similar to federal and state operating appropriations, these resources are available to support the ongoing operations of local public colleges.

Public two-year institutions were supported to the tune of $11.2 billion, which represented 20.1 percent of their total revenues.[90] Comparable amounts for public four-year institutions were only $1.1 billion and less than 1 percent.[91]

FEDERAL NONOPERATING GRANTS

Federal nonoperating grants are of significant importance to both public four-year and two-year institutions. The largest component of this revenue category is receipts for Pell Grants, the largest federal need-based scholarship program. For many public institutions—both four-year and two-year—a substantial percentage of their students qualify for Pell Grants. This is another category that has more significance as a share of total resources for public two-year institutions than their four-year counterparts.

Federal nonoperating grants at public two-year institutions amounted to $9 billion, which represented 16.1 percent of their total revenues.[92] Public four-year institutions received $11.5 billion of federal nonoperating grant revenue, which amounted to 3.7 percent of their total revenues.[93]

STATE NONOPERATING GRANTS

The revenues reported as state nonoperating grants tend to be similar in nature to Pell Grants. These are financial aid resources that are triggered either by need or merit through an established state program. The amounts available generally are small in comparison to other government resources at the state level but still important to the students qualifying to receive them.

Public two-year institutions generated $1.8 billion of revenues through state nonoperating grants, which represented 3.3 percent of their total revenues.[94] The comparable amounts for public institutions were $3 billion and 1 percent.[95]

LOCAL NONOPERATING GRANTS

The revenues reported as local nonoperating grants represent a somewhat insignificant revenue source for public institutions. These typically are one-time special-purpose grants that support a specific nonrecurring activity that is unrelated to capital projects.

The combined revenues from local nonoperating grants for public two-year and four-year institutions amounted to $383 million, which represented well less than 1 percent of their total revenues.[96]

GIFTS (OTHER THAN ENDOWMENT AND CAPITAL GIFTS)

Accounting standards relevant to public colleges and universities require distinguishing between gifts that are available for current operations and other gifts, which must be used for capital purposes or held for long-term investment as endowments. Endowment gifts must be invested, with only the earnings available for spending. Although both capital and endowment gifts are considered nonoperating revenues, they are presented in a separate category that is addressed below.

Another significant issue driven by accounting rules is the recognition of pledges (promises to give) in addition to amounts actually received. The rules governing public institutions' recognition of pledges of gifts for current (as opposed to endowment and capital gifts) are generally straightforward. Revenue is recognized when eligibility requirements have been met. This means that revenue frequently is recognized well in advance of the receipt of cash.

Gifts may be restricted or unrestricted. The former come with stipulations dictating how and when they can be expended. Although institutions value all gifts, unrestricted gifts provide the greatest flexibility because they can be spent for any institutional purpose, including current operating expenses, student aid, capital construction, payment of debt service, etc. Restricted gifts are often directed toward purposes the institution might otherwise undertake with its own resources. When gifts restricted for the same purpose are received, the institution's unrestricted resources that were allocated to the purpose may be redirected to fund other activities that may not be as well supported.

All public and independent institutions depend on gift support to varying degrees, but these revenues are not as reliable as many other sources. In years of economic downturn, for instance, personal and corporate giving often declines. Similarly, philanthropic foundations may shift priorities away from higher education and divert their support to other areas of interest. A growing trend among foundations and even individual donors is to attach increased accountability and performance measures to their support.

Furthermore, donors remain sensitive to changes in tax laws. For instance, there is widespread concern about the changes that may result from passage of the Tax Cuts and Jobs Act of 2017. The personal standard deduction has been increased significantly by the act. There is fear that this will discourage individuals from making contributions to charities, including higher education, because they may no longer benefit from a charitable deduction.

Even events on campus can affect the level of giving—either positively or negatively. The greater the reliance on private support, the more an institution needs contingency funding to protect against shortfalls.

State laws often prohibit public institutions from engaging directly in fundraising activities. In response, they have created foundations to pursue private support and facilitate activities that, though appropriate, may violate guidelines for the use of state funds or be subject to cumbersome processes. Typically, these foundations both raise and manage funds in support of the public college or university. The vast majority of gifts received are directed to the foundations rather than to the college or university.

In some cases, the public institution's governing board also governs the affiliated foundation. In this arrangement, the foundation operates almost like a department of the institution, with the central administration guiding most financial decisions. This creates a more reliable funding source because the institution controls the distribution of the foundation's resources.

In other situations, the foundation operates independently of the institution. In these cases, the institution typically requests specific support from the foundation but isn't assured of receiving it. The foundation may have established different priorities for its support. These priorities typically still benefit the institution but may be of less importance to the institution at that time. Foundations rarely decline a specific request from the institution, but there have been some isolated instances of friction between institutions and their related foundations. In a few notable cases, a public institution and its affiliated foundation have found themselves embroiled in lawsuits. And in even rarer instances, institutions have withdrawn a foundation's right to use the institution's name in its fundraising activities.

In most cases, the only gift revenue recognized by a public college or university is when the foundation transmits resources to the institution to support objectives established by the donor. The other infrequent occurrence that would result in public institutions recognizing gift revenue is when a donor requires a gift to be managed directly by the college or university.

Public four-year institutions recognized $8.2 billion of nonendowment gifts, which represented 2.7 percent of total revenues.[97] The comparable numbers for their two-year counterparts were $283 million and less than 1 percent.[98]

INVESTMENT RETURN

Colleges and universities typically have idle cash balances that they invest to generate additional revenues. In addition to cash management programs, many institutions have sophisticated short-term investment programs. Both cash and short-term investment programs are intended to use all available resources to generate additional revenues for the institution. Investment income earned on idle cash balances or through short-term investments usually can be used for any institutional purpose. (For the public institutions not authorized to locally manage investments of idle cash or other resources, the state typically invests the funds and retains the earnings.)

Many institutions also manage long-term investment programs. The majority of resources invested in long-term programs are in the form of endowments. (At most public institutions, an affiliated foundation holds the endowment investments, and the practices discussed here would also apply to them.)

Endowment income is subject to special spending rules. All or a portion of annual endowment income—which might include dividends, interest, rents, and royalties—is made available for the purpose specified by the donor or, if no purpose was specified, for the institution's general purposes. A formula, referred to as the spending or payout rate, typically determines the amount available in a given year. This rate usually is based on the endowment's historical market value and may also factor in the amount made available during the previous year. The goal of the spending rate is to provide a stable and predictable flow of resources to support the endowment donors' goals in perpetuity. Prudent management principles require that the endowment be managed and invested to ensure that it can support current purposes and those anticipated over the longer term. Balancing the needs of current objectives against those expected in the future is referred to as intergenerational equity. The goal is to establish investment and spending patterns that meet current needs while preserving sufficient resources to be able to meet needs into perpetuity.

If investment income generated by the endowment in a given year is not sufficient to meet the spending level authorized under the payout calculation, the income is supplemented from accumulated gains and market appreciation. These amounts build up when the combined value of gains, market appreciation, and investment income exceeds the amount determined under the spending rate calculation. When this occurs, the organization reinvests the funds in the endowment as a hedge against future economic downturns.

The use of a spending rate based on historical market values has a smoothing effect on payout rates. It removes some of the volatility that can occur with long-term investment returns. A typical approach relies on a 12-quarter rolling average of historical market values. This approach has proven effective over time although, in some periods, continued negative returns eventually caused the budget support from endowment income to flatten or decrease. This was the case in fiscal year 2010, when the major financial losses in fiscal years 2008 and 2009 caused the endowment income available through the spending formula to decline.

Uniform Prudent Management of Institutional Funds Act (UPMIFA)

With the exception of Pennsylvania, all states and the District of Columbia have passed a version of UPMIFA. This act builds on the foundation established in the early 1970s with development and enactment of the Uniform Management of Institutional Funds Act (UMIFA).

UMIFA provided explicit authorization for endowments to be managed using the "total return concept." The key element of this concept is distributing a portion of accumulated gains and market appreciation with cash income (for example, dividends and interest) when the income is not sufficient to meet spending requirements.

Before enactment of UMIFA, many endowments were managed under trust theory, which requires the segregation of income from principal (original gifts), gains, and market appreciation. Under trust principles, only cash income was available to support endowment objectives. This resulted in many endowments being heavily invested in fixed-income securities to maximize the value of current income. The emphasis on current income came at the expense of the long-term increase in value that could be achieved by investing in equity securities (e.g., the stock market).

Uniform Prudent Management of Institutional Funds Act (UPMIFA)

UPMIFA continues the key elements of UMIFA but adds one critical feature that proved fortuitous when financial markets collapsed during the Great Recession in 2008—the ability to spend from "underwater" endowments. Many endowments dropped in value below the amount of their original gift because of the market collapse—what's referred to as being under water. Under UMIFA, such underwater endowments could not receive income distributions in amounts greater than the cash income generated. Given the history of distributing earnings using the total return concept—that is, income plus a portion of accumulated gains and market appreciation—there now was insufficient income to meet the spending needs of many endowments.

UPMIFA takes into consideration the reality that endowments are perpetual resources that must last forever, requiring them to weather highs and lows in the financial markets. As such, UPMIFA allows the prudent use of a portion of principal to meet current spending needs. Many institutions have used the new spending authority to sustain programs supported by endowments that find themselves under water. They're carefully dipping into principal to fund programs while they wait for the endowments' market value to recover.

Endowment size varies dramatically as does the level of restrictions. The overwhelming majority of investment revenue from endowments is restricted and must be used for the purpose specified by the donor. In terms of size, Harvard University holds the largest higher education endowment—in 2018, its market value was just over $38 billion.[99] Among public institutions, the University of Texas System had the distinction of having the largest endowment in 2018 at $30.9 billion.[100] Though impressive, these endowments are not representative of higher education overall. In fact, the combined value of the 802 endowments participating in the 2018 NACUBO-TIAA Study of Endowments amounted to over $616 billion.[101] Only 104 out of nearly 4,600 institutions had an endowment valued at $1 billion or more, which represented $474 billion in total market value.[102] Of the participating institutions, 330 had an endowment valued at $100 million or less.[103] More than 9 percent of the participants had endowments valued at less than $25 million.[104] Thus, for the vast majority of institutions, endowment income was quite small.

The reporting of investment return is influenced significantly by the presence of fundraising foundations supporting public colleges and universities. Although large amounts are realized through investment operations—especially for endowments—the vast majority of these revenues are recognized in the foundation financial statements and not those of the institution. As discussed above, the primary source of investment income recognized by public colleges and universities is through the investment of idle cash balances in operating accounts. This is a relatively modest source of revenue even at the largest institutions.

The revenue from investments at public four-year institutions totaled $3.8 billion, which represented 1.2 percent of total revenues. This is a much less significant revenue source for public two-year institutions with only $155 million, which amounted to well less than 1 percent of total revenues.[105]

OTHER NONOPERATING REVENUES

Although there are a significant number of established categories within nonoperating revenues, as with operating revenues, some activities do not align with the specified categories. For that reason, many institutions choose to report some revenues in a catchall category labeled other nonoperating revenues. Though not terribly significant as a percentage of total revenues, they do provide much-needed resources for some institutions.

Public four-year institutions garnered the largest share of other nonoperating revenues with a total of $4.7 billion, which represented 1.5 percent of total revenues.[106] Comparable numbers for their two-year counterparts were $750 million and 1.4 percent.[107]

OTHER REVENUES AND ADDITIONS

CAPITAL APPROPRIATIONS

Public institutions rely on three major sources to obtain resources needed for the construction or acquisition of capital assets (buildings, major equipment, etc.): long-term debt, governments, and donors—the latter two of which provide revenues. Government appropriations for the built environment are hard to come by and nearly unheard of from the federal government—at least in recent years. Many states and some municipalities and counties (primarily for public two-year institutions) provide resources for construction of long-lived assets—either from taxpayer revenues or from bonds issued at the government rather than institution level. Without these resources, public institutions would find it difficult to accumulate resources for significant amounts of campus construction.

Public four-year institutions realized $4.7 billion of capital appropriations revenue, which amounted to 1.5 percent of their total revenues.[108] Public two-year institutions received $1.7 billion of capital appropriations, which represented 3.1 percent of their revenues.[109]

CAPITAL GRANTS AND GIFTS

As mentioned above, public colleges and universities rely on multiple sources for the resources needed to acquire or construct capital assets. In terms of revenues, nongovernmental resources come from donors—either individuals, corporations, or foundations. These take the form of outright gifts and foundation or corporate grants. Grants typically come with requirements that drive the institution to raise funds from other sources or use institutional resources to match the grants in whole or in part. Private individuals also provide gifts and occasionally require a matching component.

Public four-year institutions realized $3.5 billion in capital grants and gifts, which represented 1.1 percent of total revenues.[110] The comparable amounts for public two-year institutions was $299 million and less than 1 percent.[111]

ENDOWMENT GIFTS

As described earlier, endowment gifts are received from donors with a stipulation that the gift be held in perpetuity to generate investment earnings—current yield (e.g., dividends, interest, royalties), gains, and market appreciation through market growth. Most public institutions' endowments are held by related foundations and, therefore, do not appear among their revenues. However, there are instances in which a donor prefers to have a particular gift held by the institution rather than its foundation. In these cases, the gifts will be reported as revenues in this category.

Also relevant to this discussion is the issue of endowment types. This reporting category is reserved for additions to *permanent* endowments—those that must be held and invested forever. There are two other types of endowments, although both have become less common than in past years. One type is a term endowment, which must be invested and cannot be expended until the passage of a specified time period or the occurrence of a specified event. This type of endowment would be reported above with gifts because they do not qualify for inclusion as an addition to permanent endowments. As an example, assume a bequest is received from an estate with the stipulation that the proceeds be held for five years and, after the five-year period, the proceeds can be used to support whatever the donor specified. Alternatively, the stipulation could relate to an event occurring. For instance, a donor may make a substantial gift with a requirement that it be held and invested as a term endowment until the institution establishes a branch campus in another location. In the first case, the endowment will last for five years, while, in the latter case, the endowment will last until the branch campus is established. It is up to the donor whether the earnings on a term endowment may be spent currently for the specified purpose or are required to be added to the original gift or bequest to increase the amount of the term endowment.

The final form of endowment is a quasi-endowment, which has all the characteristics of a true endowment except that it is established by the institution rather than by a donor. As such, it is not a true endowment and can be invaded for current use. The resources used to establish a quasi-endowment may be restricted or unrestricted, and the earnings from the quasi-endowment will carry the same character as the underlying resource. For instance, the earnings on a quasi-endowment established with funds restricted for research will be restricted to that purpose. Earnings on a quasi-endowment established with unrestricted resources have no restrictions and may be used in whatever way management deems most appropriate.

Most institutions establish a minimum threshold and duration for funds to be established as a quasi-endowment. Because of the overhead of managing and investing the resources, the thresholds are fairly high and usually will align with minimums required for the establishment of a true or term endowment. Similarly, because endowments have a long-term investing horizon, it's common to require that quasi-endowments be established for a minimum of three or more years. Once sufficient resources are available that are believed to be surplus for at least three years, they will be designated by the board or management as a quasi-endowment and be pooled with true and term endowments for investment purposes. Again, as with term endowments, funds used to establish quasi-endowments would not be reported in this category because they do not represent additions to permanent endowments.

Recognizing that the majority of endowment gifts go to related foundations, the total amount of revenue recognized in this category by public institutions was very small compared to other types of revenue. It amounted to $1.1 billion and less than 1 percent of revenues.[112]

OTHER REVENUES AND ADDITIONS

As with the two previous broad revenue categories—operating and nonoperating—there are some unique resource inflows that do not fit neatly into one of the established subcategories for other revenues and additions. Generally too small to be reported as a separate subcategory, they are consolidated and presented as other revenues and additions. Compared with overall revenues, these are relatively small, but they are meaningful in some situations.

Public four-year institutions received $6.8 billion in other revenues and additions, which amounted to 2.2 percent of their total revenues.[113] Public two-year institutions generated $568 million of other revenues and additions, which represented 1 percent of total revenues.[114]

INDEPENDENT INSTITUTIONS

Table 4-4

Independent Higher Education Institution Revenues, Fiscal Year 2015-16 (amounts in billions)			
Source	4-Year	2-Year	Total
Tuition and fees	$ 71.440	$ 0.676	$ 72.116
Federal appropriations, grants, and contracts	23.414	0.043	23.457
State and local appropriations, grants, and contracts	2.155	0.006	2.161
Private, gifts, grants, and contracts	28.581	0.041	28.622
Investment return	-2.737	0.001	-2.736
Sales and services of educational activities	7.039	0.005	7.044
Sales and services of auxiliary enterprises	17.547	0.046	17.593
Sales and services of hospitals	24.108		24.108
Other	10.185	0.024	10.209
Total Revenues	$ 181.732	$0.842	$ 182.574

Source: National Center for Education Statistics

Figure 4-2

Independent Higher Education Institution Revenues, Fiscal Year 2015-16

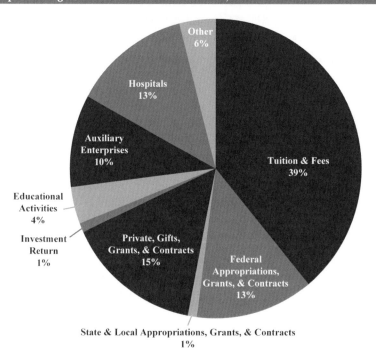

Source: National Center for Education Statistics

Independent institutions are not required to distinguish between operating and nonoperating revenues, although many choose to do so. Because the IPEDS data do not reflect this optional treatment, the following discussion focuses on revenues organized solely as reported in the order presented in the IPEDS reports. (Readers interested only in the revenues of independent institutions may still benefit from reading the explanations presented above for public institutions.)

TUITION AND FEES

As mentioned previously, independent institutions report tuition and fees net of financial aid awarded to students when the related revenue is reported elsewhere in their financial statements. This avoids double counting the revenue.

Independent four-year institutions received $71.4 billion of revenues from tuition and fees, which amounted to 39.3 percent of their total revenues. At more than a third of their total revenues, this was the largest revenue source for these institutions.[115] The situation was even more dramatic among their two-year counterparts whose tuition and fee revenues amounted to $676 million, which equated to 80.3 percent of their total revenues.[116]

FEDERAL APPROPRIATIONS, GRANTS, AND CONTRACTS

Although the independent institution revenue labels refer to the same types of revenues as for public institutions, combining them prevents alignment with reporting by public institutions and masks the fact that relatively few independent institutions receive federal appropriations. Many HBCUs receive Title III funds, and Gallaudet University—the liberal arts college for the deaf and hearing impaired—also receives an appropriation. Most others receiving an appropriation typically manage large-scale federal research laboratories on a contract basis (independent operations). Johns Hopkins University (Applied Physics Laboratory) and The University of Chicago (Argonne National Laboratory) are two examples of such arrangements. The vast majority of revenues in this combined category are for sponsored programs in the form of grants and contracts. These function in the same way at independent institutions as they do at public institutions. The grants and contracts cover both direct and indirect costs of the sponsored activity.

Independent four-year institutions' combined revenue from federal appropriations, grants, and contracts totaled $23.4 billion, which represented 12.9 percent of their overall revenue base.[117] The comparable numbers at independent two-year institutions were comparatively small at only $43 million, but this represented 5.1 percent of their total revenues.[118]

STATE AND LOCAL APPROPRIATIONS, GRANTS, AND CONTRACTS

Once again, this category includes revenues that are similar to those earned by public colleges and universities, but the accounting standards do not group them the same way for financial reporting purposes.

A number of states contract with independent colleges and universities for a wide variety of instructional services. Many of these arrangements involve purchasing student spaces in specialized programs such as health sciences. Some states support the acquisition of new facilities at independent institutions through special state grants and by allowing the institutions to issue tax-exempt debt through state or local authorities.

A small number of states provide direct support to independent institutions in the form of contracts based on full-time equivalent (FTE) enrollment of in-state students. Others appropriate funds to independent colleges and universities for capitation grants (i.e., a grant based on the number of in-state students attending a particular institution). Although state appropriations are rare among independent institutions, some states recognize that the institutions are relieving the state's obligation when they educate in-state students. Therefore, the states offer programs that provide revenues to independent institutions—both four-year and two-year—to compensate them for this effort. However, the majority of revenues in this category would be attributable to state grants and contracts.

The combined value of state and local appropriations, grants, and contracts at independent four-year institutions amounted to $2.2 billion, which represented 1.2 percent of their total revenues.[119] For independent two-year institutions, the comparable amounts were $6 million and less than 1 percent.[120]

PRIVATE GIFTS, GRANTS, AND CONTRACTS

Once again, the combination of private grants and contracts with gifts for independent institutions is not consistent with how public institutions report their revenues, but they represent the same types of revenues. A factor to keep in mind is that the category of gifts for independent institutions means all gifts—current, capital, and endowment. As such, it should be recognized that a sizable but undisclosed portion of these revenues are not available to support current operations.

Another consideration for some independent institutions with religious affiliations is the direct or indirect support provided by a religious organization. Such support would be included in this category and could take many forms. For some, it's an outright gift to support operations. For others, it represents contributed services through which a religious order compensates faculty assigned to teach at a given college or university. In other cases, the institution compensates the members of the order and then is reimbursed by the order. And for still others, the college or university operates in facilities owned by the religious organization with no requirement to pay rent.

Independent four-year institutions realized $28.6 billion of private gifts, grants, and contracts, which represented 15.7 percent of total revenues.[121] The comparable amounts for independent two-year institutions were $41 million or 4.9 percent.[122]

INVESTMENT RETURN

Investment return is a term that means the same for public and independent institutions, but it is not comparable because of the public institution practice of holding investments in related foundations. As such, the investment return for their endowments are reported by the foundations rather than the institution. Because of this, significantly more investment return revenue is reported by independent institutions during strong markets than would appear in their public institution counterparts. In the year under examination, markets did not perform as well and the losses were absorbed by the independent institutions directly rather than by a foundation.

Independent four-year institutions reported losses of $2.7 billion, which reduced total revenues by 1.5 percent.[123] Investment returns for independent two-year institutions actually were positive, albeit very small at $1 million, which represented well less than 1 percent of total revenues.[124]

SALES AND SERVICES FROM EDUCATIONAL ACTIVITIES

Sales and services of educational activities are not unique to independent institutions, but the public institution financial reporting model does not require their separate reporting and, therefore, the category does not appear in their IPEDS data. The category addresses revenues from the common practice of developing and offering salable goods and services while conducting educational activities. For instance, products developed in laboratories during instruction are sold to various parties. Many land-grant institutions operate dairy farms to educate their students in the management and operation of the farms. When dairy products such as milk, cheese, or ice cream are produced, some of it may be used in dining operations, but surplus amounts typically would be sold to the public via retail operations. Both public and independent institutions offer laboratory and other testing services, demonstration schools, hotels, theaters, etc.

Independent four-year institutions realized $7 billion of revenue from sales and services of educational activities, which represented 3.9 percent of total revenues.[125] The comparable numbers for independent two-year institutions were relatively small at $5 million and less than 1 percent of total revenues.[126]

SALES AND SERVICES OF AUXILIARY ENTERPRISES

There is no difference between the way in which public institutions and independent institutions operate and account for auxiliary enterprises. They are the self-supporting, business-like activities conducted by colleges and universities. Just as tuition and fees are reported net of any financial aid used to satisfy the students' financial obligations, auxiliary enterprises sales and services are reported net of financial aid applied to pay for their services.

Independent four-year institutions recognized $17.5 billion of revenues from sales and services of auxiliary enterprises, which represented 9.7

percent of their total revenues.[127] The comparable numbers for independent two-year institutions were $46 million and 5.5 percent.[128]

SALES AND SERVICES OF HOSPITALS

Hospitals are just as important to independent four-year institutions as they are to public four-year institutions. Similar to their public counterparts, no independent two-year institutions operate hospitals. If the institution operates a medical school, it needs access to hospitals for the applied elements of medical education. This is accomplished via either affiliation agreements between the institution and the hospital or by directly owning and operating one or more hospitals.

Independent four-year institutions generated $24.1 billion of hospital revenues, which amounted to 13.3 percent of total revenues.[129]

OTHER REVENUES

As is customary throughout all of higher education, the reporting model used by independent institutions does not identify every possible category of revenue. To the extent that independent institutions have miscellaneous revenue sources that do not warrant a separate category, they are combined and reported as other revenues. IPEDS mirrors this practice and reports other revenues in a separate category.

Independent four-year institutions' other revenues amounted to $10.2 billion and represented 5.6 percent of their total revenues.[130] The comparable numbers for their two-year counterparts were $24 million and 2.9 percent of total revenues.[131]

FOR-PROFIT INSTITUTIONS

Table 4-5

For-Profit Higher Education Institution Revenues, Fiscal Year 2015-16 (amounts in billions)			
Source	4-Year	2-Year	Total
Tuition and fees	$ 12.233	$ 3.116	$ 15.349
Federal appropriations, grants, and contracts	0.519	0.194	0.713
State and local appropriations, grants, and contracts	0.032	0.015	0.047
Private, gifts, grants, and contracts	0.014	0.001	0.015
Investment return	0.022	0.005	0.027
Sales and services of educational activities	0.304	0.025	0.329
Sales and services of auxiliary enterprises	0.255	0.057	0.312
Other	0.206	0.061	0.267
Total Revenues	$ 13.585	$ 3.474	$17.059

Source: National Center for Education Statistics

Figure 4-3

For-Profit Higher Education Institution Revenues, Fiscal Year 2015-16 (amounts in billions)

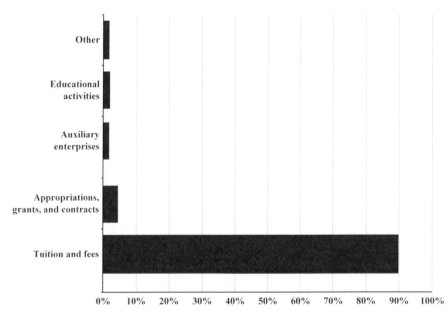

Source: National Center for Education Statistics

For-profit institutions garner a very small share of the total revenues earned by colleges and universities, which amounted to only 4 percent of total revenues. Nevertheless, it is a sector that attracts a significant number of students and warrants examination. Their reporting structure comes closest to that of independent institutions, but the differences in mission among the two sectors result in some significant variance among revenue sources. As with independent institutions, for-profit institutions are not required to distinguish between operating and nonoperating revenues. Because the IPEDS data do not reflect this optional treatment, the following presentation focuses on revenues organized solely as reported in the order presented in the IPEDS reports.

▶ For-profit four-year institutions earned $12.2 billion of **tuition and fee** revenues, which represented 90 percent of their total revenues.[132] Comparable numbers for for-profit two-year institutions were $3.1 billion and 90 percent.[133]

▶ **Federal appropriations, grants, and contracts** represented the second largest revenue source for for-profit institutions but still lagged tuition and fee revenues by a considerable margin. This category is where federal financial aid revenues are reported. Revenues at four-year institutions amounted to $519 million and 3.8 percent, while for two-year institutions, the amounts were $194 million and 5.6 percent.[134]

▶ For-profit institution participation in **state and local appropriations, grants, and contracts** was nominal—well less than 1 percent combined for both four-year and two-year institutions.[135] Their respective revenue totals in this category were $32 million and $15 million.[136]

▶ Similar to the previous category, **private gifts, grants, and contracts** were not a significant revenue source for for-profit institutions. Once again, the combined revenues amounted to significantly less than 1 percent of their total revenues.[137] For-profit four-year institutions generated $14 million of revenues in this category, while their two-year counterparts realized only $1 million of revenues.[138]

- **Investment return** was a relatively modest revenue source for for-profit institutions and represented well less than 1 percent of the combined revenues for four-year and two-year institutions.[139] The revenues for the former were $22 million and for the latter, $5 million.[140]

- For-profit institutions engage in various revenue-generating activities as an adjunct to their teaching operations. The **sales and services of educational activities** can take many forms, including clinical services in both medicine and dentistry, cosmetology services, automotive services, etc. For-profit four-year institutions realized revenues of $304 million, which represented 2.2 percent of total revenues.[141] The equivalent numbers for their two-year counterparts were $25 million and less than 1 percent.[142]

- **Sales and services of auxiliary enterprises** were reported in the same way as at public and independent institutions—i.e., net after deducting amounts for financial aid. The auxiliary enterprises revenues for for-profit four-year institutions totaled $255 million and 1.9 percent of total revenues.[143] For-profit two-year institutions earned $57 million of these revenues, which represented 1.6 percent of their total revenues.[144]

- Once again, the reporting model could not account for every revenue source in the established standard categories. For this reason, for-profit institutions employed the same practice as public and independent institutions and reported some items as **other revenues**. The amount of other revenues reported by for-profit four-year institutions was $206 million, which represented 1.5 percent of their total revenues.[145] The comparable numbers for for-profit two-year institutions were $61 million and 1.8 percent.[146]

The total revenues realized by all degree-granting institutions represent significant amounts. During fiscal year 2015-16, for public institutions, the total was $364 billion; for independent institutions, the number was more than $182 billion; and for-profits earned just over $17 billion. Collectively, the postsecondary education sectors represented a $564 billion enterprise in fiscal year 2015-16.

SHIFTING REVENUE PATTERNS

PUBLIC INSTITUTIONS

Table 4-6

Growth in Public Higher Education Institution Revenues from Fiscal Year 2010-11 to Fiscal Year 2015-16 (amounts in billions)				
Source	2010–11	2015-16	Increase/ (Decrease)	Percent Change
Operating Revenues				
Tuition and fees	$ 60.269	$ 76.595	$ 16.326	27.1%
Federal grants and contracts	29.821	27.681	-2.140	-7.2%
State grants and contracts	7.019	7.788	0.769	11.0%
Local and private grants and contracts	10.111	12.977	2.866	28.3%
Sales and services of auxiliary enterprises	23.606	27.581	3.975	16.8%
Sales and services of hospitals	30.999	45.956	14.957	48.2%
Independent operations	1.330	1.538	0.208	15.6%
Other	15.758	20.863	5.105	32.4%
Nonoperating Revenues				
Federal appropriations	1.947	1.667	-0.280	-14.4%
State appropriations	63.064	67.202	4.138	6.6%
Local appropriations	10.023	12.213	2.190	21.8%
Federal nonoperating grants	24.232	20.487	-3.745	-15.5%
State nonoperationg grants	3.405	4.857	1.452	42.6%
Local nonoperating grants	0.228	0.383	0.155	68.0%
Gifts available to support operations	6.287	8.491	2.204	35.1%
Investment return	14.216	3.938	-10.278	-72.3%
Other	6.889	5.473	-1.416	-20.6%
Other Revenues and Additions				
Capital appropriations	5.645	6.464	0.819	14.5%
Capital grants and gifts	3.746	3.756	0.010	0.3%
Additions to permanent endowments	0.965	1.119	0.154	16.0%
Other	4.913	7.362	2.449	49.8%
Total	**$ 324.473**	**$ 364.391**	**$ 39.918**	**12.3%**

Source: National Center for Education Statistics

Over time, there have been significant shifts in revenue levels overall as well as in individual categories. During the five-year period from fiscal years 2010–11 to 2015-16, public institutions' total revenues increased by

$40 billion, which represented a 12.3 percent increase at a compounded annual growth rate of 2.3 percent. Examining the changes within individual revenue categories is illuminating, especially for operating revenues.

Six of the eight operating revenue categories increased by more than the overall average revenue increase—some fairly dramatically—including several of the largest categories. The most significant percentage increase occurred for hospital revenues, which grew by $15 billion over the five-year period equating to a 48.2 percent increase. Also significant are the increases in tuition and fees and other operating revenues. The former's revenue growth amounted to $16.3 billion—27.1 percent—while the latter's was a smaller increase of $5.1 billion but at a larger percentage of 32.4.

Not surprisingly, given that the early years in this period were still being affected by the aftermath of the Great Recession, federal grants and contracts actually lost ground and dropped by $2.1 billion or 7.2 percent. Sales and services of auxiliary enterprises experienced significant growth and increased by $4 billion. But at 16.8 percent, this represented smaller growth compared with hospitals, other revenues, and tuition and fees—in that order.

Nonoperating revenues fell by 4.3 percent during the period, as the modest increases in some categories were overshadowed by significant reductions in others, resulting in an overall decrease of $5.6 billion. Both state appropriations ($4.1 billion and 6.6 percent) and local appropriations ($2.2 billion and 21.8 percent) increased substantially. Similarly, increases were seen in state nonoperating grants ($1.5 billion and 42.6 percent) and gifts available to support operations ($2.2 billion and 35.1 percent). However, these increases were not large enough to offset the significant losses in investment return ($10.3 billion for a negative 72.3 percent) and other nonoperating revenues ($1.4 billion—a decrease of 20.6 percent).

The final piece of the puzzle, other revenues and additions, realized substantial growth of $3.4 billion, which represented a 22.5 percent increase. Unfortunately, more than 70 percent of the increase ($2.4 billion) occurred in the other revenue category, so it's not clear what the influences might have been.

INDEPENDENT INSTITUTIONS

Table 4-7

Source	2010–11	2015-16	Increase/ (Decrease)	Percent Change
Contraction in Independent Higher Education Institution Revenues from Fiscal Year 2010–11 to Fiscal Year 2015-16 (amounts in billions)				
Tuition and fees	$ 60.070	$ 72.116	$ 12.046	20.1%
Federal appropriations, grants, and contracts	24.320	23.457	-0.863	-3.5%
State and local appropriations, grants, and contracts	2.165	2.162	-0.003	-0.1%
Private, gifts, grants, and contracts	22.097	28.623	6.526	29.5%
Investment return	53.574	-2.737	-56.311	-105.1%
Sales and services of educational activities	4.979	7.044	2.065	41.5%
Sales and services of auxiliary enterprises	14.798	17.593	2.795	18.9%
Sales and services of hospitals	17.521	24.108	6.587	37.6%
Other	7.608	10.209	2.601	34.2%
Total Revenues	**$207.132**	**$182.575**	**$-24.557**	**-11.9%**

Source: National Center for Education Statistics

Independent institution revenues are no less volatile than those of their public institution counterparts. The five-year period from fiscal years 2010–11 to 2015-16 saw a significant drop in revenues of nearly $25 billion, which translated to negative 11.9 percent over the period compounded at negative 2.5 percent annually. Several categories saw reductions, but one—investment return—dwarfed the others with a $56.3 billion reduction over the period, which represented negative 105.1 percent.

Both governmental categories saw reductions, with a federal decline by $863 million (negative 3.5 percent) and a state decline by a modest $3 million (negative .1 percent). The most significant gainer was tuition and fees at $12 billion, which represented a 20.1 percent increase over the period. Sales and services categories each saw significant gains: Hospitals led the way with $6.6 billion (37.6 percent), followed by auxiliary enterprises with $2.8 billion (18.9 percent), and educational activities with $2.1 billion (41.5 percent).

The final two categories helped prevent a more significant deficit but are not large enough to have a major impact. Revenue from private sources in the form of gifts, grants, and contracts achieved significant growth of $6.5 billion (29.5 percent), while other revenues increased by $2.6 billion (34.2 percent).

FOR-PROFIT INSTITUTIONS

Table 4-8

Source	2010–11	2015–16	Increase/ (Decrease)	Percent Change
Contraction in For-Profit Higher Education Institution Revenues from Fiscal Year 2010–11 to Fiscal Year 2015-16 (amounts in billions)				
Tuition and fees	$ 25.158	$ 15.348	$ -9.810	-39.0%
Federal appropriations, grants, and contracts	1.583	0.713	-0.870	-55.0%
State and local appropriations, grants, and contracts	0.157	0.047	-0.110	-70.1%
Private, gifts, grants, and contracts	0.031	0.015	-0.016	-51.6%
Investment return	0.033	0.028	-0.005	-15.2%
Sales and services of educational activities	0.402	0.329	-0.073	-18.2%
Sales and services of auxiliary enterprises	0.543	0.312	-0.231	-42.5%
Other	0.378	0.267	-0.111	-29.4%
Total Revenues	**$ 28.285**	**$ 17.059**	**$ -11.226**	**-39.7%**

Source: National Center for Education Statistics

For-profit higher education contracted during the five-year period and, therefore, joined independent higher education as the other sector with a net loss of revenues. It amounted to $11.2 billion for the for-profit sector, a 39.7 percent decrease over the period compounded at 9.6 percent per year. And every revenue category saw a decrease over the period.

The only revenue source that really matters in for-profit institutions is tuition and fees, which provided 90 percent of all revenues for the sector. Its $9.8 billion decline in revenues over the period (-39 percent) explained all but $1.5 billion of the net reduction in total revenues. The percentage drop in categories ranged from a low of -15.2 percent for investment return to a high of -70.1 percent for state and local appropriations, grants, and contracts. Again, the actual revenue loss in these categories was only $5 million and $110 million, respectively, because tuition and fees are the only significant revenue source for for-profit institutions.

KEY POINTS

▶ Higher education has three major sectors: public institutions, independent institutions, and for-profit institutions. They generally rely on the same sources of revenue, although the relative reliance on specific sources varies by sector.

▶ Public four-year institutions generate the largest amount of revenues at $308.9 billion. The next largest sector is independent four-year institutions, which realize $181.7 billion in annual revenues. Public two-year institutions also generate significant revenues of $55.5 billion, making them the third largest sector in terms of revenues. The for-profit four-year institutions place fourth, and there is a significant drop-off to $13.6 billion of revenues. Their two-year counterparts realize $3.5 billion of revenues, while the smallest sector, independent two-year institutions, top out at $842 million of annual revenues.

▶ The diversity of revenue sources is an important aspect of institutional effectiveness. Excessive reliance on any individual source places the institution in jeopardy should anything happen to interrupt the flow of those resources.

▶ There has been significant variation in revenue levels during the most recent five-year period for which data are available. The only sector that saw revenue growth during the period was public institutions with a 12.3 percent increase. Revenues of independent institutions fell significantly at -11.9 percent, while the situation was even worse for for-profit institutions that saw a -39.7 percent decline. It's not clear, however, how much of the latter can be attributed to a reduction in the number of for-profit institutions.

CHAPTER 5: ENROLLMENT MANAGEMENT

ATTRACTING AND RETAINING STUDENTS—AN OVERVIEW

Enrollment management refers to the process of attracting, retaining, and effectively serving the optimal student body in a manner consistent with the particular institution's mission, vision, and values. This effort is critical for enrollment-dependent institutions because students provide the largest portion of revenues each year. But even the wealthiest and most selective institutions must devote attention to enrollment management, or they may end up with a mismatch between the student body and what the institution seeks to accomplish.

Most members of the academy are loathe to consider colleges and universities as businesses. There is some legitimacy to this view because, unlike commercial endeavors, few colleges and universities have a single, clear widely accepted bottom line. There are too many worthwhile competing priorities to have a single bottom line that everyone accepts and agrees on. Most would agree, however, that earnings per share is a foreign concept on a public or independent institution campus (except possibly within the business school). But there is a business maxim that is directly applicable to higher education. *It is more cost-effective to keep a current customer than to find one as a replacement.* This principle is just as relevant to colleges and universities as it is to for-profit businesses. Attracting new students is costly and requires considerable effort. And there are no guarantees that they will succeed. Despite this reality, too many institutions approach enrollment management as a student recruitment effort without paying sufficient attention to helping students who are already enrolled move toward graduation.

Four specific units on campus share primary responsibility for the enrollment management operation focused on undergraduate students in a given college or university. These are admissions, financial aid, academic affairs—especially the teaching faculty—and student affairs. (Enrollment management is important for graduate students as well, but this effort typically is solely the responsibility of the department in which the student is enrolled.) Other units certainly have an impact on enrollment. For instance, facilities management's efforts to maintain an attractive and appealing campus can influence students' decisions to enroll or return each year. Similarly, the noninstructional operations that support student learning—libraries, writing centers, tutoring programs, etc.—play a major role in attracting and retaining students. And then there are the cocurricular offerings, overseen by student affairs, and their contributions to the well-being and development of students. All of these areas either support the efforts of the units primarily responsible for enrollment management—or they don't. Nonetheless, at the end of the day, enrollment management must begin with the admissions process.

Admissions is the point of entry for every student enrolled in a college or university. Whether a first-time freshman or a transfer from another institution, some facet of the admissions operation had to give its stamp of approval to the student before he or she could enroll to take classes. But the admissions process doesn't operate in a vacuum. Before recruiting the first student in the entering class, admissions must consult with various elements within academic affairs to ensure that they understand the specific types of students that should be recruited—and for what programs. This includes the majors being offered, the number of students that can be accommodated in each program, the total number of students being sought, and the caliber of students that realistically can be attracted to the institution.

After admissions and academic affairs have agreed on the academic programs and desired students, admissions turns its attention to the office overseeing the financial aid award process. (Keep in mind that undergraduate student aid usually is controlled by the central office overseeing financial aid, while nonfederal graduate student aid may be controlled by a central graduate division or the individual academic departments.) The financial aid office exists to match available resources for student aid with students who either demonstrate financial need or otherwise warrant a reduced cost of attendance.

The financial aid office oversees a budget that includes the various resources available to finance student aid. These resources include the portion of investment earnings available to provide scholarships, gifts restricted for scholarship purposes, governmental student aid or work-study funds that are under the control of the institution, and any other institutional resources available for financial aid. In making individual award decisions, the financial aid office takes into consideration several factors. This would include aid that the student is eligible to receive from external sources as an entitlement (e.g., Pell Grants, various forms of state scholarships based on high school academic performance, private third-party awards). In addition, the financial aid office will consider any restrictions applicable to specific endowment spending or gift accounts. For instance, there may be endowment spending accounts that must be used for students majoring in specific disciplines or from a given county within the state. These funds would be awarded to qualifying students before they would receive awards from other accounts that are less restricted. This approach optimizes the use of as many resources as possible. Neither the institution nor students benefit from financial aid resources that are not awarded.

The final piece of the puzzle from the financial aid perspective is loans. There are two broad categories of resources available for loans to students. The first and largest is the pool of resources provided by the federal government for either direct loans or to subsidize loans provided by the private sector. In addition to the federal loan programs, many institutions operate revolving loan programs funded primarily by gift revenues restricted for this purpose and interest earned on previous loans.

Once the total pool of resources is identified, the financial aid office must wait until the admissions office completes its efforts to recruit and offer admission to students. It's at this point that the financial aid office begins assigning aid to individual prospective and returning students to meet their demonstrated need. Once this is accomplished, the financial aid office turns its attention to distributing the remaining resources in the form of merit aid to attract the optimal student body while maximizing net revenues. After this has been done, the entire institution waits for the students to make their decisions on whether to accept admission with the aid package offered or request a larger package or one with a different mix of scholarships, loans, or work study. Of course, this is only relevant for those who have not already chosen to enroll elsewhere.

In the same way that admissions and the financial aid office have primary responsibility for attracting students, the other two units—academic affairs and student affairs—have primary responsibility for keeping students enrolled. Admissions and the financial aid office have a huge impact on these two areas' ability to succeed based on how they perform their duties to build the student body. If they pursue underqualified or underprepared students, it will be harder for academic affairs and student affairs to keep them enrolled. However, once a student has accepted the offer of admission and enrolls, there is little either admissions or the financial aid office can do to help ensure the student remains in school. (An obvious exception would be when a student's financial situation deteriorates unexpectedly and the financial aid office is able to provide additional support either via grants, loans, or work study. Another exception would be when the financial aid office fails to continue to award sufficient aid in years two through four. It's typical that aid levels do not decrease after the first year unless the student does not meet academic performance standards. Reducing aid for any other reason would be unethical and rarely occurs.)

There are many reasons why students might leave an institution before they earn their degrees. And in some cases, there is nothing the institution can do to prevent this. A student may experience serious health issues or problems at home, or simply exhaust all of his or her financial resources, including available financial aid. When any of these happen, it's important for the institution to counsel the student to ensure he or she understands all available options should his or her circumstances change. Typically, this effort will be handled jointly by representatives of academic affairs and student affairs.

There are numerous other instances when a student's departure is avoidable. For instance, he or she may be dealing with homesickness, struggling to fit in as a first-time college student, or experiencing a more serious form of emotional distress. In any of these cases, there are staff in student affairs who could offer support and identify resources to enable the student to work though the difficulty and remain enrolled. The key is having mechanisms in place to identify the situation before it becomes irreversible.

The other major preventable situation involves academic performance. Assuming a student is qualified for admission and pursuing a program for which he or she has reasonable preparation, failing grades indicate a need for intervention on the part of academic affairs (and possibly student affairs as well). In addition to the student's instructors, various software tools included in a learning management system can be utilized to identify students who are at risk of failing. It's possible that they have registered for courses that may be too advanced or that they are carrying too many credit hours. Irrespective of the reason, institutions should have processes in place to identify and assist students who are in danger of falling into academic peril. Unless a student simply no longer cares or is failing to perform for other reasons, it should be possible for academic affairs to work with the student to identify the source of the problem and provide needed assistance to enable the student to remain in school.

PROJECTING ENROLLMENT

Beyond the potential pool of applicants, pricing decisions affect enrollment. Tuition discounting refers to the practice of offering institutional financial aid to students at levels that exceed their demonstrated need. Essentially, the institution uses a combination of external resources as well as internal resources to attract students who might otherwise not enroll. By offering even a partial scholarship not tied to established need, an institution can attract students with particular skills or qualities to fill a void in the expected incoming class.

In some cases, tuition discounting focuses less on student qualities than on economics. If an institution has excess classroom and housing capacity, attracting a student by offering a partial scholarship results in increased net revenues. For instance, an institution charging $35,000 for tuition and $10,000 for room and board can realize approximately $25,000 of additional net revenue if it attracts a student with a $20,000 scholarship funded solely from institutional sources. Some costs may increase by serving that additional student, but they usually are insignificant compared to the additional revenue.

Projecting student enrollment is more art than science. The science involves determining key variables, such as acceptance rates, student-retention rates, tuition levels, and the overall attractiveness of academic programs. The art of enrollment management focuses on tasks such as recruiting students to maximize net revenue while achieving the desired student body composition and characteristics.

National and local trends affect recruitment and enrollment as well. The rates vary significantly by geographic area, but national high school graduations are projected to increase each year from the 2019–20 level of 3.41 million climbing to 3.56 million in 2024–25.[147] Things are expected to shift downward thereafter and are projected to hit a low of 3.3 million by 2030–31, followed by a slight gain in 2031–32.[148]

Numerous other factors help determine an institution's potential applicant pool, not the least of which is the institution's character and reputation. They will shape the kinds of questions that should be asked in establishing enrollment targets.

- ▶ What is the target population and what institutional characteristics help define that population?

- ▶ What information is known about the target population, and how can this information be leveraged to improve the results of student recruitment?

- ▶ Can the target population be expanded, either to grow enrollments or to enhance the quality of the student body?

- ▶ How can the institution's character be changed to make the institution more attractive to potential applicants? For instance, what new programs can be added?

- ▶ Assuming the institution's residence halls are operating at full capacity, can additional housing be built or purchased?

- ▶ Should the institution add intercollegiate athletics (or additional sports), switch from one NCAA division level to another, or abandon intercollegiate athletics and focus only on intramurals?

As the competition for students has increased, advertising and recruitment campaigns have become more aggressive. Although some states prohibit their public institutions from engaging in student recruitment advertising, others recognize that attracting the best entering students may make this practice a wise investment. Relevant questions include:

▶ Should the institution employ its own staff or contract for public relations/marketing services?

▶ What kind of advertising and marketing should be undertaken, and how should it be targeted?

▶ How can faculty, alumni, and current students become involved in recruitment efforts to enhance the overall results?

▶ What's the most effective way to utilize social media to expand on previous recruitment strategies?

Every institution has a pool of applicants that will overlap with the pools of other institutions. The objective for each institution is to attract the most desirable students within that pool. Applicants are screened by the admissions office (and perhaps by a faculty committee), which evaluates each candidate according to institutional acceptance criteria.

Because many potential students apply to multiple institutions, an institution is unlikely to admit all those who are accepted. As a result, enrollment projections must be based on a firm understanding of the historical acceptance and matriculation rates—along with confidence that nothing will prevent the institution from achieving similar results in the future. When major changes in institutional character occur—such as eliminating a requirement for lower-division students to live on campus or significantly revising acceptance criteria—the old acceptance and matriculation patterns may no longer hold true. Significant changes in economic conditions can affect patterns as well.

Enrollment projections must be adjusted to reflect overall trends in changes in student load or persistence. Questions to consider include:

▶ If the number of students offered admission is too low, are admissions standards too demanding?

▶ If the number of students offered admission is too high, are admission standards too lax?

- To what extent will more attractive student aid packages improve acceptance and matriculation rates?
- Is life experience appropriately credited in evaluating candidates for admission?
- What special requirements and obligations are associated with equal opportunity in the admissions process?
- Are transfer students encouraged to apply and appropriately supported when they are admitted?
- Are admittance rates for transfer students adjusted to compensate for changes in the admittance rates of first-time students?
- What efforts are devoted to supporting and retaining current students?
- Do course availability and scheduling practices impede students' progress toward their degrees? For instance, is it possible to complete four-year programs within four academic years?

Admission to graduate programs is usually treated differently as compared with admission to undergraduate programs. As a result, a different set of issues must be explored:

- Is admission to graduate programs administered by an office of graduate admissions or by individual departments?
- Does the office of graduate studies control the allocation of admissions slots by department and program? If not, are departments free to admit as many qualified students as they can attract?
- Who determines the criteria for admission to graduate programs? Who is authorized to make exceptions to the criteria?
- Are the financial aid or graduate assistantship packages attractive to prospective students?
- How are sponsored program training awards integrated with admissions policies to ensure that qualified students are admitted to take maximum advantage of such awards?

One aspect of projecting enrollment is estimating the number of matriculated students who will continue at the institution through graduation. Over time, a retention history evolves to guide the projections. As mentioned earlier, students remain or depart from institutions for any number of reasons, including financial need, academic performance, family demands, and their satisfaction with the quality of their academic experience—both in and outside of the classroom. Because it makes sense both financially and academically to retain as many students as possible, many institutions invest significantly in programs designed to enhance student retention. Budgeters should ask questions about these programs as well:

▶ Are the retention programs achieving the desired results?

▶ Is the program's success being examined in light of the program's relative cost?

▶ Are data being gathered for use in helping prevent students from departing before earning a degree? When the data suggest issues related to academic programming, is this information shared with faculty and academic advisors to determine what changes might be needed in the overall approach to the delivery of academic programs? When the data suggest that other factors beyond academics are the root cause of departures, is this information shared with student affairs to determine what types of intervention may be appropriate?

TUITION AND FEES

Tuition refers to the price of an instructional service rendered to students. Unlike most prices, tuition is designed to recover only a portion of the costs incurred in providing the service.

Most institutions operate under the following revenue equation: Cost – Subsidy = Price. This differs markedly from the commercial for-profit model, which uses the following equation: Price – Cost = Profit. Cost is only one factor an institution takes into consideration when setting its tuition and fee levels. Other factors include:

▶ Tuition at peer institutions

- Other revenues—especially state appropriation for public institutions—and the need to balance the budget
- Students' ability to pay, financial aid needs, and the availability of resources
- Tradition or philosophy of the institution (or state system)
- General economic conditions

In addition to tuition, institutions also charge students mandatory fees to cover various services, including technology, athletics, recreation, student activities, student government, health insurance or health services, and debt service. Price setting requires an understanding of the institution's market position and the elasticity of student demand. Demand elasticity dictates that when prices are higher, fewer students seek admission compared to when prices are lower. Some institutions may not worry about reduced demand when they raise prices because they already turn away substantial numbers of well-qualified students. On the other hand, the majority of institutions find that they have less flexibility when it comes to setting tuition—especially if comparable institutions exist within the same region.

To remain competitive, institutions must be sensitive to their peers' net student charges (Tuition + Fees - Student Aid = Net Student Charges). For this reason, institutions pay close attention to tuition pricing and student financial aid at peer institutions. And it's common for institutions to share information and discuss pricing strategies, especially within consortia and other affinity groups. However, they must take care not to share information related to specific students or general price information before it's available to the public because doing so could lead to allegations of price fixing.

Institutions use different standards to determine tuition levels. For some, tuition is set by calculating the amount of revenue needed to balance the budget within the constraints of their overall philosophy and market position. Alternatively, they may set the tuition rates and institutional aid first and drive the expense budget based on the net revenues expected to be generated.

The prevailing economic conditions when the budget is prepared come into play as well. When operating costs increase rapidly—or when other revenues decline precipitously—tuition will rise markedly. At the same time, the institution must weigh the ability and willingness of prospective students and their families to pay higher tuition.

At some institutions, traditions govern the setting of tuition levels. For many years, for instance, the California public higher education systems had a policy of charging nominal tuition and maintaining low student fees. When the state encountered economic difficulties in the 1980s, the system abandoned the policy and dramatically increased tuition to provide revenues that helped compensate for the loss of state appropriations.

There is a recent phenomenon that resurrects variations of the former California approach in different parts of the country. So-called free tuition programs have popped up in Tennessee, Oregon, New York, and Rhode Island with more on the way. The programs tend to rely on a model that provides scholarships for the portion of tuition not already covered by other forms of need-based financial aid (e.g., Pell Grants). The scholarships typically are available only to established residents who don't already have a degree. Additionally, recipients are required to maintain a minimum grade point average. In most instances, the programs are available only at community colleges and usually have established income caps. Some programs require at least part-time enrollment and/or are available only for studies in high-demand fields.

NET TUITION REVENUE

A key variable in the determination of revenues is net tuition (tuition minus financial aid awarded to students). As suggested above, tuition levels typically are established in close relationship with enrollment projections, expectations about nontuition revenues, and assumptions about overall expenses. In today's environment, another factor enters the mix: institutional financial aid.

Tuition usually is thought of as the published rate charged to students. In many cases—especially at independent colleges and universities—the published tuition rates bear little relationship to the amounts actually paid by students, due to the aid being awarded to attract students. This practice is referred to as tuition discounting.

With tuition discounting, institutions publish standard tuition rates and then award institutional financial aid to reduce the net cost of attendance for the student. As a result, the process of setting tuition prices and institutional aid budgets has become an iterative one. It requires consideration of investment returns, expectations regarding gifts available for scholarships, appropriations (for public institutions and even some independent ones), the overall budget picture, and the quality of students being recruited.

Some public institutions seek to set tuition at a fixed percentage of the estimated annual cost of education. Virginia used this policy for many years until the economic downturn of the 1990s. When state appropriations failed to keep pace with the growth in institutional costs, tuition rates had to be increased to the point that the revenue exceeded the specified proportion of the annual cost of education.

Setting tuition in the public sector often is more complicated and indirect than in the private sector. The same factors apply—but with the added drama of political considerations. Depending on the state's budget process, for example, an institution may have to delay setting tuition rates until the legislature has determined its appropriation and the governor or state-level oversight board has approved it. This situation proves problematic during strained financial times when legislatures and governors often have difficulty agreeing on the budget. Absent a budget agreement and thus an appropriation, the institution delays adjusting tuition for the fall semester and follows with a sizable increase for the second semester.

Some states take the tuition decision out of the institutions' hands completely. They set tuition either at the system level or through a state agency (or even the legislature). In states that allow institutions to establish tuition rates directly, the process is similar to what occurs in the private sector—with one major exception. While available endowment income or other investment returns may significantly influence tuition levels at independent institutions, this influence typically pales in comparison to the effect of state appropriations on tuition levels at public institutions.

A number of institutions package aid in such a way that minimizes student debt, especially for low-income students. This has been true for a number of years at elite independent institutions and, with a few notable exceptions of institutions reacting to changes in the economy and the market for students, continues to be a trend. Many independent institutions follow a "need-blind" admissions process that doesn't consider a student's ability to pay until after the admission decision has been made. The institution then packages sufficient financial aid to enable the student to attend regardless of financial resources.

Need-blind admissions practices tend to be less common at public institutions, but this doesn't prevent selected public institutions from attempting to compete with their independent counterparts on net price. A number of public institutions have opted to focus more attention toward reducing student debt for low-income students. Specific attention is paid to aid packaging that avoids debt in favor of scholarships funded first from available government programs and then from institutional sources. There are a number of public flagship institutions that have begun structuring attractive aid packages for low-income students in an attempt to enhance the diversity of the student body at those institutions.

When determining tuition levels, a key consideration is the amount of net revenue that will be realized in total and on a per-student basis. This factor is particularly important for smaller institutions, where even a modest change can dramatically impact faculty and staff positions as well as basic services. Additionally, a number of independent institutions have adopted a comprehensive fee combining charges for tuition, housing, dining, and student activities. This makes the calculation of net revenue per student much easier, although it also can produce sticker shock for some prospective students. Despite the sticker shock, it is a logical approach to pricing because it's the total cost that matters—not whether it's tuition, housing, athletics, or activities fees. Moreover, students and their families typically do not consider the costs in disaggregated fashion. It's more common for them to compare the total out-of-pocket expense when costs are a factor in the college-selection process, especially first-time attendees. They may dig deeper once the institution has been selected, and this can drive decision-making related to meal plans, housing, etc, but, at the beginning, it's the total outlay that draws the most attention.

Institutions with a strong commitment to student aid, such as those that provide considerable amounts of institutional aid, typically anticipate using a portion of the revenue generated through increased tuition to fund additional aid. If they did not adopt this strategy, institutions might risk pricing themselves out of their traditional student markets. In addition, if they are committed to providing student aid to those who qualify and demonstrate need, the institutions depend on the additional resources to sustain their commitment.

The following questions should be asked when reviewing a potential tuition increase:

- ▶ What impact is the increase likely to have on enrollments?
- ▶ Is there a price point at which a tuition increase actually reduces net revenue?
- ▶ Is it possible that a tuition freeze or even a price reduction (with a corresponding decrease in institutional financial aid) would be more beneficial financially?
- ▶ How much should competitors' practices be considered in setting tuition rates?
- ▶ How much should federal financial aid programs be considered in setting tuition rates?
- ▶ Is variable tuition pricing an option? That is, should tuition rates vary based on the demand for particular programs, student class level, or the costs of instruction—particularly for high-cost or high-demand programs?
- ▶ Assuming that a public institution has the authority to set tuition levels, how much extra, if any, should be charged to out-of-state students?
- ▶ What is the appropriate relationship between undergraduate and graduate tuition?
- ▶ How should institutional financial aid be factored into the determination of tuition prices?

▶ Should tuition be determined independent of other fees, such as housing and dining?

Fees. Most institutions set fees in combination with tuition. Setting fees for services such as dining, housing, and parking can be more complex than setting tuition because more factors need to be considered. Although competition and overall resource needs help determine tuition levels, the range of issues related to other fees assessed to students is much broader.

Operating costs obviously factor into the equation. But so do working capital reserves, facilities maintenance reserves, costs of holding inventory (especially significant for bookstores and dining), and fluctuating employment levels. For some auxiliaries—housing and bookstore come to mind immediately—competition from the private sector can have a significant impact. Institutions pay continual attention to what is happening in the neighborhoods adjacent to campus in order to be competitive while avoiding setting fees and prices too high. Student fees are the primary revenue source for auxiliary units, which operate as self-supporting businesses. Nevertheless, the business needs of an auxiliary unit cannot be allowed to push the overall cost of attendance to levels that result in decreased enrollment.

Student fees also help fund activities such as intramural sports, student government, student clubs, and student health and counseling centers. In some institutions, fees pay for student access to intercollegiate athletics events. Other fee assessments relate more directly to academic activities, such as laboratory fees for courses taken in certain programs, technology fees, and special fees for individual music lessons or models for studio art programs.

Public institutions may have a unique opportunity when it comes to setting fees. Although it is not unusual for states to control tuition rates, they frequently do not control fees. In fact, in some states where tuition is heavily controlled and fees are not, the combined value of fees assessed to students may be significantly higher than the tuition charges.

Some public institutions that have authority over the setting of fees, but not tuition, rely on fund transfers from auxiliary units for resources to help cover the costs of academic operations. This practice became quite common when states reduced appropriation support for campuses while preventing them from raising tuition rates.

Fees tend to closely reflect the actual costs of the special activity or service. Examples include fees for laboratory usage or breakage, instructional materials, health insurance or health services, and debt service. Some fees—notably technology fees—are not necessarily linked to the cost of service. Rarely does the fee come close to covering the full cost of providing technology services to students, but it helps provide resources to maintain or enhance those services.

THE FEDERAL GOVERNMENT'S ROLE IN STUDENT FINANCIAL AID

Examining the federal role in student financial aid raises the questions of who benefits from higher education and who should pay for it. Increasingly, policy makers believe that the balance of benefits has shifted from society as a whole to the individuals receiving the education. Many believe that the current system of higher education is overbuilt. A major aspect of the debate over who should pay is determining the proper balance between students and their families and the federal, state, and local governments.

Before World War II, states largely provided subsidies to public higher education to enable institutions to keep tuition low. Independent institutions received few public funds in the form of institutional aid. After World War II and the G.I. Bill of Rights of 1944 (the first of several such laws), the federal government began providing massive sums to institutions and students. Both public and independent institutions benefited from this law and the funds it made available.

The balance was altered in the early 1950s, when the Korean conflict G.I. Bill awarded funds for college directly to veterans rather than the institutions. But the federal government broadened its support for higher education in 1958 with the National Defense Education Act, which provided funds to institutions as well as to students, particularly graduate students. Beginning in the late 1950s and continuing throughout much of the 1960s, the federal government provided substantial amounts of funding for facilities, equipment, libraries, research, and training.

Federal funding shifted again, from institutional support to student financial aid, following enactment of the Higher Education Act of 1965. The 1972 amendments to that legislation established the policy of basing federal student assistance programs on individual student need.

Financial Need Formulas

To determine aid eligibility, most institutions use the Free Application for Federal Student Aid (FAFSA) provided by the U.S. government. Another option is the fee-based College Scholarship Service (CSS) Financial Aid Profile available through the College Board. Although both determine financial need, they rely on different methodologies.

Of the two, FAFSA generally determines higher need levels because of the following factors:

▶ FAFSA does not take into consideration home equity as a resource.
▶ CSS assumes a minimum level of contribution from the student, while FAFSA assumes that students may not contribute anything.
▶ CSS is tied to the CPI, while FAFSA relies on federal studies of the low standard of living.

In seeking to attract certain categories of students, some institutions modify the federal government's formula to reduce the expected family contribution. Others have revised their overall approaches to determining the amount of institutional aid that a student is eligible to receive in the form of grants rather than loans requiring repayment.

FEDERAL STUDENT AID PROGRAMS

It is impossible to consider tuition and fee revenues without also examining the effect of federal student financial aid. During the 2011–12 academic year (the latest for which data are available), 6.5 million full-time undergraduate students, representing 72.8 percent of all such students, received some form of federal financial aid.[149] The comparable number for part-time undergraduate students was 7.3 million, representing 51.1 percent of all part-time undergraduate students.[150] The major forms of undergraduate federal financial aid are described below.

Pell Grants. Established by the Higher Education Act of 1972, the Basic Educational Opportunity Grant Program—now called the Federal Pell Grant Program—provides a minimum level of assistance for students to use at any postsecondary institution eligible to participate in federal financial aid programs. The funds, collected and managed by the institution, are awarded to eligible students as an entitlement based on the national needs analysis calculation.

The needs analysis system is scaled so that the amount awarded decreases as family income increases. Actual award amounts are based on costs of attendance at a particular institution. Federal appropriations limit the total amount available to students, and individual awards are limited by provisions that establish the maximum percentage of cost that can be covered through Pell awards. Because of the program's entitlement nature, the maximum allowable award is revised downward by a reduction formula to ensure that the program has sufficient funds. The U.S. Department of Education received a $29.8 billion appropriation for Pell during federal fiscal year 2017–18.[151] The maximum award per student for fiscal year 2018–19 is $6,095.[152]

Campus-based programs. Unlike Pell, campus-based programs are operated by the institution using funds from the federal government supplemented with required matching funds. Current regulations require institutions to provide a match equal to one-third of the federal funds.

Although students must demonstrate need under the same needs analysis process used for all financial aid, campus-based programs are not entitlement programs. The institution decides which students will receive awards. The federal campus-based program funds (though administered separately) are pooled with financial aid from other sources, including the institution itself, and awarded in the form of grants or work study. (Through 2016–17, the Perkins Loan Program operated as a campus-based program, but it now has been terminated. Outstanding loans will continue to be repaid [with collected funds returning to the federal government] or canceled for borrowers who meet any of several cancellation provisions.)

Federal Supplemental Educational Opportunity Grants (FSEOG), previously known as the Educational Opportunity Grant Program, were established by the Higher Education Act of 1965 to provide federal grants for needy students as identified by the institution. FSEOG funds, distributed to institutions according to a state formula based on undergraduate enrollments, are supplemented by the institutional match and used to make grants to students. The maximum FSEOG award is $4,000 for 2018–19.[153] The U.S. Department of Education received an $840 million appropriation for FSEOG during fiscal year 2017–18.[154]

The Economic Opportunity Act of 1964 established the Federal Work-Study (FWS) Program. Funds for FWS are distributed to institutions according to a state allocation formula based on the state's proportion of higher education enrollments, high school graduates, and children in poverty-level families. Supplemented by the institutional match, FWS pays wages to needy students employed by the institution or a local nonprofit organization. Students are paid at least the federal minimum wage but may earn more based on the value of the work performed. The U.S. Department of Education received an appropriation of $1.1 billion for FWS during fiscal year 2017–18.[155]

William D. Ford Federal Direct Loan Program. The newest major federal loan program actually is a variant of previous programs. The Student Loan Reform Act of 1993 established the Federal Direct Student Loan Program. Under the program, the federal government is the lender and provides funds directly to student and parent borrowers through institutions. The program offers three types of loans:

- ▶ **Direct subsidized Stafford loans** are subsidized, low-interest variable or fixed-rate loans based on established financial need. The federal government pays the interest while the student is in school and during grace and deferment periods.

- ▶ **Unsubsidized Stafford loans** are low-interest variable or fixed-rate loans available to students regardless of financial need. The federal government does not pay interest on unsubsidized Stafford loans.

- ▶ **Federal Parent Loans for Undergraduate Students (PLUS) loans** are available to the parents of dependent undergraduate students and to graduate and professional students. The federal government does not pay interest on PLUS loans.

The U.S. Department of Education received an appropriation of $13.6 billion for the direct loan program during fiscal year 2017–18.[156]

TRIO Programs. The federal government provides these funds to institutions on a competitive basis. They are used to finance various programs and activities designed to assist and support disadvantaged students in their efforts to obtain a college education. The first program, Upward Bound, grew out of the Economic Opportunity Act of 1964. The Higher Education Act of 1965 created Talent Search. The Higher Education Act of 1968 created the third program, Special Services for Disadvantaged Students, now called Student Support Services. The U.S. Department of Education received an appropriation of just more than $1 billion for the three TRIO programs during fiscal year 2017–18.[157]

STATE STUDENT AID PROGRAMS

Many states have established competitive financial aid programs. A typical scenario is that students achieving specified levels of academic performance in high school will receive scholarships throughout college, provided the students maintain the specified level of academic performance.

Programs vary widely, but it is not uncommon for state programs to have maximum awards limited to tuition or an established dollar ceiling. Some states also award funds to students who attend out-of-state institutions. The total amount expended under state student aid programs during fiscal year 2016–17 was $9.8 billion.[158]

KEY POINTS

▶ Enrollment management entails attracting, retaining, and serving the optimal student body in accordance with an institution's mission, vision, and values.

▶ Institutions should devote as much or more attention to retaining students already enrolled as to seeking to recruit new students.

▶ Setting tuition prices involves multiple considerations, including institutional operating costs, other revenue sources, available resources for institutional financial aid, general economic conditions, and students' ability to pay.

▶ Multiple sources, including federal and state government programs, restricted institutional resources, and unrestricted institutional resources, are combined to meet students' identified financial needs as a baseline approach to awarding financial aid. Once the established needs of students have been met, remaining institutional financial aid resources are distributed on a discretionary basis to attract the optimal student body while generating the maximum amount of net revenue.

CHAPTER 6: EXPENSES AND COSTS

With a few sometimes significant variations, two- and four-year public, independent, and for-profit institutions engage in the same activities. Therefore, the types of costs they incur are fairly uniform. What varies is the manner in which costs are reported and the relative percentages invested in different categories of expense across the various sectors. Institutional character and mission dictate many of the differences observed when comparing expenses among public, independent, and for-profit institutions. Institutions focusing primarily on associate degrees and noncredit instruction will have significantly different distributions of expenses from an institution that awards graduate degrees. Research institution expenses will vary significantly from institutions that focus primarily on liberal arts at the baccalaureate level. Athletics, reported as an auxiliary enterprise by the largest institutions competing in NCAA Division I or student services for others engaged in intercollegiate athletic competition, is a nonfactor for for-profit institutions.

Two different entities establish the accounting and reporting rules applicable to higher education institutions (see Appendix A). Public institutions must adhere to one set of rules, while independent and for-profit institutions must comply with a different set. Public institutions are required to present an operating measure indicating whether their operating activities produced a net surplus or deficit. Independent institutions currently are not required by accounting standards to present an operating measure, although many opt to do so. There are no prescribed formats specific to for-profit higher education financial reporting, although the federal government requires submission of certain information on a periodic basis.

One significant reporting difference between public and independent institutions is the required treatment of three specific categories of expenses: depreciation, interest, and operation and maintenance of plant (O&M). Public institutions can present this information as separate categories in their audited financial statements, while independent institutions are required to allocate these expenses to the other categories.

One other note: The following discussion is organized by functional category, such as instruction and academic support. As discussed elsewhere, functions refer to the purpose for which expenses are incurred. The alternative method for presenting expenses, called natural classification reporting, focuses on the type of expense incurred rather than its purpose. Natural classification includes expenses such as salaries, utilities, and travel. Refer to Table 1-1 in Chapter 1 for an illustration of the interaction between functional expenses and natural classification expenses.

Table 6-1

Total Higher Education Institution Expenses, Fiscal Year 2015-16 (amounts in billions)					
Purpose of Expense	**Public**	**Independent**	**For-Profit**	**Total**	**Percent**
Instruction	$ 108.162	$ 60.202	$ 4.250	$ 172.614	30.9%
Research	36.090	18.384	0.018	54.492	9.7%
Public service	14.740	2.730		17.470	3.1%
Academic support	29.588	16.009		45.597	8.2%
Student services*	20.253	16.044	10.097	46.394	8.3%
Institutional support	34.432	24.829		59.261	10.6%
Student financial aid	15.513	0.918	0.035	16.466	2.9%
Auxiliary enterprises	31.372	16.717	0.399	48.488	8.7%
Hospitals	45.053	21.268		66.321	11.9%
Independent operations	1.689	6.210		7.899	1.4%
Other	17.805	5.387	1.210	24.402	4.4%
Total	**$ 354.697**	**$ 188.698**	**$16.009**	**$ 559.404**	**100.0%**
	63.4%	**33.7%**	**2.9%**	**100.0%**	

* *This includes academic support and institutional support for for-profit institutions.*
Source: National Center for Education Statistics

The data presented below, for fiscal year 2015-16, are drawn from IPEDS. The sequence of presentation follows the IPEDS reports and does not necessarily align with the sequence used by colleges and universities when preparing their financial statements.

PUBLIC INSTITUTIONS

Table 6-2

Public Higher Education Institution Expenses, Fiscal Year 2015-16 (amounts in billions)			
Purpose of Expense	4-Year	2-Year	Total
Instruction	$ 85.817	$ 22.345	$ 108.162
Research	36.065	0.025	36.090
Public service	13.938	0.802	14.740
Academic support	24.907	4.681	29.588
Student services	14.419	5.833	20.252
Institutional support	25.576	8.856	34.432
Student financial aid	10.402	5.111	15.513
Auxiliary enterprises	29.138	2.235	31.373
Hospitals	45.053		45.053
Independent operations	1.689		1.689
Other	14.201	3.604	17.805
Total	$ 301.205	$ 53.492	$ 354.697

Source: National Center for Education Statistics

Figure 6-1

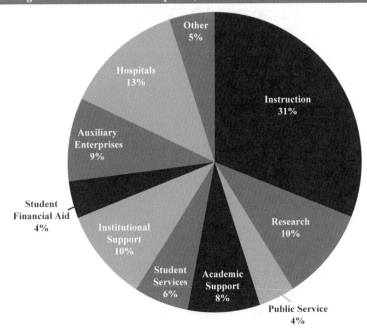

Public Higher Education Institution Expenses, Fiscal Year 2015-16

Source: National Center for Education Statistics

INSTRUCTION

All higher education institutions focus on instruction. It is considered the most important and, therefore, appears as the first expense category in any listing of higher education activities. This category includes the expenses incurred by academic units involved in teaching and directly related activities.

Instructional expenses at public four-year institutions amounted to $85.8 billion, which represented 28.5 percent of total expenses.[159] The comparable amounts for public two-year institutions were $22.3 billion and 41.8 percent.[160]

RESEARCH

Research occurs in institutes and centers as well as in traditional academic departments. Doctoral institutions typically have larger volumes of research activity than other four-year institutions. Research at two-year institutions is relatively insignificant in terms of dollars expended, but some discoveries are just as likely to surface at these institutions as at their four-year counterparts.

This category includes expenses related both to internally funded, separately budgeted, and sponsored research. Research expenses at public four-year institutions amounted to $36.1 billion, which represented 12 percent of total expenses.[161] The comparable amounts for public two-year institutions were $25 million, which represented less than 1 percent.[162]

PUBLIC SERVICE

Public service expenses encompass a multitude of activities that provide noninstructional benefits to groups and entities external to the college or university. This category includes conferences, executive training, advisory services, and other activities that deliver value outside the institution. Other examples include public broadcasting services for radio and television and cooperative extension services that support regional agricultural interests. Their mission dictates that public two-year institutions are much more likely to engage in public service activities than research.

Public service expenses at public four-year institutions amounted to $13.9 billion, which represented 4.6 percent of total expenses.[163] The comparable amounts for public two-year institutions were $802 million, which represented 1.5 percent.[164]

ACADEMIC SUPPORT

This category consists of expenses in units organized to benefit the primary missions of instruction, research, and public service. The largest academic support expenses usually are for libraries and, depending on the institution and its mission, significant expenses might be incurred for audiovisual services, museums, gardens, or academic administration.

Academic support expenses at public four-year institutions amounted to $24.9 billion, which represented 8.3 percent of total expenses.[165] The comparable amounts for public two-year institutions were $4.7 billion, which represented 8.8 percent.[166]

STUDENT SERVICES

In this category, the common theme is support for students' emotional and physical well-being, along with their intellectual, cultural, and social development outside the classroom. There are two broad types of student services activities. The first relates to the administration of operating areas that support students such as financial aid and the registrar's office. (Intercollegiate athletics is reported in this category when not operated as a revenue-generating activity presented with auxiliary enterprises.) The second type represents opportunities for student participation or interaction such as student clubs and organizations, cultural events, student newspapers, intramural athletics, career guidance, and counseling.

Student services expenses at public four-year institutions amounted to $14.4 billion, which represented 4.8 percent of total expenses.[167] The comparable amounts for public two-year institutions were $5.8 billion and 10.9 percent.[168]

INSTITUTIONAL SUPPORT

This category is sometimes referred to as the general and administrative (G&A) expense category because it represents the institution's administrative support activities other than those reported in academic support. Traditional institutional support activities include executive leadership, planning, accounting and related fiscal services, legal services, human resources, logistical services (for example, procurement and printing), most insurance, public relations, and fundraising.

Most institutions use the institutional support category to report operational expenses related to the chief academic officer and chief student affairs officer. When those expenses are not included in institutional support, they are reported in academic support and student services, respectively. This category excludes O&M, which has its own category.

Institutional support expenses at public four-year institutions amounted to $25.6 billion, which represented 8.5 percent of total expenses.[169] The comparable amounts for public two-year institutions were $8.9 billion and 16.6 percent.[170]

STUDENT FINANCIAL AID

Scholarship and fellowship expenses are reported as student financial aid. Scholarships typically are awarded to undergraduate students, while graduate and postdoctoral students receive fellowships.

To avoid double counting revenues and expenses, the vast majority of aid awarded to students is recognized as an offset to tuition and fee revenue. Although a variety of governmental, private, and institutional sources award significant amounts of financial aid to students, the expenses are relatively small compared to the total value of student aid. Only amounts disbursed directly to the student (versus applied to the student's account in the college business office) are recorded as expenses.

Student aid expenses at public four-year institutions amounted to $10.4 billion, which represented 3.5 percent of total expenses.[171] The comparable amounts for public two-year institutions were $5.1 billion and 9.6 percent.[172]

AUXILIARY ENTERPRISES

One of two major activities that fall outside the scope of academic operations, auxiliary enterprises is the collective term used to describe nonhospital activities that provide fee-based services and goods to students, faculty, staff, and—occasionally—the general public. They generally operate on a self-supporting basis and frequently must cover both their operating and capital costs from user fees and charges. Public institutions often expect auxiliary enterprise units to reimburse the central support units for services provided by these units to the auxiliaries.

The most common auxiliaries found on a campus are bookstores, dining operations, and residence halls. Other activities frequently operated as auxiliary enterprises include parking, transportation, student health, and various retail outlets (especially for computers and other end-user technology). In some cases, institutions outsource their auxiliary activities to commercial entities. These arrangements vary from campus to campus, but it's common for the service provider to share net revenues with the institution.

Depending on the magnitude of operations and the revenue generated, intercollegiate athletics is another candidate for treatment as an auxiliary enterprise. NCAA Division I athletics almost always is treated as an auxiliary enterprise at larger institutions. When not classified as auxiliary enterprises, athletics operations are reported as student services.

Auxiliary enterprises expenses at public four-year institutions amounted to $29.1 billion, which represented 9.7 percent of total expenses.[173] The comparable amounts for public two-year institutions were $2.2 billion and 4.2 percent.[174]

HOSPITALS

Hospitals represent the second major activity that is not considered part of academic operations. Teaching hospitals represent a significant activity for some universities. Although they support the academic mission, accounting standards dictate that they be reported in a separate functional category apart from traditional academic functions. A number of institutions operate multiple hospitals with different specialties as well as various clinics serving different constituencies.

In addition to reimbursing central support units for services received from them, hospitals operated by colleges and universities typically provide financial support to the institution's medical school. At a minimum, the physicians providing care in the hospitals and clinics usually have a faculty appointment in the medical school. In these cases, the hospital and the medical school share responsibility for compensating the physicians.

Although many public two-year institutions have relationships with hospitals as part of their educational efforts to train students for healthcare careers, no two-year institutions reported expenses related to hospitals. Hospital expenses at public four-year institutions amounted to $45.1 billion, which represented 15 percent of total expenses.[175]

INDEPENDENT OPERATIONS

A small number of public four-year institutions operate major research laboratories on a contract basis for the federal government. Because of the magnitude and unique nature of the operations, they are not considered core academic operations. However, their financial activities are included within the university's audited financial statements.

Independent operations accounted for $1.7 billion of expenses, which amounted to less than 1 percent of expense for public institutions.

OTHER EXPENSES

This catchall category includes expenses related to ongoing activities that do not align with standard programmatic categories. It is the final category in the IPEDS grouping of expenses.

Some institutions engage in unique activities that, while related to their mission, are not common enough to be reported in a standard programmatic category. Rather than distort data that may be used for various types of analysis, these amounts are reported as other operating expenses. One example might be the operation of historical venues that do not qualify as museums or galleries (which would be reported with academic support).

Other operating expenses for public four-year institutions amounted to $14.2 billion, representing 4.7 percent of total expenses.[176] The public two-year institutions expended $3.6 billion for other operating expenses, which represented 6.7 percent.[177]

INDEPENDENT INSTITUTIONS

Table 6-3

Independent Higher Education Institutions Expenses, Fiscal Year 2015-16 (amounts in billions)			
Purpose of Expense	**4-Year**	**2-Year**	**Total**
Instruction	$ 59.934	$ 0.268	$ 60.202
Research	18.383	0.001	18.384
Public service	2.728	0.002	2.730
Academic support	15.904	0.105	16.009
Student services	15.829	0.214	16.043
Institutional support	24.654	0.175	24.829
Student financial aid	0.914	0.004	0.918
Auxiliary enterprises	16.678	0.040	16.718
Hospitals	21.268		21.268
Independent operations	6.210		6.210
Other	5.336	0.051	5.387
Total	**$ 187.838**	**$ 0.860**	**$188.698**

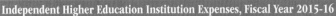

Source: National Center for Education Statistics

Figure 6-2

Independent Higher Education Institution Expenses, Fiscal Year 2015-16

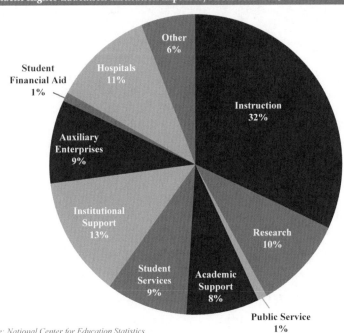

Source: National Center for Education Statistics

Due to different standards-setting bodies influencing the two sectors, public and independent institutions do not use the same expense categories when preparing their audited financial statements. However, as a result of changes in the IPEDS reporting structure, public and independent institutions now use the same expense categories when completing the IPEDS finance survey. Despite the categories being the same, there remain some significant differences in how the two sectors recognize certain expenses and measure others. For this reason, direct comparisons between the sectors or individual institutions in different sectors are not recommended. (See Appendix A for a complete discussion of the key differences.)

▶ In the category of **Instruction**, independent four-year institutions expended $59.9 billion, which amounted to 31.9 percent of their total expenses.[178] The comparable amounts for independent two-year institutions were $268 million and 31.2 percent.[179]

▶ **Research** expenses for independent four-year institutions represented $18.4 billion and 9.8 percent of their total expenses.[180] The comparable amounts for independent two-year institutions were $1 million, which represented far less than 1 percent of their total expenses.[181]

▶ Not surprisingly, given the private nature of their funding, independent institutions do not invest as many resources in **public service** as their public institution counterparts. Independent four-year institutions expended $2.7 billion for public service, which amounted to 1.5 percent of their total expenses.[182] The comparable numbers for independent two-year institutions were $2 million and significantly less than 1 percent of their total expenses.[183]

▶ **Academic support** at independent four-year institutions consumed $15.9 billion, which represented 8.5 percent of total expenses.[184] Independent two-year institutions invested $105 million in academic support, which amounted to 12.2 percent of their total expenses.[185]

▶ Independent institutions make large investments in **student services** expenses. The amount in this category for independent four-year institutions was $15.8 billion, which represented 8.4 percent of total expenses.[186] Independent two-year institutions invested $214 million, or 24.9 percent of their total expenses.[187]

▶ **Institutional support** appears significantly larger at independent institutions compared to their public institution peers, but this is influenced by the allocation of select expenses as described earlier. For instance, interest expense frequently is allocated entirely to institutional support. Independent four-year institutions invested $24.7 billion for G&A purposes, which amounted to 13.1 percent of total expenses.[188] The comparable numbers for independent two-year institutions were $175 million and 20.3 percent.[189]

▶ The amount of **student financial aid** reported as expenses is modest because most financial aid at independent institutions is treated as an offset to tuition revenue. Independent four-year institutions expended $914 million[190] for student financial aid, while their two-year counterparts invested $4 million[191] in aid. In both cases, this represented well less than 1 percent of their total expenses. Their two-year counterparts invested $4 million in aid, which represented less than 1 percent of their total expenses.

▶ In the category of **auxiliary enterprises**, independent four-year institutions consumed $16.7 billion, which represented 8.9 percent of total expenses.[192] The comparable numbers for independent two-year institutions were $40 million and 4.7 percent.[193]

▶ As with public institutions, only independent four-year institutions report **hospital expenses**. They expended $21.3 billion for hospitals, which amounted to 11.3 percent of total expenses.[194]

▶ Both public and independent institutions engage in **independent operations** (i.e., federal research centers operated under contract), but it is much more significant for independent institutions. Their expenses in this category are approximately four times larger than at public institutions because there are more of them and they represent larger operations. Independent operations expenses at independent four-year institutions consumed $6.2 billion or 3.3 percent of total expenses.[195]

▶ As with public institutions, independent institutions also engage in various activities that do not fit neatly into one of the established categories for financial reporting, yet are not large enough to warrant a separate category. As such, they are reported as **other expenses**. Independent four-year institutions incurred $5.3 billion of other expenses, which represented 2.8 percent of their total expenses.[196] The comparable numbers for their two-year counterparts were $51 million and 5.9 percent.[197]

FOR-PROFIT INSTITUTIONS

Table 6-4

For-Profit Higher Education Institution Expenses, Fiscal Year 2015-16 (amounts in billions)			
Purpose of Expense	4-Year	2-Year	Total
Instruction	$ 3.201	$ 1.050	$ 4.251
Research and public service	0.016	0.002	0.018
Student services, academic support, and institutional support	8.214	1.884	10.098
Auxiliary enterprises	0.323	0.076	0.399
Student financial aid	0.032	0.002	0.034
Other	0.788	0.422	1.210
Total	$12.574	$3.436	$16.010

Source: National Center for Education Statistics

Figure 6-3

For-Profit Higher Education Institution Expenses, Fiscal Year 2015-2016

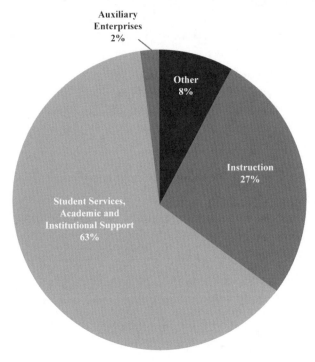

Source: *National Center for Education Statistics*

There is a third sector within higher education: for-profit colleges and universities. Though attracting significantly fewer students than either public or independent institutions, the total expenses of for-profit institutions are not insignificant. Their financial reporting model does not align perfectly with the public and independent reporting models established by the Governmental Accounting Standards Board (GASB) and the Financial Accounting Standards Board (FASB), respectively, so direct comparison at the program level is challenging except for instruction, auxiliary enterprises, and student aid. The latter two are relatively insignificant though.

▶ In the category of **instruction**, for-profit four-year institutions incurred expenses of $3.2 billion, which amounted to 25.5 percent of their total expenses.[198] The comparable amounts for for-profit two-year institutions were $1.1 billion and 30.6 percent.[199]

- **Research and public service** are combined and represent an immaterial level of expenses (barely $20 million and one-tenth of 1 percent of total expenses) for the entire sector.[200]

- **Student services, academic support, and institutional support** are combined for reporting purposes, making them the largest expense category by a significant margin. For-profit four-year institutions consumed $8.2 billion in this category, which represented 65.3 percent of total expenses.[201] The comparable amounts for the for-profit two-year institutions amounted to $1.9 billion and 54.8 percent.[202]

- In the category of **auxiliary enterprises**, for-profit four-year institutions expended $323 million, which represented 2.6 percent of total expenses.[203] The comparable numbers for for-profit two-year institutions were $76 million and 2.2 percent.[204]

- Mirroring research and public service, **student financial aid** represents a very small expense category at for-profit institutions. Combined, for-profit four-year and two-year institutions invested only $36 million, which represented two-tenths of 1 percent of total expenses.[205]

- Similar to public and independent institutions, for-profit institutions engage in various activities that do not fit neatly into one of the established categories for financial reporting while being too small to justify separate reporting. As such, they are combined and reported within **other expenses**. For-profit four-year institutions incurred $788 million of other expenses, which represented 6.3 percent of total expenses.[206] The comparable numbers for their two-year counterparts were $422 million and 12.3 percent.[207]

As these data demonstrate, higher education invests significant expenses in carrying out its primary missions of instruction, research, and public service. Public, independent, and for-profit institutions incur costs to deliver services to their most important constituency—students. But it doesn't stop there. Both public and independent four-year institutions engage in significant amounts of research on behalf of the federal government, states, foundations, and corporations.

Large sums also are invested in support services and ancillary activities to meet the needs of various stakeholders. Academic and institutional support are major categories of expense, as is student services. When the self-supporting operations, auxiliary enterprises, and hospitals are considered, it becomes clear that postsecondary education represents a significant part of the U.S. economy.

EXPENSES OVER TIME

As pressures mount on colleges and universities, the operational impacts lead to changes in the way resources are deployed. And the different sectors sometimes respond in different ways. As evidenced by the data in the accompanying tables, the five-year period ending in fiscal year 2015-16 saw varying levels of changed investment among public, independent, and for-profit institutions. Independent institutions experienced the largest percentage increase in expenses at 23.7 percent (with an annual compound growth of 4.4 percent), while public institution expenses grew by 19.5 percent (with an annual compound growth of 3.6 percent). Conversely, for-profit expenses contracted by 29.3 percent with a compound contraction of 6.7 percent annually. (It should be noted that there was a reduction in the number of for-profit institutions during the period, and this clearly would have affected total expenses. Moreover, given the substantial drop in revenues—39.7 percent—discussed in Chapter 4, it's impressive the expense decrease wasn't significantly higher.)

In terms of absolute dollars, public institutions saw the largest growth in expenses with an increase of $57.8 billion. Independent institutions invested $36.2 billion more than five years previously, while for-profit institution expenses shrunk by $6.6 billion.

Table 6-5

Growth in Public Higher Education Institution Expenses from Fiscal Year 2010–2011 to Fiscal Year 2015-16 (amounts in billions)				
Purpose of Expense	2010–11	2015-16	Increase	Change
Instruction	$ 93.091	$ 108.162	$ 15.071	16.2%
Research	33.867	36.090	2.223	6.6%
Public service	13.426	14.740	1.314	9.8%
Academic support	23.442	29.588	6.146	26.2%
Student services	16.277	20.253	3.976	24.4%
Institutional support	29.051	34.432	5.381	18.5%
Student financial aid	17.487	15.513	-1.974	-11.3%
Auxiliary enterprises	27.650	31.372	3.722	13.5%
Hospitals	29.981	45.053	15.072	50.3%
Independent operations	1.233	1.689	0.456	37.0%
Other	11.358	17.805	6.447	56.8%
Total	$ 296.863	$ 354.697	$57.834	19.5%

Source: National Center for Education Statistics

Table 6-6

Growth in Independent Higher Education Institution Expenses from Fiscal Year 2010–11 to Fiscal Year 2015-16 (amounts in billions)				
Purpose of Expense	2010–11	2015-16	Increase	Change
Instruction	$ 49.760	$ 60.202	$ 10.442	21.0%
Research	17.362	18.384	1.022	5.9%
Public service	2.255	2.730	0.475	21.1%
Academic support	13.601	16.009	2.408	17.7%
Student services	12.198	16.044	3.846	31.5%
Institutional support	20.215	24.829	4.614	22.8%
Auxiliary enterprises	14.460	16.717	2.257	15.6%
Student financial aid	0.760	0.918	0.158	20.8%
Hospitals	14.239	21.268	7.029	49.4%
Independent operations	5.376	6.210	0.834	15.5%
Other	2.275	5.387	3.112	136.8%
Total	$ 152.501	$ 188.698	$36.197	23.7%

Source: National Center for Education Statistics

Table 6-7

Contraction in For-Profit Higher Education Institution Expenses from Fiscal Year 2010–11 to Fiscal Year 2015-16 (amounts in billions)				
Purpose of Expense	**2010–11**	**2015-16**	**Increase/ Decrease**	**Change**
Instruction	$ 5.656	$ 4.251	$ -1.405	-24.8%
Research and public service	0.019	0.018	-0.001	-5.3%
Student services, academic support, and institutional support	14.854	10.096	-4.758	-32.0%
Auxiliary enterprises	0.487	0.399	-0.088	-18.1%
Student financial aid	0.087	0.035	-0.052	-59.8%
Other	1.529	1.210	-0.319	-20.9%
Total	**$22.632**	**$16.009**	**$-6.623**	**-29.3%**

Source: National Center for Education Statistics

Of greatest concern to many is the fact that the increased expenses did not translate to relatively larger commitments to the primary missions of instruction, research, and public service—at least not in a meaningful way based on percentages. Although expenses went up significantly over the five years, no primary mission in any sector saw a disproportionately higher percentage of investment. For public institutions, the increase in primary mission expense percentage was anywhere from 6.6 percent for research to 16.2 percent for instruction compared with the total expense increase of 19.5 percent. For independent institutions, public service increased the most by percentage at 21.1 percent, followed closely by instruction at 21 percent, with research increasing only 5.9 percent compared to an overall increase of 23.7 percent. Putting aside the catchall other expense category, the largest percentage increase of expenses for both public and independent institutions was for hospitals, with 50.3 percent and 49.4 percent, respectively.

Public and independent institutions saw significant percentage increases in expenses with most categories experiencing a double-digit increase. The sole category to decrease among the two sectors was student financial aid for public institutions, which dropped by $2 billion (on a base $17.5 billion), a percentage decrease of 11.3 percent. The comparable percentage for independent institutions was 20.8 percent, but this is somewhat misleading because a higher proportion of their student aid is treated as a reduction of revenues rather than an expense. Growth in independent institution student aid was only $158 million on a base of $760 million. As explained elsewhere, the amount reported as expense is only the portion that is actually paid out to students.

The for-profit sector saw significant net decreases in primary spending categories with both instruction and research and public service expense levels decreasing compared to five years ago. In dollars, the decrease in spending on instruction was significant at $1.4 billion, which amounted to a 24.8 percent reduction compared with five years ago. The research and public service decrease was nominal at $1 million, which represented a 5.3 percent reduction. Auxiliary enterprises had a sizable percentage decrease at 18.1 percent, which translated into an $88 million decrease in expenses.

The biggest drop-off occurred in student services, academic support, and institutional support, which saw a decrease of $4.8 billion that represented a 32 percent reduction compared to five years ago. Topping that on a percentage basis is student financial aid, which saw a 59.8 percent reduction during the period, but again, due to a smaller base, this amounted to only a $52 million reduction.

KEY POINTS

▶ IPEDS periodically publishes various data about postsecondary education operations. It is one of the best resources for those interested in gaining a deeper understanding of the many aspects of college and university operations and data.

▶ The expenses incurred by colleges and universities are typically presented in either of two broad categories: functional or natural classification. Functional categories include the core academic and related activities: instruction, research, public service, academic support, student services, institutional support, O&M (although independent institutions allocate these costs to other functions), student financial aid, auxiliary enterprises, hospitals, and independent operations. Natural classification expenses are presented by the type of expense such as salaries, utilities, travel, etc. and are reflected in the functional categories presented.

▶ Although public, independent, and for-profit colleges and universities conduct many of the same activities while carrying out their missions, the way in which expenses are categorized and the relative percentages reported vary significantly between the sectors.

CHAPTER 7: PLANNING FOR SUCCESS

Who should participate at each stage of the budgeting process? Is the budget merely a continuation of what was done last year? Should tuition and fees increase next year—and, if so, by how much? And how would this affect institutional financial aid? Which departments should receive increased resources next year, and which ones should remain at previous levels or experience reductions? What are the implications for fringe benefits if salaries increase by 2.5 percent?

Such questions commonly arise during the budget process. Over time, participants in the process become more skilled at raising the right questions at the right time to ensure they influence resource allocations. They learn that the best opportunities to influence the budget come during the planning stage.

Because plans guide budgets in effective institutions, planning should precede and link to the budget process. To wield meaningful influence, a participant should contribute during both the planning process and the budget process. The major decisions behind resource allocations are both process related and content related. For instance, the institutional representatives who participate in the processes can affect resource allocations just as much as the amount of resources available for allocation.

Participants generally expect that they can affect resource distribution if the institution's programs and activities are analyzed in a logical, orderly manner. The issues raised in this chapter provide a framework for analytical thinking—an essential element of planning. Still, the effect of politics on budget decisions cannot be overlooked or underestimated.

The political environment and the spheres of influence of people within an institution's community vary from one campus to another. Through friendships with trustees or legislators, for example, a department chair may have political connections that provide influence far beyond than normally indicated by such a position. An administrator or faculty member who has long participated in the planning and budget processes may gain enough institutional knowledge and political clout to become a powerful figure during budget negotiations. And some participants are simply more articulate than others and, therefore, enjoy greater success at garnering resources.

In general, the more complex the budget process and the greater the individual interconnections, the more challenging the political environment becomes. The framework outlined below enables institutions to strike a balance between rational planning and the inevitable political maneuvering. Note that an effective planning process—one that involves key stakeholders and is built on transparency—can reduce the impact of politics on resource allocation decisions.

All planning efforts should incorporate three elements: a critical review of the past, an honest assessment of the present, and careful consideration of the future. Various activities are needed to adequately attend to these three dimensions. Each requires explicit considerations, and institutions should take the time to attend to each if they hope to be successful going forward.

The wide range of planning activities undertaken by higher education fall into three main categories:

▶ **Strategic planning** takes the long-term perspective. Driven by the institution's mission and values, the strategic plan sets the agenda for major investments and guides the institution's activities over a five-year period (although some institutions favor a longer period of seven or even 10 years). The best strategic plans identify and focus on only a handful of priority areas. The typical institution cannot appropriately resource or manage more than five or six major priority areas; however, larger, better-resourced institutions may be able to expand that number slightly. When the number of priorities grows too large, however, it can develop that there are no real priorities. Stated differently, if everything is deemed of high importance, then nothing really is very important.

▶ **Infrastructural planning** fills in the gaps between the handful of major priorities identified in the strategic plan and the core functional and support areas that represent the institution's ongoing activities. Infrastructural planning's focus tends to be shorter than a strategic plan but longer than a single year. Plans typically cover a rolling three- to four-year period.

▶ **Operational planning** is tied to the institution's operating cycle—typically one fiscal year. The operating plan details the major day-to-day activities that will occur at the unit level during a one-year period. (Although the operating plan covers one year, the most effective institutions have two years of detailed operating plans available at any time.) The operating plan should drive the resource allocation decisions that are reflected in an institution's operating budget and be linked to and driven by both the strategic and infrastructural plans.

ACCREDITATION

An institution ideally integrates the various plans with one another and aligns them with the resource allocation process and ongoing assessment activities. In fact, this overall alignment is an expectation of the accreditation process to which all institutions are subject. There are six regional accreditation agencies that influence operations at nearly all degree-granting institutions. (Some institutions are accredited by special-purpose accreditation agencies, but these represent a small percentage of institutions with an even smaller percentage of total enrollment.)

Each of the regional accreditors requires evidence of various forms of planning connected to resource allocation processes, with an additional requirement that activities be assessed in a meaningful and ongoing way. Although different language may be used by the agencies, they all require a systematic, research-based approach to planning. One that is broad-based, takes into consideration a wide range of factors—both internal and external—and responds to evaluation results. A primary goal of the agencies is that institutions have mechanisms for evaluating their activities' effectiveness and use the results of those evaluations to make improvements with the ultimate purpose of providing a meaningful educational experience for students. Satisfaction of this goal is critically important in the U.S. system of higher education because it's ultimately the accreditation agencies that determine whether an institution's students have access to federally financed financial aid programs. Under rules established by the U.S. Department of Education, only accredited institutions' students are eligible to participate in the programs. Losing accreditation is essentially a death sentence for an institution because of the importance of federal financial aid to students.

A Question of Trust

Whether discussing planning or resource allocation, the institutional representatives engaged in the budget process cannot communicate too much. Stakeholders need to know not only the strategic priorities but also how to garner additional resources. Widespread sharing of information must occur at every step of the process.

An institution's desired level of openness and transparency will influence the way it communicates. Having open and transparent processes—and disseminating information about the processes and their outcomes—will create a more stable environment on campus. On the other hand, failure to disseminate information will likely create a void that stakeholders will fill with rumors—and rumors rarely are positive. Others on campus will devote significant amounts of time to speculating about the budget decisions being made and their implications.

What's more, a lack of available information also produces a lack of trust among stakeholders. If the administration or the board take actions in secret, any existing trust in the institution will erode. Trust within an organization is fragile—and very difficult to restore. To avoid this problem, communicate openly and honestly: Share both the good news and the bad.

STRATEGIC PLANNING

Strategic planning sits at the highest level of institutional planning. It is holistic—in other words, it focuses on the entire institution. Although many campus operating units will refer to their strategic plan, strategic planning does not happen at the unit level. Units can engage in strategic thinking, but their plans must be driven by the institution's strategic plan and be supportive of its established priorities and goals.

Effective strategic planning is inclusive and provides opportunities for broad participation and input. Within practical limits, the more perspectives influencing the strategic plan, the better the end result. Along with broad participation and multiple perspectives, an essential element of strategic planning—more so than other types of planning—is an external focus, along with the internal focus that will be the natural target for the plans. A routine activity during strategic planning is examination of institutional strengths, weaknesses, opportunities, and threats. Honest internal examination typically discloses the strengths and weaknesses. However, identification of threats and opportunities requires an external focus. Effective strategic planning considers the environment in which an institution operates. This includes the political, social, business, and community factors affecting the institution. External scans are critical to ensure the institution does not miss opportunities for new programming or develop plans for programs that will not appeal to the market. This scan also informs the planning process about competition and actions that may be occurring within other institutions that could impact directions the institution should take or avoid.

The process should be conducted by a strategic planning task force (SPTF) representative of the institution's diversity and championed by a senior institutional leader—typically the president, chief academic officer, or chief financial officer. Some larger institutions have a chief planning officer serving on the president's cabinet. In these situations, this individual might be the logical person to serve as the strategic planning champion. The champion does not necessarily serve on the SPTF. Instead, he or she ensures that the SPTF has the resources, cooperation, and support it needs to do its work, including access to the president and the cabinet, as needed.

By its nature, strategic planning covers a multiyear period—typically five years. Some institutions develop seven- or 10-year plans, which can be problematic because dramatic changes can occur that make pursuit of the plan impractical or misguided—especially in the out-years. A five-year plan, reviewed annually and adjusted for new realities, provides appropriate guidance while still responding to changing circumstances.

The best strategic plans focus on a limited number of strategic themes or priority areas—five or six at the most—each of which requires preestablished success measures tied to the institution's mission and linked to established milestones. Too often, especially when written to make all stakeholders feel good, plans ignore the practical realities that institutions simply can't afford to spread their resources across more than a handful of major areas. Many important activities occur on college and university campuses, but they cannot all be strategic priorities at the same time.

Strategic planning results in a written document that articulates the institution's vision five years into the future. It identifies strategic themes, which represent the handful of priority areas that support the vision and will serve as the institution's focus during the period. Finally, the plan identifies the major goals within each strategic theme. The strategic plan should be accompanied by an implementation plan that details the resources required, key participants, appropriate time frames, obstacles that may arise, and success measures.

Just as the strategic planning process requires an overall champion, each strategic theme needs an identified champion. A similar requirement applies to each of the goals supporting the various strategic themes. One senior-level official must own the goal and take responsibility for ensuring its achievement.

Financial Modeling and Forecasting

One of the more complex aspects of planning is identifying the financial implications of the alternatives under consideration. As mentioned throughout the book, colleges and universities are faced with the dilemma of choosing between good and better ideas. Identifying those that are best from a macro standpoint is incredibly difficult due to a range of factors, including anticipated enrollment, retention, faculty costs, tuition discounts, etc. Scenario planning is one way to accomplish this, and various tools have been developed to assist with this effort. In the author's opinion, the one that appears to have the greatest functionality is Whitebirch from PFM. Unlike other tools, it was built specifically as financial modeling software and offers highly sophisticated functionality capable of readily handling multiple scenarios simultaneously.

Other providers in this sector include Kaufman Hall (Axiom) and Xlerant (BudgetPak), both of which also offer forecasting capability. However, they provide this functionality as an adjunct to sophisticated budget applications. As such, they are not quite as sophisticated as Whitebirch. (See step 13 in Chapter 10 for additional information about Kaufman Hall, Xlerant, and other providers of budget solutions.)

INFRASTRUCTURAL PLANNING

Once developed, the strategic plan should guide other aspects of campus planning. Infrastructural plans, which focus on core programmatic and essential support areas, address the many ongoing activities that fall outside the five or six strategic themes addressed in the strategic plan. The plans focus on rolling three- to four-year periods and are updated on that cycle or whenever a new strategic plan takes effect. Occasionally, a strategic theme will align perfectly with a core programmatic or essential support area. More likely though, the strategic themes will address a portion of a programmatic area or touch on multiple areas. For example, a strategic theme focused on the need to alter the teaching/learning environment by dramatically increasing technology use clearly falls within the academic plan but also has significant implications for the information technology plan.

In the core programmatic areas, separate plans will be developed for academics, student engagement, learning resources, and numerous other areas. In terms of essential support activities, infrastructural plans typically address enrollment management, institutional advancement, facilities, information technology, and a wide array of other areas.

Tying everything together is a rolling five-year financial plan linking to the strategic plan and identifying its financial impacts and expectations. It highlights the costs of the various strategic themes and their related goals as well as any revenues directly tied to the strategic initiatives. It also addresses the financial impacts of the various infrastructural plans. Both the operating and capital budgets are referenced in and influenced by the overall financial plan.

OPERATIONAL PLANNING

While strategic plans typically address five-year periods and infrastructural plans usually focus on three or four years, operational plans guide what happens on a day-to-day basis during one cycle—usually a single fiscal year. More sophisticated environments have two years of operating plans available at any time. Naturally, the second year may be less detailed than the first, but it is helpful to think longer term than just the next year when engaged in planning.

The majority of colleges and universities historically have not engaged in formal operational planning at the unit level. Instead, they allow the operating budget to guide what happens, usually influenced to a significant degree by whatever happened the previous year. It's true that most activities will not change dramatically from one year to the next, but there still should be intentional effort directed to both improvement and development of new activities each year. Effective operational planning focuses primarily on one fiscal year while recognizing that some initiatives extend beyond one year. The overall objective is to establish operational plans guided by and aligned with the strategic and infrastructural plans that, in turn, guide the deployment of resources. Along with guiding the distribution of resources, operational plans should guide the day-to-day activities and decisions required to carry out the institution's mission and realize its vision.

Given this planning hierarchy, influencing how resources are allocated starts with the planning process. Anyone who wants to have an impact on how resources will be utilized should seek to participate at the earliest possible point in the process—i.e., planning.

Figure 7-1

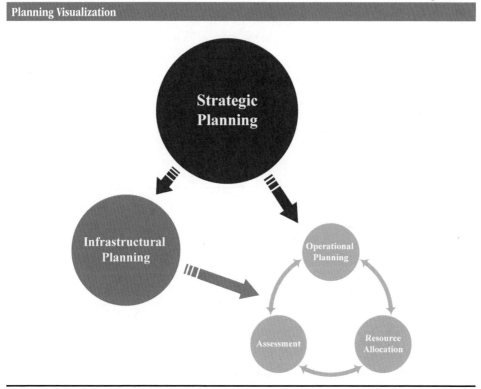

Planning Visualization

ANCILLARY PLANNING ISSUES

One issue related to planning doesn't fit neatly into strategic, infrastructural, or operational planning: the need to benchmark progress over time by internal analysis and externally through peer comparisons. In fact, higher education institutions are noted for their efforts to monitor what happens at other institutions and use it as a yardstick for comparison with their own efforts.

Benchmarking has two critical elements:

1. Identifying the comparison group. The objective is a group appropriate for comparison across the institution. Realistically, however, perfect matches won't exist. More likely, the selected institutions will match up well on some elements, such as enrollment size, operating budget, and endowment, but not well on other elements, such as the number of academic programs or specific majors offered.

Political aspects often creep into the identification of comparison institutions. Some stakeholders, for instance, will not feel comfortable with true peers and instead seek to identify institutions that clearly are better performers. Both groups will provide valuable information but generally not within the same comparison set. A better approach is to agree on a set of institutions that match up well currently—true peers—and a different set of institutions that can serve as an aspirational comparison group.

Many states assign their public institutions a set of peer institutions for comparison purposes. This works well if the institution participates in the process of identifying its peers but may prove challenging if the peers are unilaterally assigned. Too often, the state considers only quantifiable factors such as student head count, overall budget, and number of colleges and schools. If this is the approach, significant qualitative factors such as degree offerings and mission may not be given sufficient consideration in the selection of peers.

Independent institutions select their own peers or inherit them by virtue of affiliations. A good approach is to examine both the formal and informal affinity groups in which the institution participates, such as consortia, athletic conferences, or other affiliations. Of course, not all members of a particular group will represent a good fit. For instance, an athletic conference like the Big Ten provides good peers for all members other than Northwestern University, the conference's only independent institution. The remaining institutions all are relatively large public research universities, albeit with some mission differentiation. As a starting point, this makes a good comparison group for everyone except Northwestern.

2. Determining the comparison factors. Institutions have an endless list of topics for comparison. To illustrate the alternative approaches available, the examples below use two topics: benchmarking instructional costs and measuring institutional health through financial ratio analysis.

Because salaries represent one of the largest costs, institutions have great interest in determining whether their costs of instruction are reasonable for faculty engaged in teaching versus research or other activities. One way to assess this is by participating in the Delaware Cost Study—The National Study of Instructional Costs and Productivity (Delaware Study). Nearly 700 four-year institutions have participated in the study, which originated at the University of Delaware in 1992.[208] It relies on self-reported data on various aspects of costs and faculty teaching load. Study participants can access information by academic discipline and course level, sorted by type of institution. This allows them to compare their cost structure against national norms as well as customized peer sets. (There is a comparable effort focused on two-year institutions, the National Community College Benchmark Project,[209] housed at Johnson County Community College.)

As for financial ratios, one of the most valuable is the Composite Financial Index (CFI) developed by KPMG, Prager, Sealy & Co. LLC, and Attain.* The CFI consists of four weighted ratios that measure an institution's financial health:

- ▶ Primary reserve ratio: Does the institution have sufficient resources to carry out its mission?

- ▶ Viability ratio: Does the institution practice strategic debt management in carrying out its mission?

- ▶ Return on net assets ratio: How well do the institution's physical and financial assets perform financially in supporting the mission?

- ▶ Net operating revenues ratio: Is the institution able to carry out its mission without spending reserves?

---

* See: *Strategic Financial Analysis for Higher Education, Seventh Edition,* and its *7th Edition of Strategic Financial Analysis for Higher Education, Summer 2016* by KPMG, Prager, Sealy & Co., LLC, and Attain for an in-depth discussion of the CFI and additional general information about ratio analysis.

The final three ratios are supported by secondary ratios that dig deeper into the CFI's underlying factors. Sample secondary ratios include the age of facilities ratio—indicating whether an institution invests sufficient resources to maintain its built environment—and the debt burden ratio—measuring the portion of total expenditures devoted to annual debt service.

Developers of the CFI indicate that it is not intended for institutional comparisons because too many different factors affect institutional character. Instead, they recommend tracking the CFI over time and comparing to others at the level of the four primary ratios, which rely on information generally available in institutions' audited financial statements. For the most part, if one can obtain the statements, one can calculate the ratios.

The CFI authors conduct research using a proprietary database of institutions. In a recent paper focused on small to midsize independent institutions,[210] they present a scale that attaches labels to varying levels of financial health. Although the scale could extend from minus 10 to 10 mathematically, ratios below minus four are rarely encountered because an institution would cease operations well before experiencing numbers much below that level. The new scale describes institutions with CFI scores below zero as *critically unhealthy*. If something is not done immediately, the institution is in danger of failure due to a lack of financial resources, excessive debt, or operational instability. Institutions with CFI scores of zero to three are described as *barely surviving*. Absent significant structural changes, the institution's future is in jeopardy.

For years, a score of three was deemed to represent *minimal financial health*. The authors' research and conversations with institutions have led them to conclude that too many such institutions have established three as their goal, not recognizing that it is not representative of long-term sustainability. For this reason, they have described the category of CFI scores from three to six as *surviving*. Historically, scores in the upper areas of this range were deemed desirable, especially for institutions without substantial endowment resources. The current thinking is that a score below five is one that suggests the need for transformation to achieve greater financial stability. Finally, institutions with a CFI score higher than six are described as *thriving*. Most significantly, these are the institutions that are best positioned to weather short-term financial difficulties and, equally important, take advantage of opportunities requiring additional investment.

In terms of planning, ratios can be used to drive institutional performance. If the institution's financial health is unsatisfactory, the ratios can be used to direct actions that result in improvement. Depending on which aspect of the CFI lags, specific actions can be taken to improve the results. For instance, if the viability ratio is dragging the CFI down due to excessive debt for the level of available reserves, emphasis can be placed on repaying or refinancing a portion of outstanding long-term debt. If operating deficits have adversely impacted the return on net assets ratio and turned the net operating ratios revenue negative, this would indicate the need for significant restructuring of the revenue and expense portfolios to improve operational results.

The CFI and its components (including various secondary ratios) represent an important application of financial ratio analysis, focused primarily on one-year results. There are other ratios as well. In fact, for most institutions, multiple ratio assessments are needed. By design, the CFI is an annual measure that relies on audited financial statements. Other ratios focus on shorter-term considerations and do not necessarily rely on audited financial statements. For instance, monitoring cash flows can be a monthly activity. Related to cash flows is the collection of receivables, which can be represented in ratios that also can be measured monthly. Because of higher education's normal interim operating cycles, measures tied to semesters or quarters might be appropriate in some situations.

Another example of a ratio that would be relevant for a period other than one fiscal year is student retention over a four-year period. Although many students are unable to complete their degree programs in four years, this remains the norm for most degree programs. There is a direct correlation between financial aid commitments for students completing in four, five, or six years. Therefore, this would be an important metric for assessing financial health on an indirect basis.

Financial equilibrium offers yet another way to assess institutional financial health on a global level. Generally speaking, the term refers to the minimum performance to which all institutions should aspire. Financial equilibrium has four components:*

▶ **Maintaining a balanced budget.** This element ties directly to one of the four primary ratios in the CFI—the net operating revenues ratio. A balanced budget actually means a budget with at least a modest surplus from operations. Even nonprofit organizations must generate a surplus to survive. As discussed elsewhere throughout the book, the budget should address all resources available to support operations—both unrestricted and restricted.

▶ **Investing in human capital.** The faculty and staff who conduct the various operational activities are essential to an institution's success. As such, the institution must compensate them well, provide for their well-being following employment, and invest in their ongoing professional development. Unfortunately, too few institutions invest adequately in this last area, especially during times of economic difficulties.

▶ **Preserving the built environment and technology infrastructure.** Too many institutions abandon scheduled building and systems maintenance during difficult economic times, which ultimately threatens the institution's long-term financial health. Delaying essential maintenance typically occurs because so many aspects of needed maintenance are invisible to the average person. Unless a leaking roof or temperamental boiler affects people directly, they rarely recognize the problem. Similarly, technology infrastructure rarely fails in dramatic fashion except when affected by natural disasters. Instead, the infrastructure deteriorates slowly until the day it stops working completely. (See Chapter 10 for a deeper discussion of deferred maintenance related to the built environment.)

▶ **Maintaining the endowment's purchasing power.** Endowments are perpetual resources intended to last forever, so management of them should ensure long-term viability. Intergenerational equity

---

*The discussion of financial equilibrium draws on the work of: William S. Reed, *Financial Responsibilities of Governing Boards* (Washington, DC: Association of Governing Boards of Universities and Colleges and NACU-BO, 2001).

refers to the concept that an endowment should be managed so current beneficiaries are treated equitably—as well as but not better than—when compared with future generations.

Unless an institution is appropriately addressing each of the four elements, it will fall into financial disequilibrium. Financial disequilibrium eventually will threaten the institution's long-term viability if not actual survival.

ALIGNING RESOURCE ALLOCATION AND ASSESSMENT WITH PLANNING

Figure 7-2

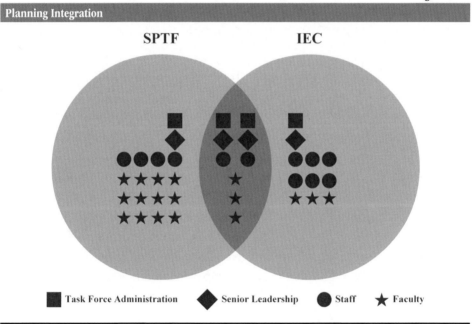

Figure 7-2 visually depicts one approach supporting the integration of planning with specific reference to the SPTF and the institutional effectiveness committee (IEC), which is discussed in more detail in Chapter 8. The SPTF naturally focuses on strategic planning, while the IEC focuses on all facets of planning—strategic, infrastructural, and operational—along with resource allocation and assessment. It is the IEC's focus on all three processes that supports the alignment that is so critical to institutional success.

After planning establishes the institution's priorities, resource allocation decisions must ensure the priorities can be carried out. It may not be possible in all situations to direct all resources to established priorities. Minimally though, institutional mechanisms should ensure that resources are not used in a manner contrary to established priorities.

Ongoing assessment represents the final element of alignment. The results identified through assessment should influence plans and drive resource allocation decisions. Assessment should be undertaken with intentionality about doing something different based on the results of the assessment. What is learned through assessment should result in an intentional decision to stay the course, alter the course, or abandon the trip entirely. Assessment that isn't intended to have an impact, unless externally mandated, should not be undertaken.

Assessment efforts should focus on what's identified as being important within the institution's plans. Management attention will be directed toward those activities whose measurement is monitored by higher levels within the organization—especially if there are consequences as a result of what's discovered. If positive results are achieved, the consequences should be in the form of rewards—increased resources, enhanced autonomy, or other benefits. Conversely, if the results are not positive, a model based on accountability would result in the imposition of sanctions such as reduced autonomy, spending limits, or reductions in resources. Keep in mind that assessment results will not always lead to rewards or sanctions. In some cases, the results will simply disclose the need to make changes in the way activities are conducted.

In too many instances, assessments are undertaken across the board because they represent "easy to calculate" outputs—not necessarily because the results are meaningful toward realization of the institution's vision. Assessment efforts should be targeted to outcomes—i.e., quality indicators— to the extent possible rather than inputs and outputs—i.e., productivity measures. It's important to measure consistently over time. Although it might seem desirable in the moment, it's rarely acceptable to change the standards because the results are not as good as what had been hoped. Instead, this is an opportunity to consider what caused the undesirable results and take steps to prevent them from occurring going forward.

As part of the planning and budgeting processes, an institution should establish success measures for all goals and major activities long before the efforts get underway. Knowing in advance what you're trying to achieve—and formally articulating it—dramatically enhances your likelihood of accomplishment.

Effective alignment of planning, budgeting, and assessment relies on common sets of data and information. This requires the institution to not only generate and disseminate information widely on the campus but also encourage extensive dialogue and interaction. Yet many institutions approach alignment activities the same way they approach routine activities in their day-to-day operations—via silos. They establish one structure for planning, another for budgeting, and still a third for assessment (if this has a structure at all).

The following sections suggest ways to achieve alignment and the roles various stakeholders can play.

SAMPLE INFRASTRUCTURAL PLANS

Figure 7-3

Infrastructural Plans

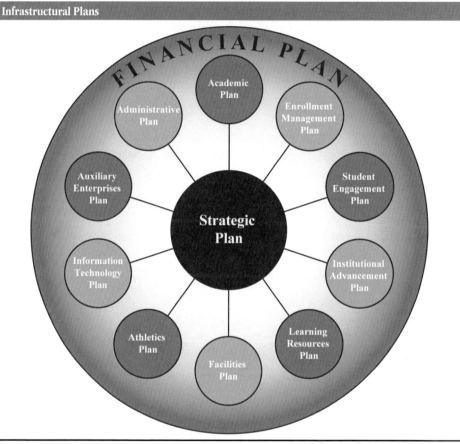

In addition to the strategic plan, infrastructural plans—for both core programmatic and essential support areas—guide a college or university. Each infrastructural plan drives operational activities and, therefore, significantly affects the budget.

PROGRAMMATIC INFRASTRUCTURAL PLANS

Three core programmatic infrastructural plans would apply in nearly every higher education institution.

Academics. The academic plan sets the tone for the entire institution by addressing the three primary functional areas: instruction, research, and public service. The plan could cover topics that range from designing a new degree program to setting the average class size within specific schools or colleges and to establishing new research institutes or centers. The priorities established for the academic plan exert significant influence over the budget process and influence other infrastructural plans, including student engagement, learning resources, enrollment management, and facilities.

Student engagement. This plan addresses issues as diverse as the student organizations that will be authorized, which intramural sports will receive support, key issues related to Greek life, and how various cocurricular efforts will be undertaken. As with most other infrastructural plans, it has close connections to other core programmatic plans—especially academic, athletics, and auxiliary enterprises—and essential support plans, such as enrollment management, facilities, and administration.

Learning resources. This plan covers the fast-changing world of academic libraries and technology. It may deal with digital media replacing traditional books and journals, critical questions about the configuration of library space to facilitate technology-enabled group study, or the implications of mobile technology. The learning resources plan links most strongly to the academic and information technology plans.

Other programmatic plans that are encountered frequently include research, community outreach, public service, etc. There is no limit to the number of plans that might be needed by large research universities. Similarly, community colleges would have programmatic plans unique to their missions. For instance, although a community college would also have an academic plan, it's entirely possible that a separate plan might be established for instructional programming conducted jointly with local high schools.

SUPPORT INFRASTRUCTURAL PLANS

Along with many others, four support infrastructural plans would be relevant to every higher education institution.

Enrollment management. This plan addresses institutional decisions regarding tuition pricing, tuition discounting, financial aid management, and retention—all of which have significant implications for a budget. It closely relates to and influences infrastructural plans for academics, student engagement, athletics, auxiliary enterprises, and others.

Institutional advancement. Activities addressed in this plan include fundraising, public relations, community relations, governmental relations, and alumni affairs. Because advancement encompasses annual giving, planned giving, and major gifts, it has the potential to interact with every other infrastructural planning area. The connections to academics could include private support for research, endowed chairs, or a lecture series. As for enrollment management, the scholarship support provided by gifts and endowment income often proves essential to student recruitment and retention. Depending on the priorities for student engagement and athletics, institutional advancement may assist student organizations with fundraising efforts, provided those efforts don't conflict with larger institutional fundraising priorities and plans.

The interactions with facilities take many forms, whether assisting with community relations related to proposed construction plans or raising funds to underwrite the cost of a new facility. The same holds true for information technology and auxiliary enterprises. Either area could have priority needs for private support. Finally, institutional advancement affects various administrative plans because accepting gifts carries both compliance and potential liability issues.

Facilities. The facilities plan includes the master plan, which addresses the long-term development of the campus, as well as management of deferred maintenance. Other topics to be addressed include space utilization, utilities, and facilities condition analysis. And because every campus operation is housed in facilities and guided by one or more infrastructural plans, the potential exists for interaction between facilities and all other programmatic and support plans.

Information technology. In addition to addressing the deferred maintenance equivalent within information technology, this plan typically outlines a reasonable life cycle for upgrading and replacing personal computing, ERPs, and other administrative systems to reflect the pace at which technology advances. Like facilities, information technology interacts with all other organizational units and, therefore, has implications for nearly all other infrastructural plans.

VARIABLE INFRASTRUCTURAL PLANS

Finally, two additional areas could appear among programmatic infrastructural plans or be considered support infrastructural plans.

Athletics. Clearly, NCAA Division I institutions will have an athletics plan. Even Division II institutions likely will treat the athletics plan as an infrastructural programmatic plan because of its operational significance. However, institutions that do not engage in intercollegiate athletics in a significant way may opt to treat the athletics plan as an infrastructural support plan. Or the institution might address athletics as part of the student engagement plan—either because the revenues are not particularly significant or because the institution focuses on intramural rather than intercollegiate athletics. If athletics warrants a separate plan, it likely will have close ties to infrastructural plans for enrollment management, student engagement, institutional advancement, facilities, and possibly auxiliary enterprises.

Auxiliary enterprises. Typically, the auxiliary enterprises plan drives how residence life, dining, and the bookstore engage with academics. For example, an institution deliberately attempting to incorporate academic activities into residential facilities or coordinate them with the bookstore will likely address auxiliary enterprises in a separate infrastructural programmatic plan that connects closely to the academic plan. If not closely connected to academics, auxiliary enterprises will be considered an essential support activity and likely be treated as an infrastructural support plan. This plan usually has significant interactions with plans for enrollment management, student engagement, and facilities.

KEY POINTS

▶ Planning is essential to helping colleges and universities focus their efforts and deploy resources effectively. Coupled with assessment and resource allocation, the three processes establish the foundation for institutional effectiveness.

▶ The way in which information is communicated, along with transparency and openness, can enhance the level of trust throughout the institution.

▶ Strategic planning provides the long-term direction for the institution, including the vision of its future. A strategic plan focuses on only a handful of major priority areas. An infrastructural plan addresses a core programmatic area or an essential support activity undertaken as the institution moves toward its vision.

▶ Strategic planning typically covers a five-year period; infrastructural planning focuses on three to four years; and operational planning covers a one-year period (although it is recommended that there be two years of operational plans available at any point in time).

▶ For institutions that fail to undertake operational planning, the operating budget functions as the de facto operational plan. The major disadvantage with this approach is its tendency to perpetuate activities resourced in previous budgets, even if they no longer contribute to institutional success.

CHAPTER 8: ESTABLISHING THE BUDGET PROCESS

In the aftermath of the Great Recession, nearly all public institutions in the United States experienced dramatic budget cuts triggered by state revenue shortfalls. Both public and independent institutions felt the effects of distressed financial markets on their investment earnings and fundraising results. And public institutions had the added complication of substantially reduced state support. Such significant changes led institutions to readjust their resource allocation patterns—sometimes in dramatic ways.

Enrollment-dependent institutions, for example, increased resources allocated to retaining existing students and attracting new ones—the latter both in the form of marketing investments and increased tuition discounting. To respond to or avoid operating deficits, many institutions dipped into reserves, reduced employee benefits (or increased the portion of premiums paid by employees), instituted travel bans, froze salaries and vacant positions, or mandated employee furloughs. Others took even more drastic actions such as eliminating programs and laying off tenured faculty and other staff.

Differences in individual characteristics dictate how an institution approaches and implements its budget process. The larger the institution, for example, the more likely it is that its budget process will include many participants and be more decentralized. Smaller institutions are much more likely to rely on a highly centralized approach using top-down directives. There is nothing to say that a smaller institution can't be decentralized, but it's more common to see greater centralization in smaller institutions because of the belief that it's easier to understand and get one's arms around a smaller operation.

Despite the fact that a decade has passed since the Great Recession ended, institutions continue to deal with its effects. The new normal was mentioned earlier, and it is just as relevant to this discussion. Detailed below are the major factors that exert the most influence on the budget process. Understanding these factors will contribute to one's understanding of how to influence or oversee the process.

INSTITUTIONAL CHARACTER

Each of the more than 3,300 public and independent degree-granting higher education institutions in the United States[211] has a unique personality shaped by its size, mission, governance structure, dominant funding sources, culture, operating climate, administrative practices, history, etc. When considered together, these various elements establish an institution's unique character.

Not all independent institutions are created or operated equally. An independent institution with a religious affiliation is not as independent as one with no such affiliation. Moreover, some religious affiliations are very loose and have only minimal impact on mission or operations. For other institutions—especially those that rely on a religious entity for financial support—some independence usually is given up in exchange for the financial support. And for other institutions, the tenets of the faith take on greater significance because of designated seats on the board even though financial support may not be significant or available at any level.

There is significant variety among public institutions as well. Public land-grant universities, for instance, often enjoy a "flagship" status that translates into strong political support in the state legislature—a highly valued asset that doesn't appear on the institution's balance sheet. In contrast, small regional public colleges with lower profiles may have more financial constraints, especially if they are "open admission" institutions with low student-retention rates. Moreover, being governed by a system office creates a very different dynamic for an institution as compared with governance experienced when there is a board of trustees dedicated solely to a single institution.

An added element of difference for public institutions is the presence of foundations. There are all manners of foundations affiliated with and/or supporting public institutions. The most common are those engaged in fundraising on behalf of the institution. These foundations typically also house and manage the institution's endowment. Other foundations have different purposes, with some existing specifically to support athletics while still others carry out major aspects of the institution's research mission. The presence of foundations adds a complicating element to governance because the foundations can be within or outside of the governance structure established for the institution.

The type of student an institution attracts will shape institutional character as well. For instance, students at an inner-city community college are more likely to have remedial needs compared to a two-year campus in a suburban setting. Similarly, the presence (or absence) of vocational partnerships with local industry will draw different types of students, as will the level of coordination with local K–12 educational systems. Then there are the elite institutions that enjoy more student interest than can be accommodated given enrollment limitations. Although financial aid plays a factor in attracting some of their students, the majority of them come from wealthy backgrounds. This can lead to different expectations on the part of the students and their parents. These expectations will have an impact on institutional character.

The presence or absence of unions representing various categories and classes of employees can have profound effects on the character of an institution. The absence of collective bargaining creates the potential for individual salary negotiations and increases the impact of individual performance on compensation. Individual salary levels may become much more significant in these situations. This is less likely to be a major issue for public institutions because it's common for individual salaries to be available via open records laws. However, at an independent institution that is required by IRS rules to disclose the salaries of only a select number of highly compensated individuals, there can be great interest and angst over individual salary levels. Great care usually is taken to keep salaries confidential at independent institutions. This type of secrecy can shape the relationships between the administration and employees as well as among employees. Unfortunately, salary secrecy tends to impair trust across the institution and lead to pitched battles over resource decisions.

Collective bargaining driven by union representation, on the other hand, introduces a different set of dynamics. There is a benefit from the standardization of compensation for all employees in given categories and classifications because there no longer are questions about how much individual faculty or staff are being paid. Additionally, collective bargaining agreements usually cover multiyear periods, which contributes more certainty to the largest portion of the budget—compensation. However, the presence of unions can lead to divisions among various groups. Some faculty are not supportive of union representation and would prefer to negotiate separately on their own behalf. Others embrace the principles represented by the union and adopt an "us versus them" attitude with respect to the administration. This can produce high levels of tension on campus, especially when contract negotiation time rolls around. It also has a tendency to engender mistrust regarding financial matters because there is a tendency to disbelieve the administration when there are claims of resource insufficiency.

One might argue that the relationship between the budget and institutional character is a "chicken and egg" proposition because they can have such dramatic impacts on each other. Institutional character frequently drives resource allocation decisions. Similarly, that character is in many ways a function of past resource allocation decisions.

Shifts in institutional character do occur, although they aren't always obvious. Nor do they generally happen over short periods. They take time, and identifying the shifts requires paying close attention to tangible factors that can be easily monitored and tracked over time, such as articulated plans, administrative priorities, revenue fluctuations, and assessment results.

A CHANGE IN CHARACTER

Large organizations typically resist change. That tendency, coupled with higher education's deep sense of tradition, often leaves institutional character mired in inertia. In other words, participants in the planning and budget processes should not expect an institution's character to change within a single planning or budget cycle. Nevertheless, they can use the budget to effect desired change as guided and shaped by the planning process.

An institution can change its character, albeit slowly, by changing the way in which it allocates its resources. Few such decisions—in and of themselves—will bring about major change, although some will provide a stronger push than others. For instance, an institution not noted for its research proficiency may make great strides in a relatively short time period simply by establishing and staffing a small office focused on sponsored programs. Moreover, if it couples this step with providing seed money to faculty interested in pursuing sponsored support, the institution can move from having little or no external support for research to measurable results within a few years.

A number of colleges and universities have attempted to change their character through intercollegiate athletics. Several have changed divisions within the NCAA classifications, with most moving to a higher, more expensive division. On the flip side, a few institutions have dropped a major sport or moved to a classification requiring less investment. Either action creates an opportunity for the institution to change its character—sometimes dramatically.

Dramatic changes in institutional character may also stem from:

▶ **Shifts in enrollment patterns or increased demand for certain programs.** For instance, current social and political events may influence students to pursue some disciplines in numbers far exceeding typical patterns. If the shifts prove more than a short-term phenomenon, the institution should realign resources to meet the demand.

▶ **Changes in employment demographics.** Now that the baby boomer generation has reached traditional retirement age, U.S. businesses are experiencing a dramatic increase in employee turnover. This is happening in higher education as well, with many senior-level positions remaining vacant (or held by interims) for extended periods of time as qualified individuals pursue other opportunities. In response, institutions have increased their nontraditional hires, such as chief financial officers hired from the private sector, government, or healthcare. Similarly, colleges and universities increasingly turn to the business and nonprofit sectors to fill the president's position. At public institutions, legislators and executives from various branches of state and local government are more frequently taking presidential positions. This influx of employees from outside higher education, coupled with looming retirements, will undoubtedly reshape institutional character.

▶ **The introduction (or discontinuation) of union representation for one or more employee classes.** The most significant change will occur if the faculty unionize, but major changes will occur whenever a class of employees moves from individual status to bargaining unit status. Unions are rarely voted onto campuses unless there is a significant employment issue causing tension between the administration and the relevant stakeholder group. It might be compensation, working conditions, or hiring practices. Irrespective of the specifics, the introduction of the union and collective bargaining dramatically changes the nature of interactions between the employees and the administration. Conversely, a decision by a represented group to decertify its union can be evidence of a significant positive shift in relations between the administration and the stakeholder group.

Whether thrust upon the institution by external forces or nurtured from within the institution, the impetus for change can be addressed through the planning and budget processes to achieve specific objectives.

An institution's character contributes to the way in which participants in the budget process interact. Moreover, the character can determine who those participants are. Some participants are essential and included in the process at nearly every institution. This would include the chief financial officer, chief academic officer, budget office staff, institutional research, etc. Other institutions take it a step further and are intentional about affording a meaningful role to various stakeholder groups such as the faculty senate, staff council, and student government. And still others establish an advisory group similar to the IEC described later in the chapter.

A key question for institutions with one or more unions is how or whether union members participate in the budget process. Some institutions establish a firewall with the unions and do not provide for specific participation by union members or their representatives. In other cases, especially when faculty automatically are members of the union, it would be impossible to have stakeholder participation without union members participating. When this situation arises, it's important for the institution to be explicit about the role for the participants. In other words, are they formally representing the union, or are they functioning solely as faculty members?

Simpler logistics typically permit smaller colleges and universities to allow more individual participation by faculty, staff, and students. Smaller institutions can involve a comparatively smaller number of participants in the budget process and yet still have broad representation from all institutional segments. This breadth of participation becomes more difficult for a large institution, which might involve an even larger number of participants but not achieve the same level of representation and, therefore, awareness.

Some community colleges and smaller four-year institutions adopt a highly centralized approach to budgeting, simply to reduce the demands placed on their smaller workforces. In institutions with streamlined management structures and fewer discretionary resources, involving a relatively small number of people in planning and budgeting can work if a high level of trust exists on the campus.

At public institutions and elite independent institutions, budget participants will ask different questions about resource allocation than their counterparts at struggling institutions. Because they typically rely on some taxpayer support, public institutions are accountable to a broader constituency than independent institutions. They must be responsive to legislators, state agencies, and the public in ways that independent institutions are not. Even states that grant a high level of autonomy to higher education will require institutions to provide information to state agencies. These demands may shape the formats for budget requests, accounting structures, and other aspects of regulatory oversight. Both public and independent institutions are subject to extensive accountability requirements for resources provided by the federal government. These resources can come directly to the institution (in the form of research grants or land-grant appropriations) or to students— through the institution—in the form of financial aid.

One unique characteristic of higher education is how much institutions share best practices with one another. Although colleges and universities compete for sponsored program funding, the most qualified students, the best faculty and staff, donor support, athletic titles, etc., they willingly share their ideas and successes. Entire conferences and symposia are devoted to the sharing of success stories, best practices, and innovative approaches to a variety of management issues.

Budgeting is no exception in this regard, and the character of the institution will influence how readily a new strategy can be implemented. Typically though, change is introduced incrementally. Few institutions have a culture that can tolerate a completely new approach to something as crucial as budgeting. As a result, institutions commonly retain the basic elements of existing budget strategies while phasing in new approaches through pilot programs or for only a portion of the overall budget. Alternatively, they introduce the new model through parallel operation with the old and new budget models operating simultaneously for a full year. The old budget model typically drives resource distribution but, while it's happening, information is available about how resources would be managed differently if the new model was in place.

ORGANIZATIONAL STRUCTURE

One of the unique characteristics of colleges and universities, especially larger ones, is the constant state of reorganization that frequently exists. An individual who spends the majority of his or her career in one institution will see numerous changes in senior leadership. Average tenures vary over time, and presidents currently are serving for an average of 6.5 years, down from seven years in 2011.[212]

Tenures for other senior leaders such as chief academic and chief financial officers tend to be longer but, nonetheless, it is probable that one of these three key positions will be turning over at least once each decade or so. (In troubled institutions, the churn may increase to one position every five years or less.) With each new hire comes the likelihood of organizational changes, especially when it's at the top level—the president or chancellor. Such changes usually shift the institution either toward or away from a centralized structure.

The more centralized a structure is, the more likely the institution is to have relatively fewer layers of management. Fewer senior leaders are needed, and each of them typically has a broader span of control. When a more decentralized structure is employed, there tend to be more management layers with larger numbers of assistant- or deputy-level executives. Either of these structures will influence the institution and how it operates. Each of the following major topics may be influenced significantly by the nature of the organizational structure, starting with the approach to decision-making.

DECISION-MAKING AUTHORITY

A continual source of tension among decision-makers in any organizational setting—but especially when dealing with resource allocation—is determining the level of authority at which to make decisions. Most budget participants will express a desire for greater autonomy: Faculty feel constrained by the department chairperson; chairpersons feel constrained by deans; deans feel constrained by the provost; and in public institutions, everyone complains about approvals required by the executive branches of government.

At what level should financial decisions be made? Most experts say the best decisions are made closest to the action. In fact, the real issue is where the organization falls on the continuum between control and accountability. A system of accountability allows greater operational latitude with respect to decision-making compared to one that relies on controls designed to prevent problems from occurring.

An accountability system can include controls as well, but they need not be the dominant factor. It might be appropriate to allow a system of accountability to operate for most transactions and decisions, with control being exercised only for selected issues that represent significant dollar or political risk. For instance, a higher authority typically is required to approve transactions above a certain dollar level or to sign off when the institution makes an official salary offer to a prospective employee. This level of control ensures that proper procedures have been followed in terms of the employee's selection and that the financial commitment fits within the institution's overall structure.

Some hiring decisions carry political risk. For example, a public institution's hiring of a former state official might be viewed as politically motivated rather than driven by the institution's staffing needs and the individual's qualifications. Academic units typically enjoy a significant amount of autonomy in the hiring process—except in situations involving positions that come with the granting of tenure. Yet it still would be appropriate to require departments to seek approval before extending an offer to a current or former governmental official.

To maintain an appropriate balance between the level of control and the amount of latitude provided to operational managers, some institutions use sophisticated systems and processes to ensure expenses are incurred in accordance with the budget. These automated systems support line-item budgeting, through which funds allocated for supplies must be spent for supplies, funds budgeted for travel can be used only for travel, and so on. Institutions that use a line-item budget system to achieve control will not process transactions that would produce deficits in the individual budget categories. This imposes a significant administrative burden on the operating units because, as resource needs evolve throughout the year, budget adjustments must be processed to align the spending with the budget.

An example of a slightly lower level of control is an aggregate nonsalary expense pool. With this approach, separate budgets are established for compensation, equipment, and nonsalary expenses. Supplies, travel, and other expenses are not represented in specific budget lines. Instead, these— along with all other expenses—are charged against the nonsalary pool expense budget. Assuming that transactions are appropriately chargeable to the nonsalary pool—meaning they're not equipment or salary charges—they are processed as long as funds remain available.

Enhanced accountability mechanisms offer an alternative to this type of control environment. Rather than relying on preventing problems, an accountability environment shifts the decision-making authority to the unit responsible for managing the budget. It also charges unit managers with addressing problems that may arise. Accountability practices are more common in highly decentralized organizational environments.

Returning to the example above, a control system would simply prevent a department from overspending its budget for travel. In a decentralized structure relying on accountability, the transaction would be processed and the department would be responsible for addressing any resulting budget deficit in a timely manner. The responsible managers might need to request additional resources from the next unit up the organizational chain, or they might transfer resources into the travel category from another category within the departmental budget. In either case, the accountability system relies on them to make the decisions that are most appropriate while still following overall institutional guidelines.

TRANSPARENCY

The degree to which the budget process is open to review by those not actively involved in the deliberations dictates the amount of flexibility decision-makers have in their negotiations over resource allocations. At the same time, the institution's character and structure for involvement will determine the openness of the process. In general, the greater the number of participants in the budget process, the more open it will be. Note that, to the extent the planning process was open and broadly participative, there usually is less concern about an open budget process because most of the key decisions have already been made and shared with the community.

Some institutions carefully control openness to prevent unintended consequences when something sensitive is under consideration. For instance, if the budget provides for changes that will result from outsourcing a portion of facilities operations, the institution will want to take great care in communicating these potential changes. Outsourcing analysis usually includes a plan to protect the employment of current workers. Nevertheless, when staff learn about the outsourcing possibility through the budget process, the news likely will alarm them—and may result in significant service disruptions until the matter can be addressed.

As a rule, budgets should not contain surprises for the campus community. Address important issues before they affect the budget—ideally, through an engaged and inclusive planning process. If difficult issues arise at the budget development stage, try to separate them from their budgetary implications. Communicate first with the affected parties and then inform the broader community before addressing the decision's budgetary implications. This approach doesn't guarantee the avoidance of acrimony or tension, but it will lessen them and may forestall challenges to the budget as a whole. If the budget contains major surprises—especially ones that could have been addressed in a more open manner through effective planning—the entire process becomes suspect.

Thanks to "open meetings" legislation and regulations, public institutions have opened their policy-making and decision-making arenas to a wider audience. On the positive side, this development enhances the accountability of people in public positions. In some situations, however, it can have negative consequences. By its nature, budget development is a process of negotiation and trade-off. So even when conducted in an above-board and appropriate manner, it can be viewed in a negative light. The negotiation process likely will result in identifying some institutional activities to sacrifice in the short term in favor of others that will provide substantial long-term benefits. Voicing this fact publicly can raise the hackles of some constituents—especially those who will be negatively affected by the loss of the sacrificed activity.

Recognizing the need for a balance between openness and privacy, some institutions have designed the budget process to allow relevant stakeholder groups to be represented even while sensitive discussions about competing priorities take place. These representatives typically are not at liberty to discuss what they learn, but the community tends to be more comfortable because it knows there was an opportunity for its colleagues to ensure that their views were heard. In this way, appropriate participation is achieved, but negative consequences are avoided. The overall communications to the broader community are structured to minimize the negative impact that budget decisions may have on individuals, programs, and activities. In these circumstances, the need for complete openness in the budget process is balanced against the need for privacy during delicate negotiations and deliberations.

Transparency is deemed to be an essential element of a budget process, but care must be taken. It's not enough to be transparent. Clarity also is required. Sharing everything that is used in the budget process may feel as if it's transparent but, if cryptic code words, symbols, and acronyms are spread throughout the material, the benefits from transparency may be elusive. Care should be taken to ensure that everyone willing to invest a modest amount of effort can understand the information that is being made available.

Neither public nor independent institutions have a lock on transparency and clarity, but they don't necessarily approach these issues the same way. Public institutions generally will be more transparent with certain budgetary information than a comparable independent institution. Independent institutions, for instance, rarely disclose individual salaries. At public institutions, compensation information usually is available in the library, if not on a website or printed periodically in the local newspaper. The bottom line with this area is to ensure that as much information as is reasonable is made available and that effort is invested to make it as understandable as possible.

LEVELS OF TRUST

Trust usually is a two-way street, and the manner in which the budget is developed both influences and grows out of trust. The more the administration, faculty, and other stakeholder groups trust one another, the more likely they are to rely on a budget process that features significant openness and information sharing. In many instances, the high trust levels enjoyed by the various stakeholders is the product of the openness. When this is present, participants don't feel as if they are being left out of important discussions or barred from seeing critical data.

In organizations lacking trust, the budget process probably involves a small group of people and produces a final product that few outside the group understand well. This type of closed process ultimately will erode whatever trust might exist. In fact, when a campus has a problem with trust, the budget process frequently is found to be a major contributor to the situation—and may actually be at the root of the problem.

COMMUNICATION

In some institutions—especially those without effective planning processes—it's common for units to submit budget requests early in the process and receive little to no feedback before the final budget has been approved by the governing board. Along the way, the departments have no idea whether they succeeded in making a case for additional resources or how their requests were perceived relative to others in the institution.

To avoid this situation, start with an effective planning process. This will result in the community understanding the likely budgetary decisions to be made. Then, throughout the budget development process, distribute information about the status of the budget—especially to lower-level units that may not have direct access to decision-makers. Given the ease of electronic communication, there is no excuse for failing to disseminate information regularly during the budget process.

Periodically sharing information throughout the budget process will help allay concerns and allow the process to proceed smoothly. Keeping the community apprised of the progress on developing the budget will help avoid rumors and the resulting distrust they engender. It also can discourage people from taking actions that may prove counterproductive in the long run. As for the amount of information to share, more is always better.

PARTICIPATION AND INVOLVEMENT

Budget development can be limited to budget staff and administrators or expand to include faculty, students, and other stakeholders. Stakeholder groups may take part in the process through mechanisms such as advisory committees and budget hearings. The effectiveness of the process will depend on the quality of the participants' efforts; their level of institutional knowledge; the support they receive from budget staff; and the budget office's willingness and ability to provide meaningful, usable data.

Opening Up

In large part, an institution's culture and organizational structure will have the greatest impact on the degree of openness in the budget process. Colleges with small faculties and staffs and a strong sense of shared governance typically have relatively open deliberations, frequently followed by a town hall meeting to discuss the proposed budget. That is, unless they have opted for a highly centralized structure, in which case, there is limited openness and information sharing. Larger institutions, because of the sheer number of people involved and a tendency toward decentralized organizational structures, will share more information while struggling to achieve the same depth of participation.

Institutions without a highly participative governance structure will more likely have a relatively closed budget process without much transparency or input from stakeholders. Even when the process is transparent and involves extensive participation by various stakeholders, the numbers represented will depict only a small fraction of the college or university's community. In these situations, widespread and frequent communication becomes paramount.

Generally speaking, the more open the process, the better—as long as there is genuine sharing of information. When there isn't, participants may develop unreasonable expectations about what is realistic in terms of resource distribution. Also important is that closed processes tend to simply perpetuate past practices—including their flawed elements. A more open budgeting process has the benefit of including new and differing perspectives. It may, however, take longer as participants raise difficult but necessary questions related to making resource allocation decisions and negotiating levels of support. The criteria for distributing resources may be more widely debated—but also more widely understood.

Role of the board. How intimately involved should the governing board be in the development of the budget? Should it influence tuition rates or the salary increase pool? Should the board directly influence the amounts allocated to Department A versus Departments B and C? Or the distribution of resources between ongoing operations and new strategic initiatives? What about participating in operational budget hearings?

The answers to these questions will vary from campus to campus. It's not possible to articulate all the possible variations or the specific factors that favor one approach over another. The goal here is to describe an effective approach that would serve the majority of institutions. Readers must recognize that it will be necessary to adapt the approach to particular campus environments and cultures.

Governing boards in higher education must distinguish between their governance responsibilities and the administration's responsibility to manage and operate the institution. Boards' governance responsibilities clearly translate into establishing major institutional policies. Management is responsible for adhering to the policies as it carries out the institution's mission.

Simply put, the governing board should focus on planning and leave resource allocation to management. Boards fulfill their responsibility to govern the institution by influencing and approving plans. In so doing, they leave to management the details—how to achieve the results specified in the plans.

That's why board members normally should not participate in budget hearings. Their mere presence will alter the nature of the conversation and potentially prevent discussion of critical issues. Nor would it be appropriate for the board to delve into issues such as the amount of resources allotted to particular departments or cost centers. On the other hand, it is totally appropriate for the board to influence the allocation of resources between strategic and operational objectives. This is a natural outgrowth of the board's responsibility to oversee planning and ensure that plans can be accomplished. These types of discussions should take place at board meetings rather than hearings that occur as part of the budget process.

The board influences and ultimately approves the assumptions on which management builds the budget. That role includes approving tuition rates and salary increase pools, plus providing the broad guidance that shapes the budget's development. The board also must approve the budget developed by management. And it must engage in assessment by periodically examining the administration's success in carrying out plans and living within the budget. The board also would be expected to review and approve any budget revisions that would affect the bottom line.

Still, the board's most critical role comes during the planning stage, when key decisions are made. Part of the planning process is confirming the appropriateness of the institution's mission. The board must validate the mission and confirm its continued appropriateness. Then, by participating in the planning process—particularly the strategic planning process—the board ensures that the plans support the mission.

Role of operating departments. Should these departments have a role in developing the budget, or should central budget office personnel have sole responsibility? In part, the answer depends on the kinds of expectations and interactions the institution wishes to encourage among departments. For example, if the institution will have insufficient revenues to satisfy requests for additional resources, involving departments without sharing the revenue details may raise expectations that cannot be met.

On the other hand, if the institution has established a culture of openness and inclusiveness, involving departments ensures that the best information about resource needs is available. Moreover, it can create the opportunity for enhanced collaboration and cooperation. With this approach, requests and justifications are based on information that might not otherwise become available to participants during the budget process. As departmental staff and faculty become aware of the constraints, their expectations may become more realistic. This creates an opportunity to build support for the direction ultimately selected.

Role of faculty and students. The level of involvement for faculty and students, in particular, significantly influences their satisfaction with the decisions that shape the resource allocations. Faculty appropriately believe that they offer unique perspectives with respect to academic program development (including new instructional endeavors), research initiatives, and service programs.

Students are not necessarily as active on campus as faculty—especially compared with earlier generations—but they still seek to influence budget decisions. As the cost of an education has risen and the federal government has increased the use of loans in lieu of grants, students have started paying closer attention to decisions that affect their costs. Even when students don't have a formal voice in budget matters, they make their views apparent through their enrollment decisions. This is one reason that program assessment should always consider market factors in addition to mission relatedness, quality, financial performance, etc. If students elect not to enroll in certain programs, for instance, the institution eventually will have to reduce resources allocated to those programs.

When faculty or students participate, there generally is a formal campus procedure for selecting representatives. Specify in advance the nature of the participation (advisory or decision-making), the elements of the budget subject to review, and the timing of the review. How each of these factors is addressed influences the outcome of the budget process. For instance, selecting stakeholder representatives by voting may yield the most active participants, but they may not be the ones best able to judge programs and activities. This is especially true if they specifically sought the role. In these situations, it's common for these individuals to have a narrow agenda to pursue. They focus exclusively on the agenda and not the greater good of the institution.

Taking a careful approach to participation calls for having effective ground rules and guiding principles in place. These especially help if someone is obsessing on a particular aspect of the budget.

Structured Participation

Different governance structures require different levels of involvement at varying stages of the planning and budget processes. A shared governance model may require a high level of faculty, staff, and student participation. These groups typically become involved at the planning stage, as budget assumptions are developed and approved, and may remain involved throughout the budget process as well. Representatives of various stakeholder groups can have significant involvement and see their views reflected in the final budget submitted to the board for approval.

Interestingly, when a process encourages meaningful involvement, stakeholders frequently adopt a wider, institutional perspective. Rather than merely advocate for the results most advantageous for their own constituency, they recognize the institution's global needs and support what's best for its long-term success.

A less participatory model may still provide opportunities for faculty and student involvement through an ad hoc budget advisory committee. Under this model, a small representative committee is established when the budget process begins and provides for the committee's input at various steps along the way. Unlike the shared governance model, ad hoc advisory committees frequently discover they do not have much impact. Sometimes, the institution seeks the committee's input on relatively few issues or only on issues that are not particularly significant. When this happens, the individual members often become advocates for their constituencies, making it difficult for the committee to agree on positions or recommendations to decision-makers.

Some colleges and universities structure formal participation in the budget process through separate faculty, student, and administrative budget committees. The most practical role for faculty and students is to help establish program and activity priorities and recommend general support levels. Faculty participation is appropriate and especially useful in evaluating proposals from deans or program heads for the allocation of faculty positions.

Factors affecting participation. Reviews that focus solely on academic budgets may not properly address the administrative and support activities essential to academic units' success. The timing of participation and the amount of time allotted for review will influence the effectiveness of the participation. Participants must have sufficient time to review the materials and consider alternative allocation decisions. The resulting recommendations will be more useful to policy makers at higher levels if available well before the time to finalize decisions.

Although beneficial from an overall perspective, the positives of an inclusive process must be weighed against the potential risk of negative outcomes. Not having input from students or faculty, for example, may lead to suboptimal decisions. On the other hand, involving students and faculty—but not accepting their input—likely will be worse. It may not be possible to accept all the advice provided but, if the advice was solicited and not followed, the institution has an obligation to explain why.

If an inclusive process is the goal, recognize that meaningful participation will necessarily take more time. In addition, a successful process includes careful explanations to manage the participants' expectations. If the process is not well understood and produces unrealistic or impossible-to-implement recommendations, the effort is likely to produce more negative results than if no involvement had been allowed.

If budgeters are willing to sacrifice the privacy of their deliberations for the sake of broader knowledge of the budget process details, they generally can be confident that the information will be communicated accurately to members of the academic community. Still, budget participants in large institutions often find that communication channels are unreliable and transmit distorted or incomplete information. Similarly, the give-and-take of budget deliberations may sometimes generate mixed signals, especially if negotiations occur over an extended time period. What was true at one stage of the process may no longer be true as the process approaches its end.

Risks of not allowing adequate participation. If not provided meaningful roles with genuine influence, departmental personnel likely will default to one of two roles: spender or cutter. The spender, or advocacy role, focuses on obtaining the maximum allocation of resources for the spender's unit or activity. The cutter, or restraining role, focuses on conserving resources, either for new initiatives or to increase reserves.

A department chairperson is a typical spender. He or she has the responsibility of protecting the resources in the current budget. If this doesn't happen, the chairperson will have failed in one of the primary responsibilities of the position—being an advocate for the unit. Remember that no unit believes it has sufficient resources to do everything it feels it could—or to achieve the quality levels to which it aspires.

Therefore, if the chairperson can't at least protect the level of resources currently being received, the faculty will have a negative reaction. On the other hand, a chairperson who garners increased resources—especially as compared with peer departments—can fall short in other areas and still be well regarded by the department's faculty. The added resources may be used for new programs, improved staffing, exceptional salary increases, or other purposes. To some extent, it may not really matter how the resources are used—just that they have been obtained.

The role of the cutter appears at various levels of the institution. For instance, the dean may seek ways to cut resources from one unit to provide resources needed by another unit—or to undertake a new college-level initiative. Although the dean clearly is an advocate for the unit, from the perspective of the department facing a reduction in resources, the dean functions as a cutter.

On most campuses, the budget office is unfairly perceived as the ultimate cutter. This really is not the case, even though the budget office is charged with development of the institution's budget. The budget office's goal is to produce a budget that reflects the institution's priorities, is fiscally responsible, and has sufficient flexibility to respond to unanticipated circumstances. In doing so, the budget office likely will be forced to reject requests for additional funds from some units while providing increased funds to others. For example, while requests for additional funds from some academic units are denied, funds may be allocated to facilities management to cover utility cost increases or to a dean to fund new faculty positions for a recently authorized graduate program.

Despite the common misperception, the budget office staff rarely has the authority to make budget-cutting decisions. More often than not, the budget office merely applies the guidance developed either through the planning process, as part of the budget assumptions approved by the board, or via explicit directions from senior management. Nevertheless, the budget office likely will be viewed as an omnipotent cutter by many on campus unless the institution makes a concerted effort to have a transparent budget process and clearly communicates various roles. This can be achieved through a broadly participative process.

In an optimal environment, individuals throughout the campus participate in the planning and budget processes in numerous ways. They serve on committees that develop the plans for the institution, analyze the information used to establish the assumptions that guide budget development, and develop the rationales to support the continued investment of resources in the mission-critical activities.

Institutions ideally have planning and budget processes best described as both top down and bottom up. The top-down aspect recognizes that institutional management is responsible for developing plans and allocating resources to support those plans. The bottom-up element reflects the reality that senior management, despite its best efforts, simply cannot be aware of the various situations in every operating unit. For this reason, the planning and budget processes, though guided through top-down oversight, must be informed by bottom-up realities. This can best be accomplished by having a broadly representative standing committee that oversees and influences the planning, resource allocation, and assessment processes.

Unfortunately, few institutions have such an inclusive process. All too often, a select group of staff working closely with the senior leaders—but not well connected to the broader institutional community—carefully controls the process. Even when institutions have advisory bodies to influence plans and resource allocation, those groups remain separate in carrying out their responsibilities with little to no interaction. As a result, most individuals on campus do not feel connected to the plans or the budgets intended to implement them. Moreover, they don't really understand the processes, which may cause them to distrust the processes as well as those responsible for establishing and overseeing them.

Managing expectations. As planning and budget processes evolve over time, involvement by various constituencies will change. People who seek to influence the amount of resources allocated to a particular activity usually find involvement at the budget stage less effective than involvement in planning decisions. When an institution plans effectively, budgetary decisions naturally evolve from the planning process. By the time the budget process is underway, many of the most critical decisions already have been made. Nevertheless, because many institutions have yet to develop effective mechanisms for linking planning with budgeting, interested parties always should seek to participate at the budget stage.

Individuals must recognize, however, that even when their involvement is solicited, the institution doesn't weigh all ideas or opinions equally. Some requests are simply pleas for more resources, with little or no evidence demonstrating the benefits to be gained from the additional allocation. Even when a strong, valid case is made for increased resources, the required allocations may not be made if the anticipated outcomes do not line up with or support the priorities established through the planning process.

Developing a budget is an arduous, time-consuming process. Participants in the process must be prepared to invest the time and effort to become familiar with the issues and the competing priorities for resources. For that reason, excessive turnover within stakeholder groups seeking to influence budget decisions will be counterproductive. People given the opportunity to participate must commit significant effort over several years to learn enough to offer meaningful input. Unfortunately, the budget process will take participants away from teaching or research, in the case of faculty, or from studying, in the case of students. Faculty, of course, will be credited with service, but the benefit to students is less tangible.

THREE PROCESSES, ONE COMMITTEE

When the goal is alignment of planning, resource allocation, and assessment, the best approach is to establish a standing committee charged with monitoring and making recommendations to senior management in all three areas. It is senior management's responsibility to make final decisions, but it is unlikely that it has the time needed for extensive analysis and dialogue on the full range of planning, resource allocation, and assessment issues. Senior management must rely on an IEC—a broadly representative group with support from relevant staff who can conduct analyses and make recommendations to senior management. Although the IEC's role is advisory, its contributions are invaluable because it gains an in-depth understanding of the issues and can present options as well as recommendations to senior management.

The committee reports to an executive champion—typically either the president, provost, or chief financial officer. The champion ensures that the committee's efforts are visible, that it has enough resources to carry out its duties, and that the senior leadership team is fully apprised of key issues. Ideally, an iconic faculty member and a well-regarded senior administrator will cochair this committee. If the cochairs do not already attend cabinet meetings, they should attend whenever planning, resource allocation, or assessment is on the agenda. Normally, the champion serves as a liaison between the committee and the cabinet, but there are times when direct participation may be warranted.

The permanent staffing for the committee should include the "chiefs" of various functional areas: accounting, budget, human resources, institutional effectiveness, institutional research, and planning. These individuals are essential participants because they usually know more about their respective subjects than anyone else on campus. Moreover, they have day-to-day responsibility for these areas. In some cases, they may be responsible for more than one area. For instance, the chief institutional effectiveness officer may also oversee institutional research, or budgeting may be overseen by the chief accounting or chief planning officer. Independent of how the institution is organized and staffed, the individuals with responsibility for these areas must participate in the committee and contribute their expertise either as full or ex officio members. Another argument in favor of their direct involvement is that they usually oversee staff with the skill sets needed to conduct analyses to support the IEC's efforts.

Beyond the staff roles described above, the IEC must reflect the institution's diversity writ large. It needs to have enough members to ensure representation from all stakeholder groups and a large array of organizational units. Representatives from the faculty senate, staff council, and—depending on institutional culture—student government should have permanent seats on the committee. A large institution with multiple schools and colleges would probably appoint one or two deans to the committee, plus several academic department heads and selected administrative/support managers from units such as auxiliary enterprises, athletics, facilities, and student affairs. To provide an institution-wide perspective, committee membership would also include faculty and staff from various units across the institution. Members should have staggered appointments lasting two to three years, so the collective body always has the benefit of new thinking and perspectives to supplement the knowledge of experienced members.

In the best situations, committee members do not serve as representatives of their home units but rather as institutional representatives, adopting a "trustee" mentality focused on serving the best interests of the institution. Their perspectives should be informed by their experience, but their greatest contribution comes when they focus on what's best for the institution overall—even when that may not always be in the best interests of their unit.

Having one committee responsible for planning, budgeting, and assessment makes sense on many levels. First, if the three processes operate independently of one another, with only limited interaction, the institution probably won't achieve its full potential. The people making recommendations on resource issues to senior management need to understand the plans being pursued with those resources. Similarly, a strong connection should exist between plans and the measures that will determine the success of their implementation. It's not enough for the leaders of separate operational planning, budget, and assessment committees to periodically communicate with one another. Even when the committee chairs do communicate frequently and well—and that doesn't always happen—the message still could become muddled when translated for the relevant committee. Having all the committee members present for all the discussions reduces the possibility of a communication breakdown. Moreover, it creates a greater likelihood of consistent communication to the broader institutional community.

Although the full committee should be present when major issues are being considered in advance of making recommendations to senior management, there are times when it might make sense for standing subcommittees of the IEC to be established. For instance, the IEC may establish separate subcommittees focused on human resources, technology, academics, etc. These subcommittees may take a deep dive into their respective areas when major issues come before the IEC. For instance, if a new academic program is being proposed and new space along with it, a standing space subcommittee may be in the best position to know whether there are other approaches that may represent effective alternatives for the program.

As mentioned earlier, strategic planning should be conducted in a broadly participative way. In satisfying this objective, the institution can ensure appropriate alignment between strategic planning and the budget by carefully selecting participants for the strategic planning process. Ideally, there would be cross-representation between the SPTF and the IEC. If this happens, there would be no excuse for the operational plans, and the resulting resource allocation decisions, not to align with the strategic plan.

INVOLVEMENT IN BUDGET MONITORING

Although planning and budget development can be a highly participatory process involving all segments of a campus, budget-monitoring responsibilities usually are carried out by one of two units: the central accounting office (sometimes referred to as the controller's office) or the budget office.

The budget office typically monitors progress on generating revenues and incurring expenses at most institutions, but the central accounting office may have this responsibility in smaller institutions with limited support staff.

Irrespective of which office has the responsibility, it monitors and reports on the progress of the institution toward generating the institution's projected revenues and expending the resources allocated to the various units and activities. Those with primary responsibility for administering specific pools of resources carry out the day-to-day activities that produce revenues or consume resources, but they see only a small part of the overall financial picture. The designated office—either budget or accounting—assembles all of the parts to create the high-level picture indicating whether the institution is on track to meet its budget targets while pursuing its many activities. If things are not on track, it is the responsibility of senior management to make the decisions that will realign expenses with revenues to achieve the budget's financial objectives. For instance, senior management is the ultimate arbiter about how and whether contingency funds will be deployed or if directives will be issued to specific budget managers to reduce expenses to stay within the established parameters.

Even when it does not have monitoring responsibilities, the budget office on every campus engages in two specific activities: reviewing requests for changes to the current approved budget and preparing for the next budget cycle. Personnel activities—unexpected retirements, resignations, extended illnesses—necessitate changes in the way salaries and benefits are deployed. When a key faculty member is seriously ill, for example, the department may request supplemental funding to pay overload to others in the department or to engage adjunct faculty to cover the faculty member's classes. Or a researcher may learn of a new grant opportunity that he or she is assured of receiving if the institution can commit matching funds. There is no end to the budget issues that arise each day on a campus. In institutions relying on an IEC, the impacts of these actions must be considered by the committee and a recommendation submitted to senior management. Ultimately, it will be the budget office staff that act on the decisions made by senior management.

When addressing day-to-day individual budget issues, the budget office staff also must consider future implications. Sometimes, the situations are temporary and will resolve themselves by the end of the fiscal year. In other cases, however, budget office staff must address the immediate changes as well as the ongoing implications. For instance, if a faculty member receives a multiyear research grant, the need for matching funds will continue beyond the current period. That ongoing commitment must be factored into future-year budgets.

Similarly, the tenure process, economic volatility, changes in the endowment payout authorized for the future, revisions to state budget policies, program expansions or contractions, and new construction all would affect future-year budgets. While others make the decisions on such matters, the budget office staff determine the decisions' impact on future budgets and communicates this information to the senior leadership team.

KEY POINTS

▶ An institution's size, mission, governance, type of funding, culture, operating climate, administrative structure, and history all contribute to its unique character. In turn, institutional character will influence how a college or university approaches the budgeting process.

▶ Both external forces and internal decisions—identified through the planning process and addressed through the budgeting process—can significantly reshape institutional character.

▶ The greater the number of participants involved in the budget process, the more open it will be. And the more transparent the process, the more faculty, administrators, and other constituents will trust one another to keep the institution's best interests in mind.

▶ Issuing regular reports on how the budget process is progressing will help allay concerns within the community and minimize rumors. The more information shared, the better.

CHAPTER 9: COMPREHENSIVE AND SPECIAL-PURPOSE BUDGET MODELS

Four comprehensive approaches typically characterize budgeting within higher education. The approaches are not mutually exclusive. Few institutions use one of the models exclusively. In fact, the vast majority of institutions have developed hybrid budget models that incorporate elements of each of the comprehensive models, frequently in combination with special-purpose models described later in the chapter.

Despite this, each of the four comprehensive approaches has unique characteristics that differentiate it from the others. They each have a distinctive focus and emphasis on the types of information used to determine resource allocations and the mechanics used to accomplish the distributions. In the discussion that follows, the models will be described as discrete approaches that are operated in a "pure" fashion. Recognize that this is not the norm. Instead, hybrid models are the rule of thumb. Also, keep in mind that an institution's budget model needs to support the allocation of resources to priorities established through an effective planning process. Moreover, whatever budget model is used must work compatibly with its culture to support the institution's operational objectives irrespective of what the model is called.

Although the labels and descriptions discussed below suggest that a particular model employs specific approaches that don't appear in other models, this is not the case. For instance, responsibility center budgeting (RCB) relies on the use of formulas but in different ways from how they are used in formula budgeting. And it is not uncommon for institutions relying primarily on incremental budgeting to couple it with initiatives-based budgeting to ensure that the results of plans are not ignored when resources are deployed.

FORMULA BUDGETING

Used primarily in public institutions, formula budgeting is a process for estimating resource requirements based on the relationships between program demand, program cost, and related factors. These relationships, frequently expressed as mathematical formulations, can be as simple as a student-faculty ratio or as complicated as the costs per student credit hour by discipline for multiple levels of instruction (lower division, upper division, master's, doctoral). Historical data, projected trends, or parameters negotiated to provide desired levels of funding can provide the bases for budget formulas, which combine technical judgment, negotiation, and political agreements. Formula budgeting is attractive to state agencies overseeing the state's higher education resources because it causes the bulk of available resources to be addressed without the need for complex negotiations each cycle. Some resources may be distributed outside the formula model, but it's a relatively small amount compared to the core that is driven by the formula model.

Budget formulas come in all shapes and sizes. Most, in some way, relate to enrollment, student-credit-hour productivity, staffing, or space. Within this overall framework, different formulas are used to address the distinct functional areas of an institution's operations. Thus, instructional resources may be allocated on the basis of average faculty teaching loads or credit-hour costs (by student level or course level) applied against historical or projected enrollment levels. Library support may be determined on the basis of enrollments and service relationships. Amounts needed for support and maintenance of the built environment may not be enrollment based because these costs tend to be a fixed expense relatively immune to enrollment shifts. More likely, the formulas used for the built environment depend upon the square footage and type of facilities, their age, and/or their replacement cost.

Rather than using distinct formulas for different functional areas, some budget formula frameworks focus on a base programmatic function's (e.g., instruction) resource needs, considering enrollments and instructional costs or workloads. It then computes amounts for other programmatic or support areas (such as libraries, academic support, O&M) as a percentage of the base. In another approach—focused primarily on staffing—the formula computes only salary expenses for the institution. Nonsalary budget requirements can be determined by various other methods—either as a function of salary expenses or based on other analyses targeted to the particular nonsalary categories.

It is rare to see formula budgeting applied holistically within a college or university, although formulas likely will be utilized in every institutional budget model to address portions of the budget. More typically, it is used at a system-wide or statewide level to give public institutions a foundation for developing budget requests and to assist the appropriate control authority with resource allocation. By their very nature, budget formulas are simplified models of how a typical institution operates—or at least is perceived to operate. This modeling role of budget formulas sometimes puzzles state officials, who assume that funds appropriated to institutions should be spent exactly as they were distributed through the formula. This concept is not practical because all formulas represent the application of an average. Only through pure coincidence would an individual institution's needs match perfectly with the results of the formula. For this reason, most institutions employ the formula when interacting with the state to obtain resources but abandon it when they make internal resource allocation decisions.

The needs justified by application of a formula routinely exceed available resources. Often, the formula is then slightly modified to yield an allocation approach more consistent with available resources. Or the state may retain the formula but simply fund it at less than 100 percent.

Either approach may be acceptable but will produce suboptimal outcomes if the formula produces results that differ dramatically from the resources available for allocation. If a significant gap exists between the resource needs identified under the formula and the amounts available for funding, the formula itself comes into question. The formula's utility and effectiveness diminish as the gap between needs and available resources grows. If the gap grows too large, the formula may prove counterproductive—simply because it cannot support the objectives that influenced its development. In other words, the formula was developed to achieve political objectives through optimal distribution of resources in support of public higher education needs within the jurisdiction or system. If the variance between the available resources and the amounts determined under the formula are too large, the policy objectives will not be met. Additionally, depending on the size of the gap, it's possible that the reliance on the formula could actually harm the institutions it is intended to support.

Advantages: The quantitative nature of most budget formulas gives them the appearance, if not always the reality, of an unbiased distribution. In some cases, formula budgeting has increased institutional autonomy by reducing political influence in budgeting. An even more significant advantage—at least in stable economic climates—is the capacity to reduce uncertainty by providing a mechanism for predicting future resource needs and potential appropriation amounts. The overall process is simplified because budget formulas tend to remain stable over long periods due to the difficulty of gaining agreement whenever proposals are offered to modify them. The competing priorities and agendas tend to result in a decision to keep things as they are.

Disadvantages. Because it tends to rely on historical data, formula budgeting can discourage new programs or revisions to existing programs. Further, given its focus on quantification, it can suffer from many of the faults identified below for incremental budgeting. For instance, if all resources are distributed to institutions using formulas, there is little incentive to conduct in-depth analyses of programs and activities supported by state resources because the formula will not be influenced by the results. This doesn't preclude analyses for internal resource distribution purposes, but it's unlikely that the state agencies would have much interest in the results for purposes of their resource distribution. Perhaps most significant, formula budgeting creates an incentive to retain programs or activities that generate funding under the formula—even if they no longer contribute to the achievement of institutional mission, goals, and objectives.

Formulas can also have an unequal or even negative impact on participating institutions. For instance, because most formulas are developed using averages, institutions experiencing increased enrollment will fare better because marginal costs for additional students tend to be lower than average costs. Conversely, the same formula will have a more negative impact if enrollments are falling. To reduce these impacts, some states have developed formulas that differentiate between fixed and variable costs. Others moderate formula results when there are abnormal enrollment swings—either up or down. Even with these practices, some institutions may suffer as the formula catches up to the enrollment change, while other institutions experience a brief windfall until the actual enrollment results are reflected in the formula distributions.

INCREMENTAL/DECREMENTAL BUDGETING

Sometimes referred to as historical budgeting, incremental/decremental budgeting is a mechanism for distributing resources in equal percentages throughout the institution. For the discussion in this section, the reader should understand that the principles apply both to incremental budgeting—when future resources are increasing—and decremental budgeting—when future resources are shrinking. The key characteristic of the model is that, in its purest application, the changes are made across the board. That is, each unit or activity receives or gives up the same percentage of its resources. Although a large number of institutions employ incremental budgeting for portions of their resource distributions, it's relatively rare—but not unheard of—to find institutions applying these principles to the entire resource pool.

Incremental budgeting measures the expected change in allocable resources from one period to the next, then distributes that percentage uniformly to each program or activity (or broad category) usually after making provision for unavoidable fixed-cost increases. This approach relies on the fact that basic aspects of programs and activities do not change significantly from year to year. And in most situations, the change in available resources in any given year represents a small percentage of the base budget. Because individuals and organizations tend to spend their resources with little variation, marginal resource additions can accommodate any needed changes.

Unlike many industries, including some equally labor-intensive ones, higher education does not experience significant workforce fluctuations over short periods. Although they contribute to this characteristic, tenured faculty represent a relatively small percentage of the total workforce at most institutions. Rather, the workforce does not change dramatically from one period to another because the number of service recipients—students and, in some cases, patients—does not change significantly from year to year. With salaries and benefits representing the largest component of any institutional budget, yet remaining relatively constant from year to year, the overall budget will remain fairly stable under normal circumstances.

Of course, significant fluctuations in the amounts of resources available—or in the demands placed on those resources—do occur from one year to the next. For example, the Great Recession significantly reduced resource availability for public institutions during fiscal year 2009 and the years immediately thereafter. And the reduction represented a very substantial drop—in many cases of double-digit proportions—that lasted several years for some institutions.

The practice of incremental budgeting varies dramatically among campuses. Some institutions use differential factors for various organizational segments. For instance, the first claim on resources usually is for the salary increase pool and other unavoidable cost increases such as utilities and fringe benefits. Once these have been addressed, the institution may specify a percentage increase for academic units and a different, typically smaller, percentage increase for administrative and support units. Alternatively, it may specify an across-the-board increase for all units. Or the institution may combine across-the-board increases for some categories with differential increases for others—and no increase at all for still others.

Regardless of the specific approach used, any institution allocating the entire pool of resources through incremental budgeting will produce suboptimal results. Because it operates only at the margins, incremental budgeting does not involve serious examination of what the base budget will accomplish. It also avoids the question of whether the institution can find better uses for some of the resources. In a purely incremental model, budgeters bypass difficult policy choices because questions usually focus on minor changes rather than on an overall approach to the mission.

In essence, this type of budgeting maintains the status quo and generally does not align well with planning. In fact, planning becomes almost unnecessary if incremental budgeting is applied to the entire resource pool. By design, planning is intended to identify priorities that will alter activities to achieve improved outcomes. Allocating all resources through any across-the-board approach obviates the need to identify priorities because everyone will receive the same percentage increase irrespective of how it aligns with priorities that might have been established.

Advantages: By far, incremental budgeting is the most efficient approach. Institutions find it relatively simple to implement, easy to apply, more controllable, more adaptable, and more flexible than almost any other approach because of the general lack of emphasis on analysis. In addition, it minimizes conflict within the institution because, for the most part, it treats all institutional components equally.

Disadvantages: Incremental budgeting carries two faulty assumptions. First, it assumes that the current distribution of resources across activities and programs is optimal—which is highly unlikely. Some units typically have more resources than they can productively use, while others are significantly under-resourced given their potential for success.

Second, incremental budgeting assumes that a standard percentage increase (or decrease) will enhance (or impair) each program or activity in an optimal manner. Again, this is highly unlikely. Neither increased nor decreased resources will greatly affect the units ces may not receive enough new resources to allow them to succeed—or the cuts may curtail their efforts to the point of hurting the institution.

Over time, excessive reliance on this approach will drive the institutional activities toward mediocrity. Poorly performing units will continue to consume resources that provide little return in terms of enhanced institutional success. At the same time, high-performing and high-potential units do not garner enough resources to leverage their efforts for better results.

Despite its shortcomings, incremental budgeting endures. Without question, this is attributable to the model's straightforward and easy application. It is practiced by the largest number of institutions throughout higher education— at least for a portion of their resource pool. Unfortunately, a small number of institutions sacrifice effectiveness for efficiency by distributing their entire resource pool through incremental budgeting.

A Quick Guide

Here are the main distinctions among the four comprehensive budget models commonly used in higher education:

- ▶ **Formula budgeting** relies on quantitative measures to distribute resources.
- ▶ **Incremental/decremental budgeting** focuses primarily on across-the-board increases or decreases to the base, rather than on analysis of the activities being supported. The implicit assumption is that the base—in whole or in part—has been rationalized in previous budget cycles.
- ▶ **RCB** classifies individual programs and units as either revenue or cost centers. Revenue centers control the revenues they generate and are responsible for financing both their direct and indirect costs as well as internal taxes assessed to them. Cost centers are funded from service charges, central revenues, and the taxes assessed on revenue centers. RCB is the sole comprehensive budget model that provides incentives that can lead to financial sustainability.
- ▶ **Zero Based Budgeting (ZBB)** examines some or all programs and activities during each budget cycle to ensure they continue to contribute to organizational success and consume an appropriate level of resources in doing so.

These four models allocate all of an organization's resources. The next two models focus on only a subset of those resources. As such, they must be employed in conjunction with one or more of the comprehensive approaches:

- ▶ **Initiative-Based Budgeting (IBB)** focuses on the identification and funding of activities that support established priorities. Resources are distributed through some type of competitive process.
- ▶ **Performance-Based Budgeting (PBB)** involves allocating resources based on a program's relative success on the achievement of specific established targets.

RESPONSIBILITY CENTER BUDGETING (RCB)

Known by a variety of terms such as responsibility center management (RCM), activity-based budgeting, revenue responsibility budgeting, incentive-based budgeting, and profit center budgeting, RCB emphasizes program performance and revenue-generation incentives rather than central budgetary control. The essential characteristic of RCB—that units manage and control the revenues they generate—contributes to this approach being referred to informally as "every tub on its bottom."

Under RCB, schools, colleges, and other organizational units become revenue centers, cost centers, or a combination of the two. In its purest form, all revenues generated by the units are attributed to the units. This includes tuition and fees, overhead recovered on research grants and contracts, gifts, endowment income, and proceeds from sales and services provided by the unit.

For instance, a college of engineering is credited with at least a portion of the tuition revenue generated by classes taught by its faculty. Additionally, the college receives credit (i.e., revenue) for students majoring in an engineering discipline and taking classes in other schools or colleges. Similarly, all overhead recovered from the sponsored programs awarded to faculty of the college count as the college's revenue. If the college's instructional or research activities lead to commercially viable products or services, the college retains any revenues generated. Essentially, any revenues that can be connected directly to the efforts of the college of engineering come under that dean's ultimate control.

In exchange for controlling the resources it generates, the college of engineering also assumes responsibility for funding all of its direct costs. This includes its salaries and benefits, supplies, equipment, travel, etc., and even space-related costs for labs and classrooms utilized by the college. In addition, the college must share in the funding for the various cost centers that serve it or its constituents. This usually is accomplished through an allocation of indirect costs for services provided by the cost centers because they do not have the capacity to generate revenues from external sources.

Typical cost centers include the library, student services, human resources, the budget office, and many others.

Some cost centers—especially those providing easily monitored and measured services, such as facilities management and information technology—rely on charge-back mechanisms for at least a portion of their resources. They charge the cost center's internal customers for the services provided to them on the basis of rates established for cost recovery. The rates, designed to fully recover all costs and balance out over time, usually are subject to a central approval process that ensures service recipients are not being overcharged to receive the established baseline level of services. Typically, the same rates apply to sponsored programs that receive services from support units. When this occurs, federal guidelines must be used to establish the rates to ensure that federally sponsored activities receive the most favorable rates. Note that services that exceed baseline levels are not included in the basic cost-recovery rates. The costs for these extra services are subject to negotiation between the revenue center and the cost center—with some appropriate central monitoring.

In addition, campuses impose a tax on the revenue centers' unrestricted revenues or the expenses they incur. The tax proceeds, combined with central revenues—such as investment income, unrestricted gifts, and unrestricted endowment income—create a subvention pool that funds cost centers as well as revenue centers that don't generate enough revenues to be self-sufficient. The combined resources available from taxes and central revenues also are used to subsidize some cost centers and provide resources that can be used in support of established priorities. Central administration collects the taxes and deploys them, along with central revenues, in a transparent manner, thereby performing a key role in the institution's resource allocation decisions.

RCB forces institutions to ask questions about how to share revenues and how much will be used to fund central services. Because all support services are fully costed and all academic units receive credit for their share of total institutional revenue, RCB forces a much broader understanding of institutional finances.

Advantages: RCB provides incentives for units to enhance revenues and manage costs. It puts them in a position to better recognize the importance of revenue sources such as tuition and overhead recoveries from sponsored programs. Also, RCB can help instill an awareness of the actual costs of relatively scarce campus resources such as space and information technology.

In models other than RCB, many overhead costs are borne centrally and consume institutional resources before allocations for other purposes are made. When costs are treated in this manner—that is, taken off the top—faculty and staff tend to lack awareness of the true cost of the services provided on campus. RCB typically operates in a highly transparent manner and results in more revenue and cost information being available throughout the institution. As a result, having access to cost information changes faculty and staff demand for services and resources. When people understand what their department will have to pay, they become more likely to pursue optimal space utilization rather than requesting additional space that may not be essential. For instance, faculty accept assigned class times during nonpeak periods to take advantage of existing space availability when they understand that the reduced space charges provide resources that can be used for other purposes such as graduate assistantships.

Responsibility for managing resources results in surpluses being carried forward from one fiscal year to the next. Deficits that materialize are covered from unit reserves or become liabilities that must be satisfied using resources from future-year budgets. RCB encourages removal of central controls and gives more attention to performance or outcomes measures. The budgeting system also drives home the reality that academic decisions have financial consequences.

With RCB, recipients of campus services become better and more demanding customers. In turn, because campus providers charge for their services, they become more responsive—especially when forced to compete with the private sector. If outside vendors can provide comparable or better services at competitive prices, the campus will turn to them. Using outside vendors may not be possible for services such as payroll, accounting, or purchasing, but internal customers will still let providers know if the service does not meet acceptable levels.

Disadvantages: Detractors complain that RCB focuses unduly on the bottom line and does not respond adequately to issues of academic quality or other priorities. Another common complaint is that decisions made by individual units—though advantageous for the units themselves—may have negative consequences for the institution as a whole. For instance, units often establish their own internal service provider operations instead of using central services. Or individual colleges or schools add courses in disciplines already available from other academic units simply to retain the revenue from those courses. And as units gain greater budget autonomy, a lack of coherence between planning and budgeting may evolve. This puts more pressure on management to have mechanisms in place to surface and address suboptimal decision-making at the unit level.

Another major complaint is the level of overhead required just to manage the model and make the necessary distributions. Simply stated, it is one of the most complex models to operate even when not fully deployed. For this reason, it is not practical for use at smaller institutions. Three is the bare minimum number of academic revenue centers needed to justify the challenge of developing and operating an RCB model. Fewer than three— and some suggest five or more—makes the benefits too costly in terms of the administrative oversight burden.

Despite these concerns, RCB remains popular and is adopted each year by more institutions. Historically practiced at a small number of independent institutions, RCB has made inroads among public institutions. By 2011, nearly half of all independent doctoral universities and more than 20 percent of public doctoral universities employed some form of RCB.[213]

ZERO-BASED BUDGETING (ZBB)

In many ways, ZBB and incremental budgeting are at opposite ends of the spectrum for allocating resources. While incremental budgeting emanates from centralized management and employs across-the-board distributions, ZBB focuses on the individual program or activity. It assumes no budgets from prior years. Instead, each year's budget begins at a base of zero. Each budget unit evaluates its goals and objectives and justifies its activities based on each activity's benefits and the consequences of not performing the activities.

This evaluation takes the form of a decision package, which includes a description of the activity, a definition of alternative levels of activity (including minimum and maximum levels), performance measures, costs, and benefits. After being ranked by priority, decision packages at one level of the organization are forwarded to the next level for review. Successively higher administrative levels rank the decision packages and then make allocation decisions for each unit.

Advantages: Proponents of ZBB contend they gain a much better understanding of their organization through the preparation and review of the decision packages. And by its very nature, ZBB eliminates a protected budget base for each activity. With no funding guarantee, each activity must prove its own worth. This can help provide information that can be used to justify eliminating programs that no longer contribute to the institution's success.

Disadvantages: The disadvantage cited most often is that ZBB assumes no budget history. Thus, it does not recognize continuing commitments—such as tenured faculty and contracts with key administrators or vendors—and cannot be easily altered in the short run. Unlike many other labor-intensive organizations, colleges and universities cannot initiate and terminate activities quickly.

Another significant disadvantage is the effort required to prepare the decision packages and the large volume of paperwork that is generated. Agreeing on priorities often proves difficult. Some contend that the centralized preaudit of lower-level decisions reduces decision-making autonomy and responsibility.

Some organizations modify ZBB and encourage managers to assume a fixed complement of activities and a corresponding base of support. For instance, they might begin with the assumption that 80 percent of the previous year's budget will continue as a base, then apply ZBB techniques to the balance of the budget. This strategy, however, compromises ZBB's ability to eliminate a protected budget base.

ZBB is often considered an all-or-nothing proposition, but this does not have to be the case. An institution can apply ZBB techniques selectively, rather than to the entire organization, or implement them cyclically. For instance, administrative and support units might use ZBB exclusively. Or each unit might participate in the ZBB process on a periodic schedule—say, once every five years. Under this approach, 20 percent of the campus would employ ZBB each year, while the remainder of the units would use a different budgeting approach.

An alternative to ZBB is program review with extensive evaluation of program activities and outcomes measured against resources consumed (see Chapter 13). There is a routine practice of program review for some types of accreditation, but what is recommended here is something less academically oriented and more focused on the comparison of outcomes achieved against resources generated and consumed. Given the recognition that so many costs are fixed or nearly fixed due to the scope of continuing operations, this type of program review probably has more utility than a full-scale ZBB approach.

It should be noted that ZBB is very attractive to some board members—especially those with a business background—because this approach is focused on continually trying to reduce resource consumption. Though not employed extensively in higher education because so much of the budget is committed to recurring activities, ZBB generates a great deal of discussion at board levels.

INITIATIVE-BASED BUDGETING (IBB)

Unlike the four comprehensive budget models described above, IBB represents a structured approach to distributing resources for new initiatives that support established priorities. To finance the initiatives, institutions typically take one of three common approaches:

- ▶ Capture centrally a percentage of the expected increase in resources for the period. This typically modest amount of revenues (for example, 1 or 2 percent) is isolated in a pool that then supports priorities established through the planning process.

- ▶ Establish reallocation targets for each unit. After examining their operations and identifying activities to discontinue or curtail, units release resources to central administration to meet the reallocation target. This approach offers the side benefit of providing a mechanism and impetus for units to review the productivity of their existing activities.

- ▶ Rely on the contingency funding included in the expense budget. If the institution does not need the contingency to cover cost overruns, revenue shortfalls, or opportunities that surface, it can devote some or all of the funds to IBB.

Reallocating to Fund New Initiatives

With the reallocation approach to IBB, the resource pool is created from resources returned to central administration. In theory, the units provide the resources by discontinuing lower-priority or unproductive activities. The funds are then redistributed in support of the priorities agreed upon during the institution's planning process.

Here's how it works. Assume that a campus imposes a 2 percent reallocation target on all campus units. Each unit identifies activities or programs it can eliminate or modify, thus reducing its base budget by the specified target. Notice that this approach focuses on base budget rather than the unit's entire budget. The base budget usually excludes nonrecurring projects, such as sponsored programs or other one-time activities that are not part of the unit's continuing operations.

To meet the reallocation target, an administrative unit such as environmental health and safety may propose changing its approach to staff training. Rather than incurring the cost of sending campus personnel off-site for required safety training, a current staff member will become certified to conduct the training on-site. Although some overtime pay may be necessary because of the trainer's shifting workload, the unit will be able to achieve the 2 percent target.

To meet its target, a college within the university might propose consolidating two of its academic departments in response to shifting demands that coincide with the retirement of one of the department chairs. The salary and benefits savings from the elimination of the chair's position, coupled with consolidation of the two departments' support staffs, will allow the unit to contribute more than the required 2 percent savings. This situation gives the dean some flexibility to take other actions to meet the school's 2 percent target.

The savings from environmental health and safety, the college, and all other units are consolidated into an initiatives pool and then redistributed based on criteria established during the planning process. Typically, redistribution entails a proposal process. All units seeking to obtain funds from the pool submit a proposal identifying the planned activities, the institutional priorities that the activities support, the benefits to be generated, success measures, and the amount requested.

A more comprehensive approach to reallocation is discussed in Chapter 13.

There may be slight variations in IBB based on whether the proposed initiative requires one-time or continuing funding. Continuing funding usually is more difficult to obtain because it reduces the funds available for initiatives in future periods. Another possible variation centers on how or if both administrative and academic units compete for funds. Funds reallocated from administrative units, for example, may not necessarily be reserved for administrative initiatives. If the institution's priorities focus exclusively on academic initiatives, the administrative reallocation may be used to fund academic initiatives.

Reallocation strategies prove particularly valuable because they enable departments to achieve the target in various ways each year. A department may meet its target one year through program reduction in response to reduced demand. The next year, it may find a less expensive provider for needed services.

Accomplishing IBB through reallocation, however, cannot continue indefinitely—especially as it relates to core academic and administrative activities. At some point, a payroll office that continually gives up 2 percent of its annual budget without successfully obtaining replacement funds will erode its ability to meet the institution's needs for payroll services. Similarly, a core academic unit attempting to meet increased enrollment demands may find it impossible to achieve a 2 percent savings. Any reallocation program must provide a mechanism for waivers and for reallocation back to core activities.

PERFORMANCE-BASED BUDGETING (PBB)

During the early development of public administration budgeting and planning, the budget was viewed as an instrument of expenditure control. PBB, which emerged in the late 1940s, signaled a shift to a management orientation by focusing on programs and activities that became ends in themselves. Specifically, PBB focuses on outputs and outcomes. The number of graduates, for example, is an output, while the number of graduates finding employment in a relevant industry or gaining acceptance to graduate school is an outcome.

This technique has enjoyed a recent rebirth of interest, particularly at the state level. The modern form of PBB:

- Relates resources (inputs) to activities (structure) and results (outcomes)

- Identifies specific outcome measures in either quantitative or qualitative terms

- Employs accounting structures that attempt to relate resources to results

- Establishes explicit indicators of input-output relationships or indices relating resources to outcomes

- Specifies goals in terms of performance measures (that is, desired input-outcome ratios)

Applying the newer forms of PBB in the public arena often proves challenging. The development of performance measures typically flows from the state to the institution and frequently doesn't reflect an understanding of the factors that influence the measures. Outcome indicators sometimes are viewed as relatively meaningless because they are linked with program budgets only at the highest level of aggregation. This may disconnect the indicators from the activities that actually drive the results. Quantitative measures are more widely employed than qualitative measures, which may be more meaningful indicators of success. Finally, performance measures at high levels of program aggregation are not easily linked with organizational divisions and departments—the structure used for resource allocation on most campuses.

As currently practiced, PBB usually applies only to a small amount of available resources—say 2 to 3 percent. It typically starts with the identification of a series of metrics for measuring performance—such as specific target scores, a specific required percentage improvement in performance, or an institution's relative ranking among peers. If the institution achieves the target scores or rankings, it receives supplemental resources. If it misses the target, it does not receive the supplemental allocation. Rarely do states assess penalties if the institution does not achieve the desired results, although this practice would not be inconsistent with PBB principles.

A few states have expanded the use of PBB, and some have considered linking the majority of an institution's state appropriation to specific performance objectives. However, this has not occurred on a widespread basis in higher education. Many of the proposals for this type of major transformation have not been adopted for fear of disruption.

KEY POINTS

▶ Higher education commonly uses two operating budget models: Comprehensive models address the entire range of an institution's operational resources and investments, and special-purpose models address only a portion of the budget.

▶ Comprehensive budget models include formula budgeting, incremental-decremental budgeting, RCB, and ZBB. The vast majority of institutions rely on a hybrid model that incorporates elements of multiple comprehensive budget models and may also incorporate features from special-purpose budget models.

▶ Special-purpose budget models fall into two categories. The first, IBB, focuses on directing resources toward the priorities established during the planning process. This model usually deals with a small portion of the operating budget, typically just a few percentage points or less. The second approach, PBB, addresses a similar portion of the budget, although some states are experimenting with distributing larger amounts based on performance results.

CHAPTER 10: OPERATING AND CAPITAL BUDGET CYCLES

Public and independent institutions tend to follow the same general budget process: People in the same positions take the same steps, in the same sequence, over roughly the same time frame. The key variant, applicable to some public institutions, is the impact the state (or local) government's budget and appropriation processes have on the timing of specific aspects of the institution's process.

The timetable for the various activities within the budget process is referred to as the budget cycle. Budget cycles typically overlap, with multiple budgets in use, in development, or being analyzed retrospectively at the same time. For example, in late summer/early fall of a fiscal year, the prior year's financial activity is being organized in preparation for the financial statement audit. At the same time, the current-year budget cycle is guiding expenditures and influencing hiring decisions. Finally, it's possible that the budget cycle for the next fiscal year has already begun.

Depending on the institution, the overall budget cycle can last up to 24 months. For public institutions, the cycle can be even longer—especially those located in states with a biennial budget cycle.

At any given time, a campus will be in the midst of both an operating budget cycle and a capital budget cycle. Both processes are complex and require a concerted effort to build on the planning work that should precede them. Each step in the process contributes to development of the budgets and, if executed properly, will help contribute to the likelihood of successful execution of the operating and capital activities addressed in the budgets.

OPERATING BUDGET CYCLE

Operating budgets address revenues and reserves, both of which may be sources for projects addressed in the capital budget. Similarly, the facilities and related projects covered by a capital budget will affect the operating budget once they are completed and placed in service. The expenses for maintaining the facilities become part of operating expenses, and if the facilities are debt financed, the interest on the long-term debt will be a claim on resources and must be addressed in the operating budget. That's one reason that operating and capital budgets cannot be developed in isolation.

Budgeting is an iterative process at both public and independent institutions. The approach may appear straightforward and sequential, but many steps may be revisited and repeated along the way. Even with this back-and-forth method, there are 16 defined steps in a typical budget process. They are presented below in the sequence in which they usually occur.

Note that various offices have primary responsibility for some individual steps, while for others, the responsibility is shared across the institution. For instance, multiple units have responsibility for ensuring that budget proposals required in step 9 are submitted to the central budget office in some form (typically electronically). Consolidating the budget, as described in step 12, normally would be among the specific responsibilities of the budget office. Finally, step 16—preparing audited financial statements—falls within the province of the controller's office.

The final point to make before delineating the steps is about multiyear budgeting (discussed further in Chapter 12). The process detailed below is presented in a logical sequence that aligns well with calendars that appear later in the chapter. With multiyear budgeting, however, some of the steps would be undertaken for the coming fiscal year with additional simultaneous work focused on the second year out. The optimal approach is one that utilizes the 16 steps and, whenever possible, focuses on the next two fiscal years.

For instance, step 5—addressing budget assumptions—can easily include assumptions for the coming year and the one following it. Obviously, it is easier to be accurate when projecting for one year versus two, so it must be recognized that the second year out will not have as much certainty. However, the 16-step process for the second year out will begin even before it is completed for the coming fiscal year. If the second-year assumptions developed during the work primarily focused on the next year prove to be off the mark, the assumptions will be updated when the second year becomes the primary focus.

1. DEVELOP OPERATIONAL PLANS ON WHICH TO BASE THE RESOURCE ALLOCATION PROCESS.

The budget development process begins with a review of the results that emerged from planning efforts, along with information about past actual results measured against the budget. The combination of these factors, along with others, will shape the budget being developed.

Areas of need should be evident from analysis of past results, while priority areas should flow from the various planning processes. Similarly, the plans should disclose areas that will be de-emphasized in the upcoming period. Along with highlighting these respective areas, the budget must be developed with contingencies in mind. There clearly are many areas to consider. The budget process requires extensive negotiations, so having well-defined plans will make the process run smoother. Not every decision will flow easily from the plans, but the absence of plans will make each decision a struggle.

Although listed here as the starting point, planning is not a discrete activity that occurs once per budgeting cycle. Planning is an ongoing process that never stops. As the budget process gets underway, participants review the cumulative results of all planning efforts, assess how they may impact the operating budget, and use the results to shape the overall process.

Effective planning processes involve participation by all campus constituencies, including the board (see Chapter 7). The board influences the overall organizational direction through its involvement in the planning process, and management uses the budget as the primary tool for carrying out the plans. Several steps in the budget process, however, require board involvement. The board, for example, reviews and approves the assumptions on which the budget is built. This is a natural outgrowth of the planning that has occurred up to the point when the operating budget cycle begins. The board also reviews and approves the final budget to ensure it aligns with previously approved plans and budget assumptions.

A Typical Budget Process in 16 Steps

1. Develop operational plans on which to base the resource allocation process.
2. Close out the prior fiscal year.
3. Analyze year-to-date results for the current year and final results for the prior year.
4. Project enrollment.
5. Establish budget assumptions for the board's approval.
6. Project central revenues.
7. Project expenses.
8. Develop and distribute departmental guidelines for preparing budget proposals.
9. Have departments develop and submit budget proposals.
10. Conduct budget hearings.
11. Analyze submissions.
12. Consolidate the budget.
13. Obtain board approval of the budget.
14. Begin budget implementation.
15. Monitor performance against the budget.
16. Prepare audited financial statements.

After approving the final budget, the board monitors the status of planned efforts and the resulting budgetary implications. If circumstances change and the budget's bottom line changes, the board should review and approve the new result. Finally, well after the end of the fiscal year covered by the budget, the board formally accepts the audited financial statements prepared by management and examined by external auditors. In preparation for the board's final budget review, management should reconcile the financial statements to the budget.

2. CLOSE OUT THE PRIOR FISCAL YEAR.

Prior-year closeout entails finalizing all revenue and expense activity in preparation for the annual audit of the institution's financial statements. The process begins well before the fiscal year ends to ensure sufficient time to conduct and conclude financial activity. Public institutions, for instance, need time to ensure they wisely spend funds that otherwise may revert to the state treasury. Similarly, departments within an independent institution that recaptures unexpended funds centrally at year-end will do their best to expend as much of their budget as possible.

Another consideration as the end of the fiscal year approaches is ensuring that transactions are assigned to the appropriate fiscal year. Although the academic calendar drives various financial cycles, many facets of an institution's operations run continuously throughout the year. Activity levels may be higher when students and faculty are present, but a wide range of operations do not shut down when the bulk of students and faculty leave campus. This means that purchasing activity continues to take place, and care must be taken to ensure that a transaction intended to provide resources for the new fiscal year is not inadvertently charged to the year that is winding down. Ensuring a proper cutoff is critical to preparing financial statements that accurately reflect the activities for the year.

Because last-minute spending to avoid returning surplus funds may result in the acquisition of unneeded goods, institutions usually have a supplemental process for reviewing transactions above a certain dollar amount that are initiated close to year-end. Similarly, campuses commonly specify that some types of purchases—particularly equipment—cannot be initiated after a certain date. These procedures stem not only from concerns about the workload for procurement staff but also from questions about the motivation behind the purchase. Yet even when an institution imposes such constraints, it typically makes exceptions for legitimate purchases such as new equipment needed for a sponsored project that begins late in the fiscal year.

3. ANALYZE YEAR-TO-DATE RESULTS FOR THE CURRENT YEAR AND FINAL RESULTS FOR THE PRIOR YEAR.

The most recently completed fiscal year will provide valuable information about actual receipt of revenues and expenses incurred throughout the period. It will highlight shortfalls and indicate programs that may be in their downward cycle. It also will identify opportunity targets for increased investment—for example, units experiencing increased demand that shows no signs of tapering off. Examining the budget for the current period will give early warning signs of potential problems and other issues that may require attention in the upcoming budget. This is the optimal time to reconsider the budget assumptions (see step 5 below) to determine whether they were valid. For example, the previous budget was built on assumptions regarding new enrollment, retention, expected philanthropy, etc. Did the actual experience align closely with the assumptions, or did they prove to be overly optimistic or too conservative? Analysis of the previous assumptions will be invaluable as the budget is developed for the coming fiscal year.

The budget analysis typically looks at past experience with diverse types of revenue—such as investment income, gifts, sponsored programs, and other revenues monitored centrally—and with expenses. To the extent possible, analyze expenses to determine whether they can be projected more accurately. For instance, if one can establish a strong relationship between a particular category of expenses and a generally available cost index, monitoring the cost index will provide an early indicator of changes in expense levels. (This technique is common with healthcare costs, which are monitored using the Healthcare Cost Trend Rate to provide early warning of significant increases in premiums.)

4. PROJECT ENROLLMENT.

A few enviable institutions cap their enrollment and enjoy excess demand, enabling them to develop a budget using the same enrollment numbers as in the past. The vast majority of institutions, however, must attempt to accurately predict enrollment for the upcoming year.

For enrollment-dependent institutions in particular, the gain or loss of just a few students can significantly impact their bottom line. Even for those less dependent on tuition as a source of revenue, the number of projected students has a ripple effect on the entire budget. Enrollment numbers affect financial aid, the number of faculty needed for instruction, inventory costs for the bookstore, the number of beds required in housing, and staffing in dining halls, to name just a few areas. For this reason, the planning process should devote significant attention to enrollment and related issues.

5. ESTABLISH BUDGET ASSUMPTIONS FOR THE BOARD'S APPROVAL.

Every budget builds upon a series of general assumptions. Plans describe what the campus intends to accomplish while assumptions create the framework for the plans.

Usually, the budget office develops assumptions with input from other offices, including planning, admissions and financial aid (or enrollment management), institutional research, human resources, housing, and the treasurer's office. Many of the assumptions are based on internal factors but also must consider the external environment as well. The assumptions address issues such as:

▶ The expected tuition and fee rates

▶ The anticipated institutional financial aid commitment

▶ The likely increase or decrease in enrollment by level

▶ The expected inflation rate for various expense categories

▶ Planned salary increases for various employee categories (faculty, administrators, staff)

Commercially available advisory services and software applications available from various firms can facilitate financial analysis to help develop assumptions. Most offer cloud-based solutions and are especially valuable for conducting "what if" analyses and scenario modeling. See step 12 below for a listing of the firms and their solutions.

The governing board should review and approve the assumptions assembled by the budget office. Doing this simplifies the subsequent step (13) of obtaining the board's approval of the finalized budget.

6. PROJECT CENTRAL REVENUES.

Departments have substantial influence over some revenue streams, especially at the graduate level. When considering other revenues—such as undergraduate tuition and fees, gifts, investment and endowment income, and even sponsored program overhead recoveries—central offices are better positioned to project revenues. As a general rule, a central office usually establishes the number of expected undergraduate students for the entire institution, recognizing that the number will be distributed among various colleges and departments. This enables the projection of tuition and fees, along with financial aid, the latter of which typically is addressed at the same time as tuition and fees.

In most institutions, it's the treasurer or controller who projects income from endowments and short-term investments. Endowment income tends to be a firmer number because most institutions employ a spending formula based on historical market values. On the other hand, several factors—including the budget itself—affect investment income.

Investment income for operating purposes usually comes from investing idle cash balances in short-term investments. Cash balances fluctuate depending on factors both within the institution's control, such as success in collecting receivables or managing the timing of expenditures, and outside its control (for example, national economic conditions).

Decisions made during the budget process also influence the availability of cash. For this reason, the treasurer typically provides both an expected earnings rate and a range of revenue likely to be earned. A budget that anticipates significant increases in reserves—institutional savings—likely will provide more investment income. On the other hand, a budget that anticipates spending from reserves usually will reflect reduced investment income. Cash-flow analyses—predictions regarding the timing of the receipt and disbursement of cash—take on particular significance when projecting investment income.

With fundraising, as a general rule, the past serves as a reliable indicator of the future. Absent major economic changes or special initiatives such as a capital campaign, development officers can use analysis of the most recently completed fiscal year, supplemented with current-year experience, to make reasonably accurate projections about giving levels, especially in the area of unrestricted support.

The vast majority of overhead recoveries for a given year will be a function of awards already received. Therefore, the starting point is the analysis of existing and pending awards. Indirect cost recoveries, however, are relatively small compared with the rest of the budget. Therefore, projecting these revenues conservatively avoids the risk of overlooking a source while still protecting the institution against shortfalls. Over time, the experience gained through analysis will pay dividends as projections become more accurate.

Projecting State Appropriations

Depending on the type of public institution (for example, research, doctoral, liberal arts) and the state's funding approach, state appropriations may contribute less than 10 percent or as much as 60 percent of all institutional revenues. In states that allow institutions to set tuition rates, the operating appropriation usually is the biggest factor affecting those rates. Even in states that have not granted tuition-setting authority, the state's support greatly affects various expense categories—especially salaries and benefits.

The process of projecting state operating appropriations will depend, in part, on the state's process for establishing its own budget. In some states—especially those relying on well-defined formulas—the campus can project revenues based on factors such as enrollment, employment levels, and usable space. Applying formulas to the projected data will yield results to incorporate into the assumptions, with the budgets developed accordingly. Other states use a more fluid process that forces institutions to incorporate more contingencies in their budget as protection against shortfalls in anticipated support.

Ignoring inflation, by fiscal year 2017, public support from the states returned to the levels experienced just prior to the Great Recession. However, even though state revenues had stabilized, things took a dramatic turn for the worse in more than one state. The most extreme situation was in Illinois, where the executive and legislative branches were unable to agree on a budget for more than two fiscal years. Although some state resources were distributed to Illinois higher education institutions, the impact of the impasse was devastating for thousands of employees and tens of thousands of students. Illinois was the most extreme case, but other states also experienced serious revenue shortfalls that, in turn, affected the states' ability to support public higher education.

During this type of turmoil, projecting state appropriations becomes nothing more than a guessing game. The same is true when states have established the pattern of waiting until after the close of its fiscal year—typically June 30—before making final decisions on the appropriation bill. Havoc is created whenever institutions have to begin a fiscal year without solid information about appropriations. Obviously, this dramatically affects the institutions' operating budgets, but it also can affect setting tuition. Imagine the difficulty for students and their families when the cost of education is not settled as the students are preparing to depart for campus.

7. PROJECT EXPENSES.

Except in institutions relying on RCB (see Chapter 9), central administration projects virtually all expense categories. Compensation, encompassing the categories of salaries and wages, along with fringe benefits, represents the largest expense for higher education institutions. Although institutions have significant investments in facilities, infrastructure, equipment, and technology, the annual depreciation and amortization charges related to these assets is modest compared with the expenses incurred for human resources.

The expenses for selected benefits can be tied directly to salaries and wages. To determine any expense assessed as a percentage of salaries—for example, the Federal Insurance Contributions Act (FICA), unemployment insurance, and workers' compensation—simply apply the applicable rate to projected salaries (while considering any ceilings that may apply). Other benefits, however, don't link so easily to salaries. For instance, rates for health insurance—usually the most expensive fringe benefit for higher education— are negotiated annually, and extraordinary increases are not uncommon.

Relatively few institutions budget fringe benefit expenses on an actual basis to departments. Instead, most use a rate to proportionately distribute the costs across the institution. When used with federally sponsored projects, these rates must be negotiated with the federal government periodically— typically at the same time the F&A rates are being negotiated. Even when federal sponsored programs are not a consideration, institutions must project the anticipated costs for fringe benefits in order to calculate the rate that will be used to distribute the costs across the institution.

Central administration also determines the inflation factor to apply to various expense categories. In the largest categories, projections reflect specified percentage increases influenced primarily by institutional decisions. Other items are subject to external influences beyond the institution's control yet still must be adjusted for inflation.

The failure to address inflationary factors affecting significant portions of an operating budget essentially imposes a budget cut on units incurring costs in those areas. If the budget process doesn't provide adjustments for this type of increased expense, the unit will have to cover the increased cost by reducing costs in other areas.

8. *DEVELOP AND DISTRIBUTE DEPARTMENTAL GUIDELINES FOR PREPARING BUDGET PROPOSALS.*

To help departments develop their budgets, the budget office should provide instructions and electronic forms (or links to a portal or cloud-based application) to everyone responsible for the accounts and activities that will appear in the final budget. This approach will minimize the likelihood of unrealistic submissions. Another critical item to include (or highlight via links) is the approved operational plans referenced above. As mentioned earlier, the approved plan represents a preliminary commitment from the administration to provide resources needed to carry out the plans. The operational plans should have been approved with appropriate consideration of the strategic and infrastructural plans (see Chapter 7).

The guidelines included with the instructions cover a wide range of issues and must provide guidance relevant for both instructional departments and support units. Examples might include enrollment trends and their implications for auxiliary enterprise units, the distribution of tenured and nontenured faculty appointments, the distribution of part-time faculty, and the distribution of instructional workload for departments. The guidelines also should highlight the ways in which the current strategic plan and its priorities will influence the approval of budget proposals. Not every budget proposal will be aligned with one of the handful of priorities identified in the strategic plan. However, every proposal should reference the strategic plan and provide some indication of how it supports the priorities, principles, and values enumerated in the strategic plan. If the institution is committed to the implementation of the plan and pursuit of its vision, extra consideration should go to budget proposals that clearly connect with the strategic plan's priorities or principles.

Additionally, there should be some indication of the new net resources likely to be available for distribution. After projecting central revenues and central expenses—with particular attention to unavoidable fixed cost increases—the institution is in a position to project the anticipated additional resources that can be made available. Some institutions are reluctant to share this information because they believe it ties their hands and puts too much knowledge out in the community. This is an ineffective approach. It is much better for the entire community to be aware of how few discretionary resources are available. As mentioned elsewhere, the most effective processes tend to be those that rely on extensive transparency and clarity. Sharing the resource realities is one way to enhance trust between the administration and the various stakeholders, and it also helps prevent the submission of unrealistic resource requests.

Nearly all institutions rely almost exclusively on electronic submissions transmitted either via email, a portal, or a cloud-based application. The online forms used for electronic submission typically incorporate various edits and diagnostics to prevent submissions that are not consistent with the instructions.

The budget process at most institutions requires approval at intermediate levels of management. As the submission moves through the applicable organizational layers, decentralized management can address unit-specific guidelines. For instance, a dean may require all departments in the college to allocate a specific percentage for curriculum development. Or a major administrative unit may require its departments to identify a portion of their budgets for reallocation to fund special initiatives. At the department level, these types of guidelines may have greater influence on the budget than those imposed by central administration.

In addition to providing budget guidelines, larger institutions often conduct online tutorials or live workshops to convey the important aspects of developing a budget submission. Interestingly, campus personnel—including faculty and academic administrators—almost always find time to attend budget-related training, unlike training on many other administrative topics. Most individuals with budget development responsibility recognize there is much to lose if they are not fully aware of the budget guidelines and procedures.

9. HAVE DEPARTMENTS DEVELOP AND SUBMIT BUDGET PROPOSALS.
Ultimately, the unit head is responsible for the budget submission. Depending on the size and complexity of the unit—and both unit and institutional policy—this individual may involve numerous others in the process or simply rely on the unit financial administrator.

The larger the unit, the more likely it is that faculty and additional departmental administrators participate in developing the budget submission. For very large departments with significant amounts of gift support and sponsored programs activity, several departmental administrative personnel will probably perform most of the work required to complete a budget submission. Conversely, in small units, the unit head may handle the entire process with clerical support from a departmental secretary. The latter approach also is typical in situations relying primarily on an incremental budget process.

Budget submissions are prepared at the lowest unit level and submitted for review and approval by successive levels of management. At each step, the responsible individual (for example, division head, dean, or vice president) reviews the submissions to ensure they collectively represent the best possible proposal for the unit. Once each level is satisfied that the combined budgets are consistent with the established plans, address all identified priorities, and comply with relevant guidelines, the budgets are submitted to the next management level and, finally, to the budget office.

10. CONDUCT BUDGET HEARINGS.

This step may be part of the planning process. Not all institutions conduct budget hearings, which can occur at the institution or unit level. At the institution level, the hearings usually involve the institutional leadership group that will make the final resource allocation decisions. Hearings at the unit level typically entail a small committee led by a senior unit leader such as the vice president for administrative units or dean for academic units.

During the meetings, individual unit heads amplify their budget submission to explain the importance of the efforts to be undertaken with the resources requested. They elaborate on the significance of these efforts and establish the connection to the institution's plans and priorities.

The appropriate body—either institution-level group or unit committee—will weigh the information obtained through the hearings and modify the budget submission accordingly. If the process operates effectively, the group will steer resources toward the activities that align with priorities established through the planning processes.

11. ANALYZE SUBMISSIONS.

The budget office reviews the various submissions from the units to ensure they comply with the established guidelines and to assess how well they align with planning priorities. To the extent anomalies emerge, the units are required to submit revised budgets. Some submissions may be returned because they outline unrealistic proposals. (This is less likely to occur if a planning process is in place to help manage expectations.)

The overall budget process cannot continue until all unit submissions comply with the guidelines and are aligned with the established priorities.

12. CONSOLIDATE THE BUDGET.

After accumulating all unit and central account budget proposals, the budget office develops the consolidated institutional budget, usually using budget software. Automating the process enables the budget office to produce a consolidated budget as submissions are received. It then can assess how things are coming together and spot any problems that materialize.

While ERPs (e.g., Banner, SAP, PeopleSoft, Workday) are excellent transactional systems, they provide only limited analytical capability. The embedded reporting applications are unsophisticated and lack flexibility. This leads to the need to extract data from the ERP for use in a report-writer or spreadsheets. Customizing the ERPs to meet analytical needs becomes expensive because the customization must be repeated each time the vendor releases a new version of the software.

Complex organizations increasingly are adopting the use of dedicated budget applications referred to as business performance management (BPM) systems. These systems assist institutions with analysis and the development of capital plans and budgets, strategic plans, operating plans and budgets addressing tuition, financial aid, enrollment, and many other relevant topics. Typical BPMs provide:

▶ Standardized templates, methods, and processes for developing budgets

- ▶ A single source for all financial and budget data that can provide both real-time and end-of-period data as well as multiyear budget-to-actual comparisons
- ▶ Standard report and query templates with access to data based on user authorization

BPM systems enable decentralized users to access, view, revise, and report budget and planning data—often via the cloud. Central offices can utilize this information when building and/or monitoring budgets and when analyzing the impact of potential resource allocation decisions. The firms providing BPM services and solutions include Adaptive Insights, Anaplan, Host Analytics, KaufmanHall, Oracle, PFM, Prophix, Questica, SAP, Strategic Planning Online, and Xlerant. Each offers technology solutions, and many supplement this with consulting services. Although most of the applications were not designed with higher education in mind, many of them have been adapted to facilitate managing the budget process by making high-level adjustments, forecasting, and providing analytical tools useful to senior management.

These tools are more likely *interfaced to* other administrative software such as the accounting system rather than *integrated with* it. For this reason, stand-alone software may include only summaries of historical information and not include historical transaction details unless it is intentionally uploaded to the application.

Institutions without the capacity to employ commercial solutions must manually load budget details into whatever tool (for example, Excel) is used to produce the consolidated budget—a time-consuming and labor-intensive process. These institutions are less likely to produce preliminary consolidated budgets. Instead, they focus on entering all source information and produce the consolidated budget once after everything has been received and processed. A manual process is more likely to yield mistakes that require correction before production of an accurate budget. As such, significantly more time is required for manual processes—both for input and error correction.

Once the consolidated institutional budget has been produced, it must be analyzed to ensure it is consistent with the institutional plan, addresses all established priorities, and meets the target developed during the assumptions phase (step 5).

13. OBTAIN BOARD APPROVAL OF THE BUDGET.

Next, management submits the budget to the board for review and approval. Assuming the board was consulted during development of the institution's plans and approved the assumptions used to develop the budget—and the budget is consistent with those plans and assumptions—board approval should not be a problem.

The board usually seeks assurance about specific issues identified during the planning process or asks about special risks embodied in the budget. Three issues routinely arise when boards review budgets:

- The impact of the tuition increase
- Contingency built into the budget
- Compensation increase

Management should anticipate these questions and provide supplementary narrative information. After hearing answers to its questions and discussing the budget's implications, the board generally gives its stamp of approval.

If, however, the board determines that the budget deviates from approved plans or assumptions in some way, it may withhold approval. In that case, management typically directs the budget office to make the changes necessary to address the issues raised by the board. This may entail asking selected units to submit revised budgets. Everything comes to a halt if the board remains unwilling to approve the budget. If the budget is consistent with the plans overseen by the board and with the budget assumptions it approved, this suggests a serious problem. The board and management need to invest the effort required to resolve the issues that stand in the way of finalizing the budget.

14. BEGIN BUDGET IMPLEMENTATION.

Once the board has approved the budget—ideally, well before the beginning of the new fiscal year—the accounting system must be updated to reflect the new resource allocation decisions. This step is necessary because various administrative processes must occur to be ready for the fiscal year. Depending on how soon the academic year will start, for example, it may be necessary to process new hires into the payroll system, issue purchase orders, or execute leases for rental space.

Many ERPs allow activity for a future year to begin in the current fiscal year. In fact, some systems will allow multiple fiscal years to operate simultaneously. This feature is beneficial in one sense but also problematic. Care must be taken to ensure transactions are processed in the appropriate fiscal year. The earlier the budget can be finalized and implemented, the better prepared the campus will be for the next academic year.

15. MONITOR PERFORMANCE AGAINST THE BUDGET.

To ensure it carries out the plans represented by the budget, the institution must track the progress of revenue generation, along with the expenses being incurred. The responsibility for this activity varies among institutions. In some colleges and universities, the budget office monitors revenues and expenses to ensure they remain on track throughout the fiscal year. For others, this responsibility is carried out by the controller's office.

Unlike some other enterprises, higher education revenues are not received evenly throughout the fiscal year. Some revenue categories are more stable, such as investment income and selected auxiliary enterprises, but tuition and fees typically arrive in large chunks usually at or just before the beginning of the term. Most institutions have two major resource inflow spikes: the start of the fall and spring semesters, which each bring in significant amounts of tuition and fee receipts within a short time. A third potential spike comes with summer school tuition.

Many expenses—particularly faculty salaries—are committed before the academic year starts, although the actual expenses tend to be incurred evenly throughout the year. A large expense like faculty salaries will drop off during the summer at most institutions, but this can be mitigated when faculty have the option to spread their salary over 12 months. At research institutions, it's common for faculty to have their summer salaries covered by sponsored research programs. Irrespective of these options, expenses should be monitored continuously throughout the year to ensure things remain on track.

Revenues that do not materialize as planned, or expenses that run higher than expected, may call for action. If the deviations can be accommodated through the contingency incorporated in the expense budget, management usually can make the adjustments without board involvement (although notification is advisable). If the bottom line is affected, however, the board will likely need to review and approve the budget revisions.

16. PREPARE AUDITED FINANCIAL STATEMENTS.

Well after the fiscal year has ended and the institution has turned its attention to the new budget, the institution needs to close the door on the previous year. The audited financial statements—the last step in the budget cycle—facilitate this process.

At this stage, final revenue and expense numbers are available. Some analytical effort will be required by the budget office, controller's office, or both to reconcile the budgetary and financial statement reporting. Once this has occurred, the board can compare the budget as approved by them—both initially and as revised throughout the fiscal year—with the audited financial statements.

Figures 10-1 and 10-2 illustrate the operating budget cycles for a large public institution and a large independent institution. Because a public institution must integrate its approach with the state's budget process, it must take additional steps linked to state submissions. The nature of the state budgeting cycle requires campuses and other state agencies to meet various deadlines and, in most cases, to submit information on a somewhat piecemeal basis.

Figure 10-1

Sample Public University Operating Budget Development Cycle (for a state utilizing a biennial budget cycle)	
June 30	Prior fiscal year ends.
September	*In odd-number years, submit base operating budget and activity-based budget for the upcoming biennium to the state.*
September–October	Present operating and capital budget requests (odd-number years) or amendments (even-number years) to governing board for approval. Governing board accepts audited financial statements.
October	*Submit biennial budget request. In even-number years, the request represents amendment to existing biennial budget; in odd-number years, the request is for the upcoming biennium.*
December	*Governor submits proposed budget to the legislature.* Distribute upcoming fiscal year budget development instructions and templates to vice presidents for distribution to reporting units (after applying any unit-specific revisions). Process all modifications that will affect target budgets for the upcoming fiscal year. Tuition, housing, and board fee increase requests for upcoming fiscal year due for designated programs.
January	*Submit budget amendments to the legislature for items not addressed by the governor's proposed budget.* Distribute internal budget targets to the vice presidents for distribution to reporting units (after applying any unit-specific adjustments). Application, activity, and other fee increase requests for upcoming fiscal year due. Begin development of tuition proposal and financial aid allocations.
February	*Cross-over of state budget bills from House and Senate.* Mandatory fee increase requests for upcoming fiscal year due. Full budget submissions due from auxiliary enterprise, selected other self-supporting units, and various academic units. Present upcoming fiscal year housing rates and budget development assumptions to the governing board for approval.
March	*Joint conference committee forwards legislature's budget bill to governor.*
April	All remaining budget submissions, including addenda requests, for upcoming fiscal year due. Present dining, tuition, and mandatory fee proposal to governing board for approval. *Appropriation act approved by legislature and governor.*
May	Carryforward requests for current fiscal year budget due. Present budget to governing board for approval. Distribute approved budget and addenda to vice presidents. Update financial system with new fiscal year budget.
July 1	New fiscal year begins.

Items in italics represent submissions to the state or activities that occur at the state level.

In contrast, the independent university's process appears to flow in a more natural sequence. Despite the differences, the basic tasks must occur on both campuses. Although smaller, less complex institutions may rely on a more streamlined budget process, the general flow presented in Figures 10-1 and 10-2 could be adapted to any public or independent institution.

Figure 10-2

Sample Independent University Operating Budget Development Cycle	
June 30	Prior fiscal year ends.
October	Board of trustees budget committee meets to review final budget performance results for prior fiscal year and the planning schedule for the upcoming fiscal year's budget development process.
	Board of trustees accepts audited financial statements.
October– November	Planning and budget advisory committee meets to:
	‣ Review and discuss budget planning strategies and procedures
	‣ Review and discuss program priorities
	‣ Review and discuss preliminary revenue planning assumptions
	‣ Set planning parameters for upcoming fiscal year
December– February	Central administration staff (including planning office, budget office, finance office, and provost's office) meet with deans and other unit heads to review and update strategic plans (preplanning meetings).
	University administration meets with deans and other unit heads to discuss strategic plans (planning and budget meetings).
February	Preliminary allocation materials distributed.
	Board of trustees budget committee reviews preliminary budget performance report for current fiscal year and receives status report on upcoming fiscal year budget planning.
	Trustees review and approve tuition and room and board rates for upcoming fiscal year.
March	Faculty salary planning guidelines distributed to schools.
April	Upcoming fiscal year budget allocations are finalized.
	Budget office prepares and distributes final budget allocation materials and detailed budget preparation materials for upcoming fiscal year.
	Faculty salary plans due to provost's office.
	Detailed upcoming fiscal year appropriated budgets due to budget office.
	Faculty hiring plans for all schools due to provost's office.
May–June	Budget office reviews upcoming fiscal year appropriated budget detail and reconciles with final budget summary.
	Budget office prepares budget summary for upcoming fiscal year for review by the president and trustees.
	Exempt and nonexempt staff salary plans due to human resources.
	Board of trustees budget committee reviews and endorses final upcoming fiscal year operating budget and receives status report on current fiscal year budget performance.
	Upcoming fiscal year budget detail entered into financial system.
	Upcoming fiscal year budgets are distributed to units.
July 1	New fiscal year begins.

OPERATING BUDGET CALENDAR

The budget calendar must have sufficient flexibility to allow for the routine reexamination of individual components. It details deadlines for key deliverables that must be completed in order to develop the budget and obtain the board's approval. Some units may need to revise their budget proposals to adhere to guidelines or targets, and the board may request revisions as well. To the extent that effort is devoted to planning prior to working on the budget, the need for revisions should be diminished. Nevertheless, the entire budget process can take anywhere from six to 12 months at midsize independent institutions and appreciably longer at large independent and public institutions—particularly because of the influence of state agencies in the latter case.

The end point usually is keyed to the board's meeting schedule, so it's good practice to include a month or more of cushion within the budget calendar. Otherwise, the board may have to convene in a special meeting for the sole purpose of reviewing and approving the budget. When this occurs, the board may want to examine the budget in greater detail than would have been the case under the normal schedule.

Every institution should aim to have the budget approved well before the fiscal year starts. Approval for nonfaculty positions ideally should happen sufficiently early to allow the recruitment process to be completed well in advance of the expected start date for these positions. Faculty recruiting requires even more lead time—as much as an entire fiscal year. Sufficient lead time is essential, especially if new faculty will be teaching sections in the fall semester or if any other approved positions are expected to generate revenues during the year. Unless the revenue projections contemplate hiring delays, revenue shortfalls are likely if the new positions are not filled early in the fiscal year.

Beginning with the Great Recession, legislatures and governors often struggled to agree on a state budget, making it difficult (if not impossible) for some public institutions to finalize their own budgets in advance of the new fiscal year. As mentioned elsewhere, this problem rose to epic proportions in Illinois during the period between 2015 and 2017 when no state budgets were developed and enacted. Like the federal government, several states have operated with continuing resolutions, executive orders, or similar administrative stopgap measures to enable state government, including public higher education, to operate without the benefit of an approved statewide budget. Although temporary authorization allows public institutions to conduct most routine operations, it impairs effectiveness, stifles innovation, and creates anxiety about the possibility that cutbacks may be needed later in the fiscal year. It also frequently interrupts progress on construction projects, especially when the capital appropriation is provided on a fiscal-year basis rather than on a project basis. When this occurs, project completion costs typically rise because of inflation in the construction industry.

Some states use biennial budgets, which forces institutions to project far into the future—sometimes more than two years from the latest completed period. The discipline that accompanies a multiyear model can be beneficial when a public institution chooses to use it internally to manage operations more effectively. When imposed by the state, however, it can become a hardship.

When projecting two or more years into the future, budgeters typically reduce the uncertainty by using current experience as a base. Adjustments are made at the margin to reflect anticipated changes in revenues and expenses, which in turn are determined by such variables as program mix, enrollments, market factors affecting the availability of job candidates, inflationary influences, and investment yields.

Scheduled changes such as the introduction of a new degree program or tighter admissions standards can be planned. But it is difficult to predict more extreme events, such as new environmental regulations, dramatically changing interest rates, changes in federal student assistance programs, or the impact of an international crisis. As a result, public institutions in states with biennial budgeting may be forced to rely excessively on incremental budgeting and to include significant contingencies as a protective measure.

CAPITAL BUDGET CYCLE

The typical capital budget cycle includes fewer steps than the operating budget cycle but lasts appreciably longer. Although individual programs may continue for years (for example, a multiyear-sponsored research project) and activities such as instruction will occur as long as the institution exists, an operating budget covers only the activities occurring within a single fiscal year.

In contrast, the capital budget extends over several years. It covers physical assets such as buildings, roads, and parking lots, and the dollar magnitude of individual projects usually dwarfs items in the operating budget. Even a very large sponsored project usually will not represent as large a financial commitment as the typical project addressed in a capital budget. The latter may range from the acquisition of a single major item of equipment to the renovation of a laboratory or to the acquisition or construction of a campus building. Similarly, it's not uncommon for an individual capital project's budget to exceed the combined annual operating budgets for a number of academic departments.

Figure 10-3 provides a detailed capital budget cycle for a large public university operating within a six-year capital planning cycle. The general flow presented in Figure 10-3 could be adapted for use at any public or independent institution.

Figure 10-3

Sample Public University Capital Budget Development Cycle for Fiscal Years (FYs) 4–9 (for a state utilizing a six-year capital planning cycle)	
Items in italics represent interactions with the state or activities that occur at the state level.	
May FY 1	Distribute call to vice presidents for FYs 4–9 six-year capital plan.
July FY 2	Project initiation forms due for each new project.
	Prepare six-year capital plan.
August FY 2	Present six-year capital plan to governing board executive committee for review and approval. Emphasis is on 1) biennial plans, 2) project justifications, and 3) funding (state general fund, bond, gift-funding proposals for each biennium, and impact on student fees).
October FY 2	University architect's office completes project formulation documents for proposed projects.
November FY 2	Vice president for finance completes business plans and debt assessment impact for proposed capital projects.
December FY 2	Present six-year capital plan, business plans, and debt assessments to governing board executive committee for review and approval.
February FY 2	*State planning and budget department notifies agencies of submittal schedule for FYs 4–9 six-year capital plan and unfunded projects from FYs 1–6 six-year capital plan eligible for the preparation of detailed submissions.*
March FY 2	Six-year capital plan presented to governing board building and grounds committee for final review and approval.
April FY 2	*Six-year capital plan submitted to state planning and budget department.*
June FY 2	*Detailed documents for projects approved by state in February submitted to state planning and budget department.*
	Notification by state planning and budget department of six-year plan projects approved for detailed submittal.
	Notification by state planning and budget department of maintenance reserve subprojects that meet required criteria.
August FY 3	*Detailed documents for projects approved by state in June submitted to state planning and budget department.*
	Annual maintenance reserve plan documents submitted to state planning and budget department.
September FY 3	Complete financial feasibility studies for revenue bond projects.
November FY 3	*Governor submits six-year capital improvement plan to legislature.*
December FY 3	*Governor submits FYs 4–5 biennial budget to legislature.*
May FY 3	*FYs 4–5 appropriation act approved by legislature and governor.*
July 1 FY 4	Approved FYs 4–5 project authorizations take effect.

Depending on institutional policies and procedures—and the volume of capital activity underway at any time—the capital planning and budgeting processes at large institutions can be as complex as those for the operating cycle. At institutions with few resources available for capital activities, the processes may be relatively informal and include minimal formal planning. Instead, the institution might maintain a wish list of projects to undertake as resources become available or in response to operational problems.

Regardless of the type of institution, the most desirable way to address both new projects and ongoing maintenance involves a formal process for identifying and addressing capital needs. Outlined below is a recommended seven-step process.

1. ESTABLISH THE NEED FOR SPACE.

The need for new space—or significant renovations to existing space—is first identified at the department or school level. The unit develops the rationale for additional space, citing the specific activities that will occur there. The request might focus on increased sponsored programs activity, the introduction of a new academic program, improved faculty-student interaction because of technological upgrades, or enhanced campus-corporate training partnerships.

The request usually includes an analysis of existing space resources and an explanation of why they are not sufficient to accommodate the new activities.

2. SEARCH FOR EXISTING SPACE.

Once the need has been identified and shown to be consistent with the institution's plans and priorities, the search begins for other space on campus that could be reassigned without adversely affecting other institutional activities. If no existing space is available, efforts begin to acquire or construct space.

Depending on the activity's importance and urgency, an interim arrangement to rent space might accommodate the identified need temporarily.

3. REVIEW THE CAMPUS MASTER PLAN.

After the addition of new space has been approved in concept, review the campus master plan to determine the appropriate location for the space. Master plans address long-term facilities and infrastructure needs and identify how the physical space will be developed over time.

An effective master plan typically covers a 10- to 20-year period. Its purpose is to guide a campus as it develops its built environment to maximize the programmatic benefit and aesthetic value and also ensure that all capital investments provide the maximum benefit. Plans typically are reviewed and revised regularly and rewritten approximately every five years.

Campus master plans identify specific areas reserved for academic expansion, along with the designated location for any new residential facilities, administrative space, athletics and recreation venues, and other buildings. Within the constraints of the institution's political climate, a master plan also indicates potential boundary expansion for the campus.

This sensitive issue is usually not addressed in the master plans of independent institutions. Public institutions, however, typically must disclose expansion plans even though doing so may complicate relationships with the local community. Unlike most independent institutions, public institutions are subject to open meeting and open records laws and regulations, which require that official actions taken by the board or management be open to the public.

This burden is somewhat offset by the fact that a public institution may be able to invoke eminent domain to acquire land in support of its mission. Under eminent domain, the public institution directly, or through the local government, forces the transfer of privately owned land to the institution (with appropriate compensation to the owner). This is a last resort. It is much more typical for public institutions to acquire land through normal competitive purchase.

4. ASSESS FEASIBILITY.

Rarely will a campus undertake space acquisition or new construction to address a single need for space. More typically, several identified needs will be combined to determine the best overall solution. It may be desirable to acquire an available commercial facility, or it may make more sense to construct a new on-campus facility.

The decision to buy, lease, or build considers such factors as:

▶ Suitability of available commercial space

- Overall cost comparison between building/leasing new space and acquiring/renovating commercial space
- Availability of space to rent until a permanent solution can be implemented
- Time needed to construct the new space

5. OBTAIN APPROVALS.

As a general rule, approval of land or other significant capital acquisitions—such as those above a certain dollar threshold—by independent institutions occurs only at the board level. Rarely does anyone outside the institution need to authorize the institution's acquisition of capital assets. (Sometimes, an independent institution seeking to acquire land locally must obtain approval from the local municipality. The approval usually is linked to concerns regarding the property tax implications that arise when a tax-exempt organization acquires property and removes it from the tax rolls.)

Public institutions have a more substantial approval process that requires significant lead time. Most states, for example, have statutory requirements related to the acquisition of land and buildings. Various state agencies will be required to approve the acquisition or construction of new facilities. In some states, this occurs only if state funds will be used to finance the acquisition or construction. Other states, however, require approval by various state agencies for all transactions of a capital nature.

Along with concerns related to demonstrated need, states may raise environmental concerns (such as asbestos or ground contamination), building and related construction code regulations, and other issues related to public policy. If the transaction requires debt financing, additional approvals will be required from various state financial offices.

6. SECURE FINANCING.

Once all (or the essential) approvals have been obtained and the project is ready to proceed, funding must be secured. For large projects, it is common for existing institutional resources to be used to fund the start-up efforts related to initial project planning and permitting. In some cases, gifts will have been raised for the project, and these can be used to finance these early costs. Eventually, however, most major projects will require the borrowing of funds to finance construction. This can take the form of various short-term or temporary financing arrangements to address just the period of actual construction with bonds eventually replacing the temporary arrangement. Or the bonds can be issued at the outset of the project with no temporary financing arrangements employed.

7. *ACQUIRE OR CONSTRUCT.*

Once funding has been arranged, the purchase is consummated or the actual construction begins. Depending on the nature of the project, this step may take several years. During this period, the capital budget will be reviewed regularly to ensure the overall capital portfolio is being managed effectively.

Cost overruns are common with construction projects, and it is not unusual for an individual project budget to have a sizable contingency factor. Although the amount will vary by project, a 5 percent contingency is customary and a 10 percent contingency is not uncommon.

CAPITAL BUDGET CALENDAR

Due to the types of projects included in a capital budget, its cycle will be much longer. Several years may elapse from the time a project is conceptualized until it has been completed, placed in service, and removed from the capital budget or added to the operating budget. The capital budget extends through the end point for the longest-term project that has been formally approved within the institution. Because multiple projects may be in different phases at any point, capital budgets tend to stretch out for years—especially at public institutions.

Because of the lengthy capital project approval process in some states, and the fact that many states employ a biennial budget cycle, a single project could have a six- or eight-year life. For instance, the institution could internally approve a project in year one and then embark on a two- or three-year process to obtain approval for the project from the relevant state departments and agencies. Once approved by the state, the project will wait until resources become available. Depending on debt markets and competing priorities, this process easily could take one or two years.

Once funding has been secured, the process begins to program the project specifics and issue invitations to bid for the various project components. This will lead to the awarding of contracts followed by actual construction. It's not uncommon for major projects to require two or more years for construction.

DEFERRED MAINTENANCE

Deferred maintenance refers to the scheduled routine repair and maintenance of facilities that is postponed, thereby creating a backlog. Every campus has some amount of deferred maintenance resulting from various operational considerations. A particular classroom facility may be due for interior painting but, because of increased demand for the program housed in the facility, the decision is made to postpone the painting until spring break during the following academic year. Or a roof scheduled for replacement must continue in service because the specialized materials it requires are temporarily unavailable. Such situations are not problematic when they are short term and exceptional in nature.

On the other hand, many institutions have large backlogs of deferred maintenance that developed because of financial stress. In other words, revenue shortfalls or expense overruns in prior years prevented the institution from making the repairs or conducting the maintenance in accordance with the established schedule. A modest deferred maintenance backlog may be manageable, but once it grows too large to address within normal operating cycles, facilities begin to deteriorate rapidly. Even relatively new facilities will not operate optimally if not properly maintained. And of particular concern is the reality that poorly maintained facilities are more expensive to operate and more prone to additional problems.

For these reasons, institutions seek to quantify the deferred maintenance backlog so they can address it through the operating budget, the capital budget, or both. There are various methods for doing this. One that is popular within higher education is the Facilities Condition Index (FCI), a simple formula that is very difficult to calculate. It is structured as follows: FCI = Cost of Maintenance and Repair Deficiencies / Current Replacement Value of the Facilities. Notice that there are only two variables. Moreover, it can be applied to an individual facility, a sector of a campus, or the campus as a whole. Where the challenge arises is gaining agreement on the definition of the variables.

For some institutions, the calculation can be pretty straightforward. When an institution has established maintenance schedules for all major components and systems of the built environment and good records, they are in a good place to begin calculation of the FCI. If the maintenance is not conducted as scheduled, a deficiency exists and its value can be estimated in dollar terms using current rates for the relevant type of maintenance.

The calculation of current replacement value (CRV) is subject to some debate, but there are at least a handful of formulaic approaches that, when applied consistently, give institutions reliable information that can be utilized to calculate the FCI. One approach utilizes original construction cost by type of component and escalates the cost to current levels. When aggregated, the result represents the CRV for a given component, facility, or combination of facilities. Alternatively, the relevant current unit construction costs can be multiplied by either gross or net square feet of a given type to produce the CRV for the indicated space. Still other methods are available and, depending on the desired level of sophistication, can be costly to employ. The most important consideration may be less focused on the specifics of the methodology than on the consistency of its use over time. It's important to know whether the campus is keeping pace with deferred maintenance, falling behind, or—somewhat unlikely—making great strides to address the backlog.

Normal repairs and maintenance are considered operating expenses. As such, they typically are managed by including an amount in the operating budget to address at least a portion of the backlog. And if the institution ends the year with unanticipated surpluses, it may allocate a portion of the surplus to addressing the backlog.

When the operating budget (or surpluses it generates) cannot accommodate the backlog, the institution usually turns to its capital budget, which includes a special category to address critical aspects of deferred maintenance. The major concern for such projects is the funding source. It is rare that bonds can be sold to finance deferred maintenance projects, so other sources must be found. Many public institutions receive special appropriations for this purpose. Independent institutions, however, must generate the funds themselves through operating surpluses or fundraising.

Trade-offs are necessary between demands for new or enhanced space and the need to maintain and repair existing space. Some institutions rely on outside firms to assist with the analysis required to determine the appropriate mix between routine scheduled maintenance, facilities renewal/upgrades, and new construction.

Unlike many indicators of financial stress—such as reduced enrollment resulting in declining revenues or bad debts from students unable to pay their bills—deferred maintenance backlogs do not appear in the audited financial statements. Some effects of deferred maintenance may be visibly apparent, but nothing in generally accepted accounting principles (GAAP) requires disclosure of the amount of the backlog. Stakeholders must ask the right questions to ensure that the backlog does not become unmanageable.

Attending to existing backlogs poses a financial challenge—one that can become worse as institutions add new facilities. The campus building boom of the late 1990s and early 2000s has resulted in significantly increased deferred maintenance burdens. One strategy being employed by a number of institutions is to place a moratorium on new facilities projects unless they come with a dedicated renewal and replacement reserve for the facility. In other words, the source of ongoing maintenance funds must be identified at the start of any new capital project to ensure the new facilities do not contribute to the deferred maintenance backlog.

Obviously, this approach addresses only part of the problem because it does not generate funds to address the existing backlog. Still, it represents a step in the right direction.

KEY POINTS

▶ An operating budget covers activity occurring within a single fiscal year. A capital budget addresses projects related to major physical assets such as buildings and extends over several years.

▶ A typical operating budget cycle consists of 16 steps, while the corresponding capital budget cycle usually has seven steps.

▶ Key steps in the capital budget process include identifying the funding sources and uses of funds for each project.

▶ Public institutions must perform the same budgeting steps as independent institutions, along with whatever steps are added in order to satisfy the expectations of various state agencies.

▶ The calendars for the operating and capital budget cycles typically are not linked because of the differing objectives for the two budgets. The operating budget calendar usually begins well before the start of the fiscal year it pertains to and ends when the board approves the audited financial statements. The capital budget calendar has a much longer time line. It begins with the internal approval of a capital project and continues as long as any approved project remains incomplete.

CHAPTER 11: BUDGET FLEXIBILITY

Inevitably, things will not always play out as projected. Or as a colleague put it, "The budget is obsolete the day it is published."

There is no guarantee that revenues projected in the budget will actually materialize. Enrollment targets, for example, might fall short because students offered admission chose to enroll elsewhere, or previous students did not return for another year. Alternatively, more students than expected may accept financial aid packages exceeding the amount budgeted. Financial markets may not deliver the investment income anticipated when the budget was developed.

Conversely, some expenses might prove larger than expected. The renewal rates for health insurance may be significantly higher than expected. Major winter storms could drive snow removal costs beyond anything considered possible. The contracted internet service provider may go bankrupt, forcing the institution to rely on a backup provider with rates initially set only for short-term consumption.

Any of these situations could wreak havoc on resource allocation plans. Building flexibility into the budget enables institutions to better respond to such changing circumstances and conditions—and the financial implications that accompany them. In fact, one mark of a well-managed institution is its ability to take advantage of unforeseen opportunities and respond to unanticipated problems.

Ultimately, flexibility comes from having adequate resources to conduct the institution's activities—academic programs and the supporting operations. One way to provide flexibility is through **contingency funding** to cover revenue shortfalls or expense overruns. Unrestricted revenues—such as tuition and fees, unrestricted gifts and endowment income, most state appropriations, and surpluses in auxiliary enterprises or other self-supporting activities—can provide the resources that cushion an institution against unforeseen events. The challenge comes in identifying the cushion and preserving it until it is absolutely necessary to use it—while still addressing the demands of daily operations.

Apart from contingency funding, **maneuverability** is a key element supporting flexibility. For example, funds with the fewest restrictions on their use can be held back and not allocated at the outset, making them available to address unanticipated needs. All institutions must deal with the reality that some donated funds carry donor-imposed restrictions. In fact, today's donors are savvier and tend to provide restricted versus unrestricted giving. In these situations, the donor explicitly states what the funds may be used for—either specific programmatic objectives (e.g., research, student financial aid) or specific types of expenses (salaries, library materials, etc.). When managing budgets during tight financial times, it's desirable to have a comprehensive understanding of the restricted resources and the specific stipulations attached to them. In some cases, the restrictions are so specific that the institution has no latitude to use them for anything else. In other cases, however, the restrictions may be very broad and provide flexibility to displace previously committed resources, which then can be spent for other purposes.

Not all unrestricted funds are equal. When a donor makes an unrestricted gift, the only constraint on using those funds is that they be used for lawful purposes consistent with the institution's mission. Although state operating appropriations (general funds) are considered unrestricted, regulatory requirements frequently cause them to be managed as if they carried restrictions. For instance, the state may have established rules requiring special approvals when state general funds are used to pay for a personal services contract. Or it may be necessary to utilize an established procurement contract when acquiring certain commodities. In other words, even when the state doesn't identify the particular program that must be supported with the funds it provides, it may dictate how to support whichever program is chosen.

Public institutions can establish flexibility by allocating state general funds to qualifying activities while preserving completely unrestricted resources for other uses. Resources such as gifts and endowment support—when not restricted—and any other resources with no strings attached, usually are preserved to support activities that are not eligible for state funding.

Risk tolerance also impacts flexibility. The greater the institution's aversion to risk, the more important the need to develop a budget that provides maximum flexibility through contingency funding and maneuverability. Not allocating all anticipated revenues to expenses or investments helps avoid the risk that resources will be insufficient to meet all commitments. A budget that allocates all anticipated revenues runs the risk that some planned expense or other investment will have to be deferred due to revenue shortfalls or cost overruns.

FIVE CHANGE FACTORS

One of five factors typically causes significant changes in an institution's revenues or expenses. All are major reasons for building cushion into the budget.

1. Enrollment fluctuations. If enrollments fall below expected levels, institutions will lose tuition revenues and, in the case of public institutions, may lose state appropriations as well. Unless the expense budget contains a cushion, the institution will face a deficit for that year. This is especially likely at smaller independent institutions with high tuition. Even a modest shortfall in expected students can have a devastating effect on revenues without a commensurate reduction in expenses. If the average net tuition revenue from students (after financial aid) is $25,000, missing the mark by 20 students is a half-million dollars. The more reliant on tuition, the greater the likelihood that significant forced expense reductions will be required to offset the revenue loss.

Similarly, excess enrollment can create budget problems. Additional class sections may be required to accommodate the unanticipated increase in enrollment, but the revenue generated from the additional students may not cover all additional costs. Unanticipated enrollment increases may also affect auxiliary units. Dining operations can probably accommodate more students, but bookstores may not have adequate textbook inventories to meet demand. Or the institution may not have enough residence halls to accommodate the additional students seeking campus housing.

Sometimes, enrollment patterns do not follow historical trends. For instance, enrollment may shift dramatically among majors, making it impossible to reallocate resources. The institution may need to engage adjunct faculty or identify additional graduate students to serve as teaching assistants to meet the increased demand, even though no savings can be realized in the programs experiencing the enrollment declines.

2. Revenue fluctuations. Revenue shortfalls occur in sources other than tuition and fees. There is a very strong correlation between success in attracting philanthropic support and conditions in the U.S. economy. When the economy suffers, so do institutions' fundraising results. This can be particularly troubling if the situation also affects financial markets. Investment income, though not large for most institutions, may not achieve the financial targets set for them. Similarly, economic problems might affect state revenues, thereby causing the state to reduce appropriations to public institutions. If the problem develops late in the fiscal year, the state may even require the institution to return funds already distributed.

3. Expense fluctuations. An unanticipated utility hike, increased insurance costs due to a spate of natural disasters, or price increases for required repair materials are examples of expense increases that collectively could create the potential for an operating deficit. Campuses are like small- or medium-sized cities. Unexpected price increases in almost any commodity can affect the bottom line. If the increase relates to a widely used commodity, the impact can be significant.

4. Financial emergencies. Although most campuses have several types of insurance, a natural disaster can strike at any time and lead to significant unplanned expenses to meet policy deductibles or cover costs not protected by insurance. Other emergencies might range from paying dramatic midyear increases in healthcare premiums to repaying the federal government due to an audit of sponsored programs. In the latter case, institutions often deem it more practical to negotiate a financial settlement than aggressively challenge the federal government, even when they have followed all the rules governing the sponsored research. This practice resolves the issue more quickly but also provides less time to plan for the financial impact of the settlement.

5. Unforeseen opportunities. Say a faculty member needs a substantial commitment of institutional matching funds to secure a major research project that will raise the institution's profile. Or perhaps another college or a corporation suggests collaborating on a new initiative that dovetails with a priority area identified through the institutional planning process. Rather than pass up such opportunities, an institution with a discretionary or contingency fund could take advantage of them.

A Three-Tiered Approach

One institution's approach to contingencies relies on multiple funds. The first category, known as the president's discretionary fund, provides resources to deploy when unique opportunities arise. The second level, a tuition reserve fund, solely addresses revenue shortfalls caused by unexpected drops in enrollment. Finally, there is a contingency fund for use in an emergency situation. If none arise, the contingency amount will be added to reserves at year-end.

CREATING THE CUSHION

At each level of the budget process, participants have the opportunity to allocate every potential resource to its fullest or maintain a cushion for responding to expense overruns, revenue shortfalls, or opportunities. Although modest, a cushion created at the department level will allow the unit to respond to issues that might arise.

More cushion is needed at the highest levels because of the greater magnitude of issues to deal with. A cost increase for a special laboratory supply may affect only one or two units and probably can be accommodated with a modest amount of cushion. On the other hand, a major spike in healthcare premiums can absorb an institution's entire contingency reserve.

Some people view financial flexibility as a sign of inefficiency and poor administration, even referring to contingency funding in an institutional budget as "fat." One extension of this philosophy is the notion that a leaner budget translates into greater accountability or improved efficiency. In fact, the most effective organizations can readily marshal their resources to respond to challenges or take advantage of opportunities. Such institutions intentionally avoid committing all resources and, instead, program a contingency into the budget as a cushion against unforeseen circumstances.

There is no prescribed level of contingency from an authoritative body. The CFI (see Chapter 7) indicates at least 2 percent of operating revenues as the smallest amount to achieve minimal financial health at an independent institution. The comparable number for a public institution is 4 percent (or 2 percent if the institution limits endowment income counted in its operating measure to the amount available for spending currently). Keep in mind that these are minimums. The maximum value counted toward the CFI is 7 percent for independent institutions and public institutions limiting the amount of endowment income counted toward the operating measure and 20 percent for other public institutions. One can infer that the desirable level is something more toward the lower middle of the range—say 3 percent for independent and qualifying public institutions and something closer to 8 percent for other public institutions. This means that the contingency must be set at a level to ensure the desired surplus can be achieved. It usually is expressed as a percentage of total revenue or total expense. The volatility of the operating activities will be a significant factor in the establishment of the contingency. The more volatile operations are, the larger the contingency.

Recognizing the importance of flexibility, most budgeters will protect the budget contingencies from those above and below in the hierarchy. They must take care, however, not to go to extremes and forget that contingency funds exist for use when needed. The funds should not be spent unwisely, but neither should the institutions miss opportunities because of a misguided desire to build reserves at all costs.

Managers typically seek to shift uncertainty to others. Department heads routinely turn to deans or central office personnel for resources needed to respond to emergencies or opportunities. For instance, a department that encounters unanticipated price increases for needed supplies or higher-than-expected salary demands by an adjunct filling in for a temporarily disabled faculty member may expect the provost to provide funding to address the situation.

Alternatively, deans and central administrators may assume the burden of closely monitoring departmental spending to anticipate or prevent problems or use contingency funds to address problems within departments rather than use them for opportunities at the college level. At the state level, officials often shift uncertainty to public higher education systems or individual campuses by establishing regulations that prohibit operating deficits.

Flexibility changes from one budget cycle to another as circumstances change. New resources must be found to adapt to different conditions, and new strategies must be utilized to create contingency funding in the budget. Although budgeters at all levels seek to include cushion in their portions of the budget, they are reluctant to label it as such for fear that others may seek to claim the amounts—with good reason. It's not uncommon for presidents and provosts to seek to spend the cushion, occasionally even attempting to spend the same dollar multiple times.

To avoid deficits, senior management ideally should establish an institutional-level contingency fund to address significant revenue shortfalls and expense overruns. The chief financial officer must ensure the president and provost understand the nature of the cushion and what it is intended to cover. The optimal level of cushion for most institutions is in the range of 2 to 4 percent of the operating expense budget. This is large enough to address most situations that might arise but small enough to realistically incorporate into the budget.

On rare occasions, an institution will receive an unanticipated windfall—such as a large bequest with no restrictions—and it should know immediately how to deploy such funds. In fact, plans at the institutional level should include a list of priorities to address if resources become available, either through unanticipated savings or a windfall. Truly effective institutions take it a step further. They develop a complementary list of areas that will experience resource reductions if expenses must be curtailed. This approach protects high-priority areas when revenue shortfalls or expense overruns occur.

Fewer Restrictions on Endowment Spending

Nearly all states have enacted versions of UPMIFA, which loosened prohibitions on spending from underwater endowments. These are endowments whose current market value has fallen below the level of the gifts originally received from donors. The previous restrictions were deemed impractical given that true endowments have a perpetual life.

Two major features of the act benefit colleges and universities. The most significant is the provision for prudent spending from underwater endowments. This provides institutions with the flexibility to spend a portion of principal to support the endowment's objectives.

The other provision establishes a streamlined process for addressing smaller endowments whose restricted purpose no longer is relevant. Following procedures established in their state, institutions can consolidate such endowments and use them for a purpose consistent with the donors' original intent.

HIDDEN COSTS THAT LIMIT FLEXIBILITY

No one—especially someone with budget responsibility—likes surprises. To reduce the impact of surprises, institutions should budget contingency funding that can be reallocated to meet unanticipated expenses, provide funds to take advantage of new opportunities, or allow the institution to withstand revenue shortfalls.

Even with contingency funding, however, some policy decisions carry hidden costs. Here are some common examples.

New facilities. Institutions rarely fail to acknowledge the costs of constructing or acquiring a new facility. Occasionally, however, they ignore the ongoing O&M costs incurred when the new facility is placed in service, erroneously assuming that existing budgets will absorb these costs. In addition to ongoing operating costs for routine maintenance and utilities, a new facility will need funds for equipment and furnishings. Again, so much attention usually is focused on the building or space itself that its related costs are ignored or underestimated.

One institution has taken the progressive action of phasing these costs into the budget whenever a new construction project is undertaken. Recognizing that facilities management will require more resources to properly operate and maintain the new space, they begin incorporating the amounts needed even before the facility is ready to open. This avoids significant shocks once the building is placed in service, and it helps add to the cushion needed to protect against unanticipated budgetary impacts.

New academic programs. Typically, the obvious costs—salaries and benefits for new faculty and staff, space needs, workstations, supplies, and so on—are anticipated and factored into the budget. But the less obvious items—the ancillary cost and revenue impacts of the new programs—may not be addressed.

If, for instance, the new program attracts more students, complementary programs will probably experience increased demand for their courses and need to hire additional instructors. Or rather than significantly increasing enrollments in existing departments, the new program may prompt students to transfer in from existing departments. The net result may be that courses in existing departments become undersubscribed, causing those departments to be overstaffed.

The question becomes: Who should provide the resources to meet the increased or shifted demand for instruction? More than one department must bear the burden of curricular changes that affect several programs. Although the question has no single correct answer, the obvious implication is to consider all additional costs—and lost revenues—before making programmatic changes.

Making the Case

Whenever a new program, activity, or facility is being considered, institutions should borrow a standard practice from the corporate sector and develop a written "business case" to support the decision-making process. The documentation for each initiative should include:

- ▶ **Rationale.** Describe what the effort will accomplish, how it aligns with established priorities, and how it will contribute to institutional success. Also, identify any anticipated ancillary impacts—both positive and negative—that might occur if the initiative is pursued.
- ▶ **Estimated financial impact.** Project both costs and resources for at least three years (and, when possible, for five years). With a capital project, the business case must identify the total project cost, even if it extends beyond five years.
- ▶ **Project details.** If the initiative relates to a support program, the analysis typically is more straightforward because there usually are fewer issues to be examined. What are the anticipated impacts on the institution—positive and negative—and how will other units be affected?

Projections tend to be more complex for academic programs. For instructional programs—the most common academic programs—estimate the projected number of students, faculty, and support staff. Explain any anticipated involvement or participation by other organizations and any dependencies—other things that must occur for the initiative to succeed. Also, address how students will be attracted to the program. In other words, will they be new students who will contribute additional revenue or students already registered in other programs? Finally, at a minimum, the business case must detail the anticipated impacts on institutional operations (e.g., library, information technology, registrar, accounting).

In short, a business case presents all relevant factors in one place. This puts decision-makers in the best possible position to make the most appropriate choice for the institution based on what is known and can be reasonably expected. It also provides the basis for accountability if the effort does not achieve expected results.

Elimination of activities or programs. Hidden costs have the potential to erase some or all of the anticipated savings. For example, continuing academic programs that require courses or services from the program being eliminated will have to find substitutes or provide the services themselves.

If program curtailment results in the release of personnel, reduction-in-force policies may require that the personnel displace other less senior staff or receive significant severance payments.

Space usually is at a premium on campuses, so vacated space will be in high demand. Nevertheless, a unique single-purpose space may be abandoned when a program ends. Even if the vacant space no longer requires ongoing maintenance costs, at some point down the road, the institution will have to incur costs to convert the space for an alternate use.

Human resources. Positions protected by tenure policies or job security established through individual contracts or collective bargaining agreements can greatly affect budget flexibility. In some institutions, the tendency toward job permanence for certain employment categories makes it difficult to reallocate positions from one activity to another or to reduce the number of positions assigned to an activity. As for tenured positions, an assistant professor may receive tenure at age 30 and continue working until age 70. If the professor earns a modest average salary of $100,000 plus benefits throughout his or her career, the decision to grant tenure represents a financial commitment approaching $5 million.

Tenure. Tenure, as practiced throughout higher education, is a unique and cherished aspect of employment—one rarely seen outside of colleges and universities, at least using the traditional college format. How and where tenure is awarded to a faculty member is not always given the attention it should though. Many institutions award tenure to deserving faculty without specifying a program, department, or other organizational unit. When this happens, one can argue that tenure has been granted at the institution level. Essentially, the employment guarantee may exist as long as the institution continues to operate. This can be a costly mistake, as it ties the institution's hands when demand for a given program disappears.

When tenure is granted at the more appropriate program level, it's a relatively easy, though potentially painful, decision to close programs and terminate affected positions when circumstances warrant such actions. When tenure is granted at the institution level, closing the program still may be possible, but the elimination of tenured positions may be called into question.

Seed funding. Grants or other temporary sources can help launch a new program or activity. Once operational, however, the program or activity may require support from other resources—unless it generates resources on its own through gifts, service fees, or tuition.

Higher education is not noted for its ability to terminate programs or activities, so an established program is likely to continue even if anticipated revenues do not materialize. Prepare for the possibility of a new program not generating sufficient funds to sustain itself by recognizing and accommodating these potential costs at the outset.

STRATEGIES TO INCREASE FLEXIBILITY

Flexibility is structured according to the portion of the budget to which it pertains. Compensation costs can represent as much as 70 percent of college or university budgets with fixed expenses, such as utilities and facilities maintenance, absorbing another 10 to 15 percent. The balance usually is spent for other operating expenses such as technology, supplies, noncapital equipment, etc.

Constraints on the use of funds differ from one expense category to another. For example, policies may prevent unexpended amounts budgeted for compensation to be spent for other operating expenses. Instead, such amounts are captured centrally for reallocation or, in some public institutions, must revert to the state. Strategies for creating flexibility tend to be tailored to the activity, the expense policies affecting the institution, and the nature of operations within the institution.

Outlined below are specific strategies an institution might employ to increase financial flexibility. Not all will work in every situation, but they offer the potential to achieve enhanced results from the budget process.

(Note that success with these strategies might backfire at public institutions. Accumulating unrestricted balances as a cushion against economic difficulties can create a juicy target for state officials looking for more resources. In some instances, states have recaptured what they perceive as excessive fund balances or simply reduced appropriations and directed institutions to spend down their existing balances. Public institution officers and appropriate state officials should talk about what actions can be taken to protect needed reserves developed through prudent management.)

Change the framework. The potential for operating and budgetary flexibility may simply disappear through atrophy. In other words, budget practices will become stale if not examined and modified regularly. The same activities will take place year after year, with the participants comfortably replicating what had been done the year before—which had also been done the year before that, and the year before that, and so on. Absent a comprehensive approach to examining the budget process, participants tend to allocate resources as in years past, usually with little to no substantive change. This is especially true in institutions that do not employ a rigorous planning process to drive budgetary decisions.

Ample evidence suggests that budget practices remain static. For instance, the historical employment growth driven by program expansion rarely has a corresponding reduction resulting from program contraction. Focusing on new programs or activities that might enhance the operating environment or make the institution more appealing to its applicant pool comes easily. It proves much harder to identify programs and activities that no longer contribute to success.

An institution may be able to capture excess resources by analyzing the way they are currently being distributed. Taking a holistic approach that focuses on the entire operating budget—addressing both academic programs and support activities—affords the opportunity for an in-depth review. An alternative approach focuses on activity clusters. It simultaneously examines a particular academic program and all of its related activities, both those for academic and student support.

Not all budgeting models are created equal. (See Chapter 9 for a discussion of the differences among budget models commonly used in higher education.) Some are more adept at supporting flexibility than others. Incremental models are relatively easy to change because of their reliance on straightforward formulas to distribute resources. If circumstances change, the formula can change. (Note that the ease with which the resource distributions can be changed does not necessarily correlate with how easy or hard it is for units to adapt to those changes.) Many believe that RCB provides relatively greater flexibility because of the creation of incentives at the unit level—especially for revenue responsibility units.

On the other hand, formula-based models have difficulty supporting flexibility because—unlike the straightforward formula used with incremental budgeting—the various formulas employed in a formula-based model can be very difficult to change. ZBB and its variants entail in-depth assessment of activity costs in comparison with what is accomplished to determine whether the investments are reasonable. The time required to conduct the analyses suggests that it also doesn't react well to changing circumstances.

Examine cost structures. In general, academic programs have many fixed costs—costs incurred no matter how many students are served. As an example, every institution, no matter its enrollment, has some form of chief academic officer. Every institution also has a registrar for managing student records and determining when a student has met the requirements for a degree. For a third example, consider the faculty member who teaches biology courses. Whether that faculty member is tenured or adjunct is irrelevant. As long as the institution intends to offer a biology program, it will have fixed costs related to faculty for those courses.

The alternative to fixed costs is variable costs—costs that rise or fall based on levels of service. When a community college offers multiple sections of algebra, the number of faculty becomes a variable cost. There may be some fixed costs for algebra because a minimum number of faculty are needed each term. Overall, however, this represents a variable cost once that fixed number has been exceeded. If eight sections of algebra are offered with a standard class load of four, two faculty members will be needed. If student demand dictates that the college offer 16 sections, two additional faculty will be needed.

A further refinement of variable costs is known as step-variable costs. These costs do not vary proportionally as volumes increase or decrease. Instead, they remain steady until a specific threshold is reached. In the previous example involving sections of algebra, it's likely that a step threshold is established. If the objective is to limit each algebra section to 25 students, the step threshold is 25. A new class section will be offered for every 25 additional students seeking to take a class in algebra. Another step variable threshold would be established for the number of faculty teaching algebra. If the established teaching workload results in a faculty member teaching four sections of algebra, one additional faculty member will be added for each four additional sections.

In reality, of course, the numbers don't necessarily work out. What happens if 12 additional students instead of 25 want to take algebra? Do you add a section for the 12 students or distribute them among existing sections, thereby increasing the student count beyond the standard of 25? Similarly, what happens if 18 sections are needed? Presumably, four faculty will teach the first 16 sections. Will the additional two sections represent overload for existing faculty, or will they hire one or two adjuncts to meet the additional demand? Such situations arise routinely on campus, so the institution needs to have policies and practices in place as a decision-making guide.

Fixed or Variable?

It's not unusual for participants in the budgeting process to make erroneous assumptions about a cost's true nature. Too often, costs are assumed to be fixed when they actually are variable. Just because a cost has been incurred every year for as long as anyone can remember does not mean it can't be eliminated.

Resource allocation decisions must be informed by financial analysis to determine whether costs truly can be eliminated without adversely affecting the program or activity. The lower the fixed costs incurred by a program or activity, the greater the flexibility an institution has over its operating budget. And when program and activity planning are aligned with the budget process, costs become much more variable.

Conduct an in-depth revenue analysis. Revenue analysis focuses on the individual activities (such as programs, courses, and projects) that actually generate revenue. Among other things, such analysis will reveal which academic programs generate the most revenues and which provide the least.

Some individual courses produce significant amounts of net revenue because they rely on a single faculty member lecturing to large groups of students without the need for significant capital investment (psychology, business, and English are three examples). Unless variable tuition pricing applies, these revenue-generating courses subsidize more labor- or capital-intensive programs, such as nursing, music, or engineering. Linking the analysis to productivity indicators, such as numbers of students served, student credit hours generated, and number of course sections offered, provides even greater value.

The point of the analysis is not necessarily to encourage the institution to invest more in courses that provide greater returns, although that may be appropriate in some situations. Instead, the goal is to develop an understanding of cost and revenue structures so that informed decisions can be made. If results show that a particular program produces significant net revenues but is frequently under enrolled, it would make sense to align recruitment efforts in this direction. Conversely, it may make sense to establish enrollment caps for other high-cost programs to avoid incurring marginal costs to accommodate anything less than a full (or nearly full) cohort of students.

The analysis will help identify which programs might be attractive targets for competitors from the for-profit education sector. For the most part, these organizations are not interested in competing to offer instruction in the physical sciences or engineering because those programs require substantial investments in facilities and equipment. Instead, they want to capture the high-volume, high-return programs and courses to generate profits for their investors.

Gaining an in-depth understanding of cost and revenue structures is also crucial for campus business operations such as auxiliary enterprises and charge-back units (e.g., central stores, facilities management, copy centers).

Through the analysis, various units will know whether they are pricing goods and services appropriately to recover all costs.

Build reserves. Perhaps the simplest strategy for creating a pooled reserve of resources at the institution, college, or department level is to withhold a small percentage of the funds that otherwise would be available for distribution within that level of the organization. For instance, the president may withhold 2 percent of the anticipated overall increase in revenues to create a discretionary fund under his or her control. The fund might finance new initiatives, respond to emergencies and opportunities, or cover expense overruns in central budgets. Similarly, a dean may divert a small percentage of the school's unrestricted resources to provide funds for cross-cutting initiatives that will benefit the school as a whole.

Operating budgets at every level should include at least a modest amount of contingency funds. The pooled reserve goes beyond such contingencies. It provides resources—at whatever level it is created—to enhance the operational flexibility enjoyed at that level. Reserves might fund establishment of a research laboratory, for instance. Working with his or her senior cabinet, the president may decide the research laboratory represents the best use of the funds that otherwise would have been dispersed throughout the institution.

By drawing on the reserve, the institution can pursue initiatives that individual units probably can't afford. Reserves, however, represent a one-time special use of resources. Once they have been deployed, they are no longer available until they can be replenished through annual operating surpluses. Additionally, although reserves can be used to offset revenue shortfalls budgetarily, the institution will report an operating deficit whenever the current year's operating revenues do not equal the corresponding operating expenses.

Capture savings from position vacancies. It's a fact of their existence that organizations employing large numbers of people will routinely experience turnover. Rather than impose specific targets for salary savings on operating units, an institution may require all (or a portion of) position vacancy savings to be captured centrally. Under this "lapsed salary" approach, whenever a position becomes vacant and the salaries and benefits are not expended as originally planned, the funds revert to a central pool for reallocation within the institution (or for addition to reserves).

It is not always possible to capture any savings though, either because a replacement is hired immediately at a comparable salary or the savings must cover the payout of accumulated vacation and sick leave. When this is not the case, however, the savings generated by midyear departures or the delay in recruiting a replacement can enhance institutional flexibility.

Reduce the grade or rank of vacant positions. A college or university can capture some surplus resources centrally by simply downgrading positions that become vacant. In essence, this forces the hiring of replacements at lower salary levels with the savings used for other purposes.

This strategy won't work in all situations. For instance, if a senior-level administrative position becomes vacant because a long-serving incumbent departed, the marketplace has likely changed. The replacement may demand an even higher salary. Similarly, if a senior researcher retires, the overall research mission may dictate recruitment of an equally accomplished researcher as a replacement.

Employ part-time or temporary faculty. Temporary faculty hired on a course-by-course basis are significantly less expensive than tenured faculty or even permanent contract faculty. Some departments routinely hold certain faculty lines vacant so that the unspent funds can be used to employ temporary faculty, thereby increasing the department's budget flexibility. This practice also is customary when faculty are on sabbatical or leave without pay. The salary savings generated can be used to meet other departmental needs such as travel or small equipment.

While appealing from a flexibility standpoint, this strategy has drawbacks. Temporary faculty often become academic nomads, moving from one temporary position to another each semester or each year because they are unable to find permanent positions. And though these faculty may be well qualified in the classroom, they may not be as accessible to students and colleagues as permanent faculty. Their presence can also have a negative impact on the morale of the permanent faculty, who see positions being filled by people who may not be as committed to the institution or the discipline.

Withhold some salary adjustment funds. Public institutions commonly receive funding for a specified percentage of total budgeted salaries to cover salary adjustments. This is true even when some positions remain vacant. Therefore, it is possible to gain increased flexibility at central or school/college levels by withholding the salary adjustment for any position not currently filled. Resources captured in this way can then be applied to other campus or unit priorities.

Carry over balances. State systems or independent institutions that permit the carryover of year-end balances from one fiscal year to the next have a natural source of budget flexibility. This liberal use of year-end balances reduces the pressure on units to spend all of their resources before year-end and encourages the saving of resources for major purchases or projects. It imposes additional burdens on central administration to ensure that the overall amount carried forward is reasonable.

In states that do not allow balance carryover, the institution must monitor the level of resources that units seek to carry forward, along with the amounts by which other units are prepared to overspend their budgets through accelerated purchases. This process would begin in the latter part of the fiscal year and continue through year-end. By matching up these situations, the institution can avoid either a surplus or a deficit for a portion of the budget while still achieving unit objectives.

The situation will be reversed in the subsequent year with the prior year's overspending units reducing their budgets by amounts equal to the previous overspending. This enables the previously underspent units to spend more in the current year. While this process provides flexibility, it also creates a significant administrative burden on the central offices that must solve what can be a complex puzzle.

Pursue sponsored research and training activities. Grant and contract awards include many direct costs (such as salaries, graduate student support, travel, and supplies) that enhance the financial position of the institution.

External support also provides financial relief for committed research activities.

Recover overhead costs. F&A costs charged to sponsored projects are based on actual expenses incurred to support all projects. When collected from the sponsor, however, there is no requirement to use the funds for purposes related to the specific sponsored projects generating the recoveries. With some modest limitations established by federal policy, the institution can use the funds for any purpose it deems appropriate.

In most independent institutions, overhead recoveries represent another revenue source similar to tuition or investment income. For some public institutions, however, state guidelines may require return of the funds to the state treasury—the source of funds for the original investments in support costs. Or states may impose specific rules about how the institution can utilize these funds.

A number of states allow institutions to retain and use overhead recoveries to support research. For instance, the funds might be used to make internal grants to young investigators to help them start their research. Alternatively, the funds might be allocated to cover the cost of travel to professional meetings at which faculty present their research findings.

Enhance fundraising efforts. The financial support received from alumni, foundations, corporate allies, and friends is invaluable in helping meet institutional or constituent needs. Yet while all gifts provide value to institutions (or they should not be accepted), unrestricted gifts bring the added benefit of flexibility. With that in mind, institutions should work with donors so they understand the importance of gifts that carry no restrictions.

Engage in technology transfer. Technology transfer refers to the practice of leveraging an institution's intellectual property for commercial gain. Essentially, it involves licensing the use of inventions or discoveries to share knowledge and generate revenues.

At research institutions in particular, faculty and graduate students are continually engaged in the pursuit of knowledge. Many undergraduate students engage in research activities as well. Research sometimes results in a commercial application for which companies will pay substantial sums. Many institutions rely on a third party to commercialize discoveries, although others have established related foundations or internal units for this purpose. In these situations, revenues come either from a one-time sale or ongoing royalties from use of the discovery.

Some campuses elect to commercialize the discovery directly, and the resulting revenues represent a return on investment. Various models can apply to leveraging the discoveries, including a distribution of net revenues to the institution, the home department, and the researcher(s)—whether faculty, technicians, or students.

KEY POINTS

▶ The most effective institutions incorporate significant flexibility into their budgets. Recognizing that plans will not always achieve the desired outcomes, they remain prepared to adapt and change course.

▶ Enrollment, expense, or revenue fluctuations; emergencies; and unforeseen opportunities all drive the need for budget flexibility.

▶ Building contingency into the budget is the most important strategy for enhancing flexibility.

▶ Additionally, policies can contribute to or impair budget flexibility.

CHAPTER 12: INSTITUTIONAL POLICY IMPACTS ON BUDGETING

A variety of institutional policies—not just those directly related to finances—carry financial implications. Based on the policies they adopt, for example, institutions can enhance or impair budget flexibility. While some policies are imposed on institutions, others reflect conscious decisions made by management to achieve specific operational objectives or for compliance reasons.

One way to influence budget decisions is to alter the policies and procedures related to resource allocation and use. Along with the specific issues addressed in this chapter, readers are encouraged to carefully consider Chapter 7 addressing planning—especially infrastructural planning.

ENTERPRISE RISK MANAGEMENT (ERM)

Before exploring various policies on the academic and support sides of the institution, there is one overarching issue that applies across the institution. The concept of risk tolerance was introduced in Chapter 1 in the context of an institution's comfort level when allocating resources. The higher the risk tolerance, the greater the likelihood that all anticipated revenues will be allocated. Conversely, institutions with lower risk tolerance are more inclined to protect against unanticipated financial impacts by establishing contingencies within the expense budget.

Beyond the issue of risk tolerance and its impact on contingencies is the issue of ERM. ERM is the term used for the collection of activities and efforts designed to acknowledge risks and take actions to mitigate or eliminate them. In most cases, the only way to eliminate a risk is not to participate in endeavors that expose the institution to that risk. There are many different ways to mitigate risks, and many of them have budgetary implications.

ERM is intended to focus on risks in several categories, as described below:

▶ Strategic risks: Risks to an institution's ability to achieve its goals
▶ Financial risks: Risks that could result in the loss of assets

- Operational risks: Risks that affect the institution's ability to carry out the day-to-day tasks of providing instruction, conducting research, and delivering services
- Compliance risks: Risks related to external laws, mandates, and regulations as well as internal policies and procedures
- Reputational risks: Risks to the institution's brand and reputation

ERM seeks to mitigate the impact of risks that an institution chooses not to avoid. Risk mitigation can take many forms and starts with risk assessment followed by the prioritization of risks based on potential severity and frequency. Once this is completed, specific actions can be taken, which might include the procurement of insurance, establishment of policies to limit exposure to risks, and implementation of a risk-monitoring program as part of ERM.

Questions to ask as part of ERM include:

- How much risk is your institution willing to tolerate in each of the categories specified earlier?
- What is the institution's approach to testing its emergency preparedness?
- Recognizing that risks frequently are accompanied by opportunities, how does your institution identify opportunities that arise? When opportunities arise, what is the procedure for obtaining a decision whether to pursue the opportunity?
- How frequently does the institution conduct a comprehensive risk assessment?
- Where does responsibility reside for overseeing the institution's ERM?

Answering the questions above can help an institution manage the budgetary impacts related to risk.

THE ACADEMIC SIDE

Policies, procedures, and practices related to an institution's academic mission typically fall into the following categories.

Programmatic directions. The planning process that feeds into the budget process establishes priorities for academic and support activities. The infrastructural plans, influenced by the strategic plan, provide the framework for allocating resources to encourage or promote selected activities. For example, if research is identified as a priority activity, departments that attract external research funding may receive increased allocations for positions and funds to allow increased faculty release time. Alternatively, if the research productivity is low because of insufficient resources within a department, the addition of a grant writer may be warranted.

If higher enrollments are the objective, academic departments that increase their enrollments may receive additional faculty positions or increased support costs per FTE faculty position. If the objective is to increase the use of instructional technology, at least two actions are likely. First, the units supporting faculty in these efforts will receive additional financial resources. Second, the individual faculty members utilizing technology in their teaching will receive enhanced staff support from the instructional technology unit (and likely go to the top of the list for upgraded personal computing). In each of these examples, the budget provides the mechanism for encouraging activities consistent with established priorities.

Programmatically, globalization has raised the need to accommodate different constituents' interests. First, study-abroad programs have risen in popularity among American students. Coordinating these programs not only requires specialized administrative systems and processes but also raises risk management concerns—all of which carry attendant costs (for example, travel insurance, healthcare, security).

At the same time, substantial numbers of international students study at American colleges and universities each year. The presence of students from many diverse cultures can strain programs and systems designed to accommodate domestic student needs and interests. For example, accommodating unique dietary restrictions in the dining hall, offering enhanced options within student life, and recruiting faculty with the requisite experience all have budgetary implications.

As budgeters consider program priorities, they must also identify a means for measuring operational progress. The measures typically combine **quantitative indices** (such as student-faculty ratios, student credit hours per FTE faculty position, and square footage maintained by facilities management) and **qualitative indicators**. The latter might include the quality of a department's faculty, national reputation of a department, or service orientation of support units.

Input measures (such as the average ACT/SAT score of entering freshmen) and output measures (such as the number of students graduating) no longer provide enough information to constituents. The emphasis has shifted to outcome measures, primarily in response to the rising cost of an education. Rather than measuring the number of graduates, for instance, students and their parents want to know whether the graduates found jobs in their desired fields or gained admission to graduate school. Not all indicators lend themselves to quantification, increasing the need for professional judgment.

Each policy and procedure related to academic programming should be evaluated using the following measurements (and others, when appropriate):

▶ The extent to which the quality of the activity or program is being improved

▶ The extent to which the activity is responding to a change in workload or demand

▶ The extent to which the purpose of the activity is being altered (diminished, expanded, or redirected)

Making Changes

Four factors come into play when considering changes in a budget.

▶ Price/cost changes resulting from inflation (or deflation). Inflation or deflation factors reflect changes in the prices of goods and services, including cost-of-living adjustments to salaries and wages.

▶ Increases or decreases in workload related to operational changes. Shifts in enrollment, the demand for course offerings, the number of courses and sections taught, and the volume of sponsored activity all can lead to changes in faculty workload. Changes in support staff workload mean a different level of service provided or more (or fewer) activities undertaken. This can be driven by various factors such as shifting demand for campus housing, increased mandates from regulators, or the availability of new technology. Any of these can cause a workload shift for staff.

▶ Improvements in, or deterioration of, the quality of a program or activity. This factor accounts for qualitative variations among programs and activities. A decision to decrease average faculty instructional workload might be made with the expectation of either enhancing the quality of instruction or improving the volume of research. Another approach might be enhancing technology to improve instructional quality or faculty effectiveness.

▶ Introduction of new or elimination of existing programs or activities. Changes in academic programs may lead to the need to add faculty or reassign existing tenured faculty. Similarly, different types of activities may call for different administrative and support services.

Considering all of these factors enables decision-makers to be more discriminating when adopting budget strategies and more accurate in projecting the consequences of those strategies.

Allocation of faculty positions. Decisions about the distribution of vacant faculty positions, or which dollars to earmark for faculty hires, take on greater significance if support money automatically follows the faculty position. Before decision-makers can allocate faculty positions, they must have a systematic way to establish them.

An institution can create a new position at any time but can't hire for it unless sufficient resources are available to cover the compensation. The resources might come from tuition, endowment income, state appropriations (occasionally tied to enrollment), or other sources not otherwise committed. Nonendowment gifts typically do not support a new faculty position because the salary related to the position usually represents an ongoing commitment. Unless the situation is unique (for example, a visiting scholar), most institutions require identification of an ongoing revenue source, such as tuition or endowment income, before creating a new position. Existing faculty positions can be vacated through retirement, resignation, death, tenure denial, or a decision not to renew a non-tenure-track position's contract.

Most institutions have a hierarchy of decision-making authority for the allocation of faculty positions. In one model, the chief executive or chief academic officer controls all faculty positions. All new and vacant positions are pooled, and units must submit requests with appropriate rationale if they seek additional faculty resources.

In some cases, faculty positions are controlled at the school or college level. The department heads or research directors submit requests for faculty positions to the dean of the college or school. These requests usually relate to vacancies because new positions require approval from the highest level—either the president or the provost. Occasional exceptions involve endowed chairs, but even in these cases, the central administration must authorize acceptance of the gift that provides funding for the position.

Teaching loads. Most institutions consider some measure of instructional workload when allocating resources to departments. Four of the most common indicators are student-faculty ratio, average student credit hours per FTE faculty position, faculty contact hours (weekly time spent in the classroom or lab), and number of courses taught. Departments with larger credit-hour loads have higher student-faculty ratios and generate, on average, more student credit hours per FTE faculty position. To determine the policy implications of these ratios, one must also consider the effect of the learning space availability and class size on teaching loads (and, more important, on learning outcomes).

Class size and instructional methodology also dictate the relationship between faculty contact hours and student-faculty ratios. The advent of more effective online instructional delivery has dramatically altered the way in which contact-hour measures and student-faculty ratios are used. The indicators generally are best used as a basis for initial analysis of the teaching/learning process, not as the sole basis for allocation decisions.

Additional considerations arise when online instruction is a significant factor. Some of these affect faculty, while others affect staff. It is now recognized that relying on sophisticated technology for instructional delivery affects more than the technology itself. There are implications for pedagogy and for the ancillary activities that support the instruction. For instance, advising must be available during nontraditional office hours because students are not always engaging during those times. Similarly, online help centers must be staffed when classes and classwork are taking place, again not necessarily during traditional office hours.

Departments that depend heavily on labor-intensive laboratory or studio instruction will have lower ratios than departments that rely on large lectures. Questions to ask include:

- ▶ Is there an opportunity to alter the mix between laboratory instruction and large lecture?
- ▶ Does the discipline require individualized instruction (as in the case of studio training for musicians)?
- ▶ Do accreditation standards mandate certain instructional methodologies?
- ▶ Is it possible to respond to increased student demand by relying more heavily on instructional technology as opposed to adding additional faculty positions?

Individual faculty teaching loads vary widely, even within a single department. Within a given department, the following issues can be examined:

- Are faculty with lighter teaching loads given reduced loads as a matter of tradition or policy—or because they are more active and productive as scholars or more engaged in service activities?

- Are faculty teaching loads skewed by rank? For instance, are senior faculty required to teach only six courses per academic year, while assistant professors must teach seven? If so, does this practice prevent the junior faculty from competing effectively for sponsored research funding, thereby adversely affecting their likelihood of obtaining tenure?

- Do faculty members with equivalent credit-hour production actually have comparable workloads? For instance, does one individual teach large lecture sections of only two courses, while another teaches several different courses with fewer students per class?

- Do some faculty teach the same courses year after year, or are course assignments rotated throughout the department?

In addition to answering questions like these and making interdepartmental comparisons, conduct a trend analysis of departments' workload over time. An appropriate balance may have deteriorated, either because of increased demand without additional resources or reduced enrollments without a corresponding reduction in staffing.

It also is beneficial to consider a wide range of factors when making interdepartmental comparisons. Legitimate reasons may support major differences between seemingly similar departments. For instance, some disciplines enjoy increased opportunity for sponsored support. If some faculty in those departments attract grants, their success will affect instructional ratios for the whole department.

Weighting factors for teaching loads. Faculty positions frequently are allocated based on measures of instructional load. The measures typically consist of elements weighted by level of instruction or level of student. Weighting is skewed in favor of advanced levels of instruction and students under the theory that effort at higher levels is more time-consuming for faculty and, therefore, more expensive.

The relative difference among weights also may reflect institutional priorities regarding instruction at various levels. For instance, lower-level undergraduate courses might be weighted at 1.0, upper-level undergraduate courses at 1.5, graduate instruction at 2.0, and graduate research at 3.0. These particular weights, which may be totally arbitrary, assume that a faculty member engaged in research involving graduate students invests three times as much effort as a faculty member teaching a lower-level undergraduate course. Although instructional effort varies by discipline and even course, these variations usually are ignored and weighting is applied uniformly across the curriculum.

If the weighting used to compute teaching load reflects institutional priorities, any revision in the weighting should result from a change in priorities. If resources are allocated based on weighted student credit hours, for example, a change in weights will lead to a change in the distribution of resources. Table 12-1 demonstrates how a change in weighting in favor of graduate instruction and research can alter the distribution of resources.

Table 12-1

Illustration—Faculty Staffing as Determined by Weighting Factors						
(Assume 1.0 FTE faculty position carries a load of 600 weighted credit hours.)						
	Credit Hours by Level of Instruction	Weighting Factor		Weighted Credit Hours		Net Increase
		Current	Revised	Current	Revised	
Department A						
Lower division	3,000	1.00	1.00	3,000	3,000	
Upper division	4,000	1.50	1.50	6,000	6,000	
Graduate instruction	1,500	2.00	2.50	3,000	3,750	
Graduate research	500	3.00	3.50	1,500	1,750	
Total	9,000			13,500	14,500	
Divide by full-time load				600	600	
# of FTE faculty positions				22.5	24.2	1.7
Department B						
Lower division	2,000	1.00	1.00	2,000	2,000	
Upper division	3,000	1.50	1.50	4,500	4,500	
Graduate instruction	2,500	2.00	2.50	5,000	6,250	
Graduate research	1,000	3.00	3.50	3,000	3,500	
Total	8,500			14,500	16,250	
Divide by full-time load				600	600	
# of FTE faculty positions				24.2	27.1	2.9

Under the existing weighting, even though Department A produces more unweighted credit hours, Department B is entitled to more faculty positions because it produces relatively more hours at the graduate level. Changing the weighting in favor of graduate effort results in an even greater disparity in the number of positions assigned to Department B. This change could be the result of a change in priority or the result of analysis indicating that the revised weighting more accurately reflects the relative effort required at the various levels.

Distribution of faculty ranks. Departments with a higher proportion of junior faculty typically are less expensive to support because salaries are lower. In addition to the fiscal implications of the distribution of faculty by years of experience and rank, there are several academic considerations:

▶ Is the proportion of tenured faculty low enough to provide for the periodic addition of new blood?

▶ Are the guidelines for promotion clearly established and communicated?

▶ Do tenure and promotion criteria differ significantly from one department to the next? How are exceptions handled when the opportunity arises to recruit a faculty star?

▶ Is the distribution of faculty expertise within a discipline or department appropriate for its instructional and research missions?

▶ Are vacant positions filled at the same rank as that of the former incumbent?

Even dramatic changes in policies and procedures cannot quickly change faculty demographics—especially when a substantial percentage of the faculty are tenured.

Distribution of faculty salaries. The salary distribution issue typically arises when a department seeks to fill a vacant faculty position, especially one in the senior ranks. One common strategy—filling vacant senior professorial posts from among current junior faculty—has the benefit of upward mobility, which encourages junior faculty to remain at the institution. This also enables the institution to invest salary savings elsewhere. Finally, replacing the junior faculty with an outside hire thereby introduces new blood into the department.

The biggest drawback to this approach is the potential for a leadership void. Unless the junior faculty member being promoted can provide the leadership lost with the senior faculty member's departure, the department may suffer. A department staffed primarily with junior faculty needs senior leadership to respond to the challenges that arise. If the person promoted cannot provide it, any benefits from salary savings or improved morale among junior faculty may be offset.

Use these questions to guide consideration of salaries:

▶ Does the distribution of faculty salaries correspond to faculty ranks?

▶ Is the distribution of faculty salaries more closely aligned with seniority or with the faculty's contributions and professional accomplishments? What incentives and disincentives result?

▶ How large (or small) is the gap between salaries for new hires and those with long service? What factors have influenced this gap, and what are its effects on faculty job satisfaction or the ability to recruit qualified faculty?

▶ Do the differences in faculty salaries across disciplines reflect market conditions?

Salary compression occurs when only a negligible difference exists between the salaries of junior and senior faculty members. The problem typically surfaces when the salaries for current employees have not kept pace with the market due to resource challenges. When new employees are hired at competitive rates, the gap between the two groups shrinks and the premium for experience erodes. In extreme cases, salary compression can become salary inversion, which occurs when the starting salary for new hires exceeds the salaries of current employees.

Faculty at all ranks want to know how the salary adjustment pool is determined. In the aggregate, salary adjustments are tied to the expected increase in institutional resources (a combination of tuition, endowment income, appropriations, and gifts). The salary increase usually consists of two components: a merit pool (for high performers) and a cost-of-living adjustment (available to everyone performing satisfactorily). Many institutions add a third component to be used for special recruitments, retaining a faculty member recruited by another institution, or providing salary increases to promoted faculty.

There is no accepted standard for the size of the salary adjustment pool or the split between merit and cost-of-living adjustments. In some public institutions, the state determines the cost-of-living adjustment applied to all state employees, including faculty. Within the constraints of collective bargaining arrangements, institutions striving for improved effectiveness tend to invest more dollars in the merit pool so they can reward individual performance. Many institutions find it easier to distribute increases pro rata, thereby avoiding decisions on how to distribute merit-based increases.

When resources become available, an institution that has been unable to provide competitive salaries will attempt to remedy this situation quickly. Similarly, if an institution wants to increase its salary ranking among peer institutions, it likely will invest more in salaries than in other operating expense categories. In most cases, the merit adjustment pool is calculated as a percentage of total salaries and distributed to each academic and support unit for assignment to individual faculty and staff.

If the chief executive officer, chief academic officer, or deans reserve a portion of the total salary adjustment pool so they can address recruitments and promotions or match offers, this necessarily reduces the merit pool. The merit pool also will shrink if it is used to supplement departmental allocations to remedy disparities in terms of market conditions or institutional priorities.

Use of part-time and temporary faculty. As budgets have become tighter, departments and institutions have resorted to stretching their dollars by hiring increased numbers of part-time and temporary faculty. This has been a continuing pattern since the 1970s and has occurred in nearly every year since 1970. Comparable data are available going back to 1987 when full-time faculty represented two-thirds of faculty employed across all sectors of higher education. By fall 2015, the latest year for which data are available, full-time faculty had decreased by 20 percent to only 52 percent.[214] Generally, part-time faculty members receive considerably less compensation and fewer benefits than full-time faculty members. They frequently are ineligible for certain benefits, thus increasing the institution's savings. In addition, they tend to have significantly less job security due to their employment usually being governed by short-term contracts (e.g., one semester or one year). Another benefit to management exists because departments have the flexibility to hire part-time faculty only when student demand or other factors dictate that more faculty are needed. For instance, this happens frequently to cover for a full-time faculty member away on sabbatical.

Excessive reliance on part-time or temporary faculty has several disadvantages. First, although many adjuncts are excellent instructors, some are not as skilled as permanent faculty. However, because of the relatively low compensation they receive, they have little incentive to enhance their skills. In addition, adjuncts typically have relatively heavier course loads on average than permanent faculty, leaving little time for their own scholarly pursuits. Part-time faculty also tend to be less available to students and colleagues because of their other employment activities. The institution's lack of commitment often prompts part-time faculty to find the highest bidder for their services as they jump from one temporary position to another. Finally, accreditation agencies may question the quality of instructional efforts when an institution relies excessively on part-time and temporary faculty.

There are institutions that have resisted the trend toward reliance on temporary and part-time faculty. Such institutions frequently establish policies dictating that part-time faculty may be hired only with funds budgeted for that purpose or with savings from vacant permanent faculty positions. Other institutions prohibit using permanent faculty position vacancy savings to hire part-time faculty. Collective bargaining agreements sometimes drive these policies. In other cases, they evolve from an institutional desire to rely on full-time faculty to the maximum extent possible.

Some states closely monitor the status of permanent employee positions at public colleges and universities. If a department attempts to stretch their compensation budget by holding full-time faculty positions vacant in order to hire part-time or temporary faculty, the state might simply eliminate the permanent position in a subsequent budget cycle.

Public institutions may also draw criticism if they appear to put dollars ahead of academic quality by hiring an excessive number of adjuncts. Reacting to undergraduate complaints about overuse of part-time or temporary faculty, some states limit the number of faculty who can be employed in a given period. Other states set a cap on the overall faculty head count. Hiring too many part-time faculty may cause an institution to exceed the cap.

Many policy questions relate to part-time and temporary faculty. They include:

▶ Should departments have the latitude to hold faculty positions vacant solely to divert resources toward temporary hires?

- What is the proper balance between instruction provided by permanent full-time faculty versus temporary or part-time faculty, especially at the undergraduate level?

- How are savings from the reliance on part-time or temporary faculty used? Are they captured centrally, or are they available to support the department's instruction, research, or service activities?

Sabbatical leaves. Many institutions have a policy that provides one year of leave at half salary or one semester at full salary to faculty for every six to 10 years of full-time service. Some institutions award one-semester sabbaticals every seventh semester.

For one-year faculty leaves, departments use the salary savings to employ part-time instructors to cover the permanent instructor's courses or pay overload to other permanent faculty. Any surplus is used to cover other departmental needs or is captured centrally. Arrangements that allow for full pay during one-semester sabbaticals prove costly for departments because no savings are available to pay part-time faculty.

Common questions related to sabbaticals include the following:

- Are sabbaticals guaranteed for all faculty meeting the minimum service requirements?

- What expectations regarding scholarly accomplishment have been established for faculty members who are granted sabbaticals?

- Are faculty expected or required to seek outside funding to cover part of the sabbatical leave?

- If one-semester sabbaticals at full pay are permitted, are the faculty member's courses canceled, or are other arrangements made (such as temporary instructors employed to teach the courses or overload payments to other permanent faculty)?

Graduate assistantships. Graduate assistantships offer significant flexibility in staffing departmental responsibilities. Departments might use graduate assistants as graders, tutors, lab section coordinators, instructors of independent sections, or research assistants. Various models govern how assistantships are allocated throughout the institution and within departments. They may be based on seniority, on the percentage of teaching load represented by large lecture classes, or on scholarly or research productivity. Another approach is simply to allocate the positions evenly throughout the institution based solely on enrollment.

Budgetary questions related to graduate assistantships include the following:

- ▶ Is the assistantship an entitlement such that all graduate students enrolled in certain programs receive one?
- ▶ How are graduate assistants compensated—tuition remission, stipends, salaries, etc.?
- ▶ Do graduate stipends and salaries vary? If so, on what basis?
- ▶ Are assistantships limited in duration or available as long as the graduate student remains in good academic standing?

Academic support staff. The distribution of academic support staff—such as clerical workers, laboratory technicians, and grants specialists—may vary significantly from one department to the next. The differences may result from specific instructional methodologies, the nature and extent of research activities, instructional loads, service commitments, or historical patterns.

Beginning in the 1990s, increased use of technology—especially personal computers that brought word processing and email capability—dramatically reduced the need for clerical support, leading to the elimination of many support positions. Once the hardware and software costs have been covered, what happens to the savings represented by the elimination of the positions? Keep in mind that the technology acquisition costs represent a periodic expense that won't reoccur annually. The position savings, after covering the technology costs, become permanent.

Typical questions related to academic support staffing include the following:

- ▶ Do all departments have a need for support staff?
- ▶ What is the basis for allocating support staff across departments?

▶ Is it possible to share staff across departmental lines due to the sporadic nature of some workloads?

THE SUPPORT SIDE

The academic portion of the institutional budget cannot be understood without analyzing its relationship to the administrative and support budgets. If the academic mission (instruction, research, and service) is paramount, administrative and support budgets should be designed to facilitate activities in the academic arena. Over time, however, these activities can become ends unto themselves. For this reason, some campuses require periodic reviews of support units to ensure they continue to support the academic mission effectively. (Although reviewing support units is more common— especially during challenging financial times—it is strongly recommended that a holistic review of all institutional activities take place periodically. Ideally, this should occur as a precursor to strategic planning (see Chapter 13 for additional discussion on this point).

Policies, procedures, and practices related to an institution's support activities typically fall into the following categories.

Administrative support. This category includes activities such as human resources, finance, and advancement as well as other areas that support academic activities either directly or indirectly.

Here are relevant questions to ask about each activity:

▶ Are the activities self-supporting? If not, what effort is devoted to ensuring that subsidies are at appropriate levels?

▶ Is the service essential to the campus?

▶ Does the service that is provided by the support unit duplicate services available from other units?

▶ To what extent are new technologies (such as automated systems) or approaches (such as outsourcing and shared services) being utilized to reduce the overall cost of the service and/or improve its effectiveness?

▶ Have performance standards for the service been established? If so, are they monitored on a regular basis?

AUXILIARY ENTERPRISES

A different set of questions is appropriate for these operations:

▶ Have the activities been assessed to determine whether they should be self-operated, outsourced, or discontinued because they no longer contribute to institutional success?

▶ Are they expected to pay a fair share of the institution's operating expenses, such as utilities and central support services (payroll, accounting, purchasing)?

▶ Are the units able to generate and maintain reserves adequate to meet operating needs, including facilities maintenance, as well as future program expansion?

Facilities management operations. Higher education finds itself in the unique position of being both labor-intensive and capital-intensive. Unlike many other labor-intensive industries, higher education invests substantially in facilities and other physical resources. Even institutions that favor online delivery of their academic mission invest heavily in technology infrastructure.

Questions relevant to facilities management operations include the following:

▶ Does the campus conduct ongoing space-utilization analysis?

▶ Has the campus achieved all possible savings related to energy usage and efficiency?

▶ Has the campus examined whether enhanced effectiveness can be achieved by self-operation, outsourcing, or a blended approach to service delivery?

▶ Do all campus facilities have a preventive maintenance plan?

▶ Is deferred maintenance measured regularly and assessed with respect to its appropriateness given the current operating environment and resource availability?

- ▶ Does the unit have a process for determining when a facility has outlived its usefulness, given current demands, resource availability, and operational costs?
- ▶ Has the unit devoted appropriate attention to issues related to environmental sustainability?

Information technology. This category has registered explosive spending, whether for instructional technology, ERPs, wireless infrastructure, networks, or new/updated administrative applications. Staying current with technology is challenging at best. Most institutions make incremental progress.

The relevant questions for information technology include the following:

- ▶ Does the institution ensure that its use of purchased software is as effective as possible? Does it take advantage of all functionality provided by purchased software when it would benefit the institution?
- ▶ Does the institution install updates and new releases for purchased software as they become available?
- ▶ Are staff trained to fully utilize and appropriately maintain systems that are employed?
- ▶ Has the institution established a strategy to guide decisions on whether to use homegrown, purchased, or outsourced applications?
- ▶ Has the institution considered pursuit of cloud-based and open-source solutions to address technology needs?
- ▶ Has the campus examined whether enhanced service effectiveness can be achieved by self-operation, outsourcing, or a blended approach?
- ▶ Does one unit oversee all technology, or are separate units established for the various broad categories of technology such as academic, administrative, and medical?
- ▶ Has the institution established life-cycle standards for the various categories of technology to ensure that resources are not being

wasted by supporting outdated or obsolete technology or abandoning hardware or software too quickly?

Student affairs. This support area is unique because of its direct involvement with an institution's primary constituents—the students. When reviewing student affairs, answers to the following questions may prove enlightening:

▶ Do on-campus housing policies support enrollment plans and contribute to auxiliary units' success? For instance, are freshmen required to live on campus and, if so, also required to purchase a campus meal plan?

▶ Are the offerings for student entertainment and other activities attractive enough to encourage students to stay on campus, thus avoiding potential problems with the surrounding community?

▶ Does the campus use residential colleges, led by faculty principals, or language houses to supplement formal instruction with extracurricular activities?

▶ Are services available to support and supplement what students experience in classrooms and labs to further their education and personal development?

▶ Are appropriate support systems in place to assist international students, first-generation students, students with disabilities, etc.?

Operating expenses. Both academic departments and support units can be evaluated in terms of how effectively they use their resources to cover day-to-day operating expenses, such as travel, supplies, and services as well as to acquire small equipment. The following questions might help assess performance in this area:

▶ Are units held accountable if they overspend their operating budgets?

▶ Does the institution enable units to carry forward unspent funds from one fiscal year to the next (to avoid creating an incentive for units to waste money late in the fiscal year rather than appear not to need it)?

- Are units experiencing imposed annual budget cuts due to inflationary increases not being addressed for continuing costs?
- Are unit operations periodically examined to determine whether a portion of their existing budgets can be reallocated to a central pool to provide funds for higher-priority initiatives?
- Are travel funds allocated using a clearly defined methodology?

Multiyear budgeting. The number of budget cycles influences the perspective taken during the budget process. Attention to one budget cycle focused on a single fiscal year leads to short-term thinking, primarily related to incremental changes from the current year's budget. Expanding the process to focus on multiple years encourages a more proactive approach—and has the added benefit of being encouraged by some accrediting agencies.

Understandably, the out-years will have fewer details, but they can still highlight shifts in priorities and broad institutional changes. For instance, an academic program being phased out over time will eventually free up resources for allocation to other units or for other purposes. The preliminary budgets for the transition years can reflect this decision.

Budget format. In most public institutions, the state dictates the format for the submission to the state. Although it may be more efficient to use the same format for internal budget purposes, the state's prescribed format may not match well with the institution's needs. For this reason, most public institutions use higher-education-specific formats for internal budgeting and then aggregate the detailed information to comply with the state's prescribed format.

Both public and independent institutions should periodically assess the budget structure and the types of information it contains. As with financial statements, budgets tell different stories. A budget that has functional or programmatic expense categories, such as instruction, research, and institutional support, will not have the same structure as one that displays expenses in natural categories such as salaries, benefits, and travel. Although these are the two primary budget formats used for the entire institution's budget, it is common for another format to be used when the focus is less than the entire institution. The budget may then focus on a division such as academic affairs and show separate aggregations for its organizational units, which could include the various colleges and schools, library, academic centers, institutes, etc.

The combination of the two primary formats generally is recognized as the most beneficial for decision-making. The easiest way to combine the formats is with a simple matrix. The columns present the natural expense categories, while the rows present the information sorted by functional category (see Table 1-1 in Chapter 1). Another common budget format is one that presents the revenues and expenses by organizational unit. This format can be presented using the same matrix approach to disclose both natural expense and functional categories. This approach is useful for highlighting accountability for the various budget components.

Other questions about budget format focus on issues related to all-funds budgeting versus unrestricted funds only. Undoubtedly, it is easier to focus only on the unrestricted funds when developing budgets, but this approach is distorting and tends to result in suboptimal spending and management decisions. Moreover, when restricted resources are essential to achieving the institution's aspirations, it's very misleading not to proactively manage these resources.

All-funds budgeting focuses on all resources available to support the institution's operations. It allows an institution to concentrate on the full magnitude of its operations, not just those financed through tuition and state operating appropriations. By relying on a single consolidated budget and a comprehensive process to manage and control operating resources, an institution will have the best opportunity to ensure its priorities are established effectively and funded adequately.

This approach also has the benefit of focusing on the full range of resources, allowing an institution to monitor its use of restricted resources more effectively. This can be especially important at public institutions and independent institutions with decentralized departments that manage significant levels of gift or endowment income accounts. When the resources are not budgeted and monitored centrally, departments might hoard those funds rather than deploy them in support of established priorities. To prevent this from occurring, some institutions have established policies that encourage (or even require) the use of restricted resources when both restricted and unrestricted resources are available.

Table 12-2

All-Funds Budget Illustration (amounts in millions)	Unrestricted Resources			Restricted Resources			
	General Funds						
Revenue Sources	State Op. Approp.	Local (Nonstate)	Designated Funds	Sponsored Agreements	Endowment Income	Gifts	Total
Operating Expenses							
Instruction	$89.439	$327.512	$12.051	$20.000	$54.153	$14.332	$517.487
Research		67.159	7.012	271.206	32.265	15.500	395.182
Public service	12.154	7.510	21.541	37.040	1.921	2.139	82.305
Academic support	74.145	117.812	32.158	20.593	11.459	11.581	247.155
Student services	28.596	17.412				4.392	50.400
Institutional support	37.185	5.312	1.237	16.458			60.192
Operation and maintenance of plant	78.512	22.656	1.854	9.347		2.157	114.526
Student financial aid	11.371			24.175	89.587	29.129	142.891
Auxiliary services (including athletics)		147.617	16.427		4.118	19.432	187.594
Other		32.916	12.485		11.576	6.431	63.408
Total	$331.402	$745.906	$104.765	$398.819	$205.079	$105.093	$1.861.140

REVENUE POLICIES

How revenues are projected, how institutional priorities are set, and what institutional policies and procedures are in place all influence the budget and the budget process. In both public and independent institutions, here are the primary determinants of revenue.

Research. For some institutions, research yields a significant percentage of total revenues, especially when overhead recoveries are included in the measurement. Most research support, however, must be used for the purposes specified in the award and is not available for general operating purposes.

For the most part, overhead recoveries are an unrestricted resource, but they usually are committed for specific purposes related to research. Some constraints relate to the portion of recoveries attributable to facilities (versus administrative support), although these funds are not classified as restricted. The federal government requires that major research institutions be able to demonstrate they are investing at least as much in facilities as the amount of the recoveries attributable to facilities.

Tuition and financial aid. These are key considerations for all colleges and universities. See Chapter 5 for a complete discussion of these subjects.

Endowment income. Though significant for some institutions, this represents a modest portion of total revenue for the vast majority of colleges and universities. Even in the wealthiest institutions, endowments rarely contribute as much as 25 percent of total operating revenues.

The typical budgeter does not have direct involvement with endowment management. This usually is handled by the chief investment officer (or treasurer), a board committee, an external manager engaged by the institution or—in the case of many public institutions—staff at an independent fundraising foundation affiliated with the institution.

Nevertheless, many policies related to endowments and endowment income concern budgeters.

- ▶ What are the investment objectives for the endowment? Are they focused primarily on current yield or long-term growth? (Too much emphasis on either one can be problematic. Current yield is needed to provide resources for operating expenses, but growth is essential to maintaining the endowment's purchasing power over time.)
- ▶ Is there a clearly defined asset allocation strategy?
- ▶ What is the rate of return on the portfolio? How does this rate compare with the returns for endowments of similar size?
- ▶ What is the spending rate, and how is it calculated?

- Are procedures in place to ensure adequate support for programs and activities, even if the endowment returns are negative in a given period?
- Are endowment gifts taxed to provide resources to underwrite the costs of managing and investing the endowment?

Other policy issues relate more specifically to the income generated by the endowment.

- How is income from endowments without purpose restrictions used? Does it primarily support continuing operations, or is some or all of it used as seed money for new initiatives?
- How much of the endowment income is set aside to respond to contingencies?
- Has the institution established a program that results in the matching of gifts (or earnings) from new endowments to serve as an inducement for units to pursue such gifts? (Note that some states have established programs of this type.)
- How much restricted endowment income is made available for spending each year, and how are these resources taken into consideration when unrestricted revenues are allocated throughout the institution?
- When does a new endowment gift begin participating in the distribution of spendable income—at the next distribution or only after one full year?
- Is an underwater endowment eligible to participate in the income distribution?

Gifts. The majority of colleges and universities receive significantly more revenue from annual giving than from endowment income. By comparison, gifts are less predictable than endowment income because the amount of endowment income available for spending in a given year is based primarily on historical data—i.e., already known facts. Nevertheless, an effective development operation can predict gift revenues with a reasonable degree of accuracy using analysis of past giving patterns and known plans for future periods. Key questions include:

▶ Does the institution have a process for measuring the cost of fundraising? If yes, does the institution measure the success of fundraising against the investment made to generate gifts?

▶ Does the institution pursue multiple gift strategies, including annual giving, giving societies, major gifts, planned gifts, and other methods?

▶ Do policies exist to guide the acceptance or rejection of gifts with excessive restrictions, from donors with whom the institution prefers not to affiliate, or that would impose a costly burden on the institution?

▶ How much fundraising effort is expected of individuals not working directly in development? For instance, are deans, department heads, and individual faculty members expected and/or encouraged to participate in development activities?

▶ Are gifts taxed to provide resources to help finance the development operation?

▶ Does the institution maintain an alumni affairs office? If so, how closely is this office integrated with development operations?

▶ For religiously affiliated institutions, is the church a significant source of revenue?

▶ For public institutions, what is the relationship to the affiliated fundraising foundation?

▶ Does the foundation determine how it will support the institution, or is this responsibility shared with institutional management?

Sponsored program funding. Sponsored support is another category that can be difficult to predict with a high degree of accuracy. Nevertheless, institutions for which sponsored programs represent a significant revenue source typically develop sophisticated models for predicting the volume of revenue to be received. In most cases, awards are received before the funding itself. This is especially true with multiyear awards, which may be for as long as five years.

With a sponsored activity, the funds are committed to a particular project and may not be used for other purposes. Accurate predictions are still important, however, because amounts funded from sponsored sources may provide budgetary relief for other committed resources. In addition, indirect cost recoveries usually accompany such funding. In most instances, this revenue represents unrestricted funds that the institution can use for any operating purpose.

In theory, the overhead recovery funds are intended to reimburse the institution for overhead expenses incurred in support of sponsored activity. In practice, however, recoveries sometimes are used for a variety of purposes. These might include seed funding for young investigators, lab equipment, stipends for graduate assistants, supplemental funding for research libraries, and other objectives that aren't necessarily connected directly to sponsored activities.

The questions to be asked regarding sponsored support focus on two general areas. The first includes policies governing activity outside the institution—particularly those involving the federal government, the largest sponsor and the most influential participant from a regulatory standpoint. The second area includes policies related to the conduct of research and the use of overhead recoveries.

- ▶ What are the current federal research priorities?
- ▶ Are the institution's academic activities aligned with those priorities? If not, is it possible to shift priorities to compete more effectively for this funding?
- ▶ How significant is the institution's technology transfer activity, and does it lend itself to partnerships with business, industry, or governmental entities?
- ▶ Does the institution have a mechanism to support investigators' pursuit of nongovernmental sources of sponsored funding (such as foundations and corporations)?

- What are the institution's practices with respect to overhead recoveries? Are they captured centrally and treated as another revenue source? Or are they allocated throughout the institution to support additional research initiatives or related activities? (For instance, some institutions routinely allocate a percentage of overhead recoveries to the principal investigator or his or her department as an incentive to stimulate additional research.) Or are they controlled by the units conducting the research that generated the overhead?

- What are the practices with respect to the waiver of overhead? (Many researchers believe that they will be more competitive for awards if overhead is lower or nonexistent.) Along the same lines, what are the policies for accepting sponsored agreements from organizations that limit the payment of overhead? For example, some federal agencies, corporate sponsors, and nonaffiliated foundations cap the percentage of overhead they will pay. Does this influence the institution's willingness to conduct research for these entities?

- Does the institution allow overhead waivers to reduce the cost to sponsors when unique circumstances justify them? Is it clear to researchers how such waivers can be obtained?

OTHER OPERATIONAL POLICIES AND PRACTICES

Independent institutions have more control over internal policies and procedures than public institutions, which usually must adhere to the same guidelines established for state agencies even though their missions are significantly different. Even with the flexibility enjoyed by independent institutions, the combination of professional standards and federal guidelines tend to mitigate any competitive advantage they might otherwise enjoy in these main areas.

Accounting. The vast majority of higher education institutions continue to rely on fund accounting to manage their resources, although some have adopted a more traditional commercial accounting system with special accommodations to handle the unique requirements for restricted resources. The complex structure of accounts used by many institutions is designed to ensure that funds can be managed effectively and used only for appropriate purposes. For example, colleges and universities—especially many public ones—are precluded from using funds budgeted for salaries and wages for purposes other than compensation. Other categories of operating expenses may enjoy greater spending flexibility, especially in situations that do not rely on line-item budgeting.

Accounts or funds frequently are established to ensure certain revenue sources are spent for their specified purposes. For instance, sponsored agreements have special rules related to the use of the resources. Similarly, proceeds from bond issues typically must be spent for specific capital projects. Some institutions assess special fees for activities such as laboratory work, student activities, or technology. In such cases, the institution may require that these revenues be accounted for in specific funds so they can be matched against investments in these activities.

Internal, independent, and—in some cases—federal auditors assess the degree to which faculty and staff actually comply with accounting policies and procedures. Auditors examine not only the accuracy of management reports and financial statements but also the appropriateness of expense transfers, the documentation supporting expenses, and the overall internal control structure.

Anyone with budgetary responsibility must understand several aspects of the accounting structure. Selected topics include:

▶ The nature of the expenses that represent appropriate charges to a specific account

▶ The extent to which funds or expense charges may be transferred between accounts

▶ Constraints on the use of resources imposed by the fund structure within the institution

Financial and budgetary reporting. All institutions have financial and budgetary reporting systems to monitor the flow of funds and support compliance efforts. Commercially available software provides large-scale integrated applications with modules focused on accounting, budgeting, procurement, payroll, fixed assets, and many other financial areas. This integration can reduce the amount of manual effort required to ensure compliance with regulatory requirements and ease the preparation of financial reports.

The most modern (and expensive) systems—ERPs—use a standard architecture to address a multitude of functional applications. These powerful systems also can be customized to include embedded controls and edits, which can prevent inadvertent noncompliant actions.

ERPs rely on integrated databases with multiple applications accessing the same data, thereby allowing the data to be entered in the system only once. Numerous institutions have implemented data warehouses to provide some of the benefits of an ERP or to extend the ERP's utility and value. The data warehouse draws data from multiple operational systems and makes it available for reporting and analysis. The reliance on ERPs and data warehouses has increased management reporting capability and created an opportunity for improved decision-making and compliance.

Human resources. Because salaries and wages account for so much of an institution's budget, it is reasonable to expect that a large part of a budget's flexibility will be influenced by the institution's human resources policies and procedures. Tenure obligations represent long-term financial commitments. The manner in which faculty salary structures are established—and the ease with which adjustments can be made—strongly influence the institution's competitiveness in recruiting faculty. Similarly, support staff salary structures, whether based on market conditions, union pay scales, or statewide public employee scales, affect the ability to hire and retain qualified staff.

Contractual and tenure policies specify the lengths of probationary periods, the amount of advance notice required for termination of an appointment, schedules for performance reviews, and grievance procedures. In some states, these schedules are prescribed by regulation, and budgeting clearly depends on them.

Moreover, the policies governing the appointment of temporary and part-time personnel will determine some constraints on budget flexibility. Faculty research appointments frequently may parallel tenure-track appointments but not require a tenure commitment. This flexibility is beneficial in the area of sponsored programs when time frames may dictate quick-response hiring.

Collective bargaining. The existence of a collective bargaining agreement will restrict the actions that the administration may take during the budget process. Collective bargaining agreements usually specify salary increases, pay rates for various activities, and required employee benefits.

These agreements may be modified only with the consent of the designated representatives for those covered. Previously negotiated compensation increases are rarely rolled back or deferred to a future period. When this has happened, it almost always has been done to avoid the need for layoffs.

The existence of these agreements makes it somewhat easier for the administration to project compensation costs into the future. Most agreements cover multiple years and tie future salary increases to objective criteria such as inflation, enrollment, or state appropriations. Collective bargaining agreements covering faculty employment also establish faculty workload standards. This aspect of the agreements impairs the administration's flexibility.

Agreements typically prevent the administration from increasing workloads even when revenue shortfalls occur. Though part-time faculty are not necessarily covered under the contracts, their employment circumstances frequently are affected. For instance, an agreement may specify the circumstances under which part-time faculty can be hired as replacements for permanent faculty. Agreements also typically cover the conditions under which early retirement programs can be implemented for faculty.

A standard feature of most collective bargaining agreements is coverage of the issue of retrenchment—major financial cutbacks (see Chapter 13 for an in-depth discussion of retrenchment). Most agreements specify the procedures to follow, the expense categories to address before making personnel cutbacks, and the levels of severance required for faculty whose positions are eliminated. All of these elements reduce the institution's flexibility in responding to a financial crisis.

Because of varying campus practices and differences in state laws, collective bargaining agreements can include a range of clauses addressing issues related to employment and factors only indirectly related to compensation. For instance, the agreements typically specify promotion and tenure criteria. Some go further to include prohibitions against tenure quotas. Others address the way in which salary adjustments will be balanced between merit and cost of living. Still others address incentives for faculty to pursue sponsored support.

Collective bargaining agreements may apply to multiple staff categories as well as faculty. For instance, one agreement might be in force for clerical personnel, another for public safety personnel, another for custodial workers, and still another for skilled trades workers in facilities management. In each case, the agreements reduce the administration's flexibility in managing the institution.

The bottom line on collective bargaining agreements is that they are a mixed blessing for both the institution and the employees they cover. The institution gains some degree of certainty about future expenses but gives up flexibility in terms of its operational environment. As for employees, they are able to negotiate from a position of strength because they are united in their approach to the administration. The downside for some employees is that they might receive better compensation and perks if they negotiated as individuals.

Procurement. Procurement regulations are intended to facilitate the efficient and economical acquisition of goods and services while preventing abuses or wasteful spending. As with most bureaucratic procedures, their complexity makes it hard for faculty and staff to appreciate how chaotic procurement activity would be without such a framework. Nevertheless, procurement regulations do limit flexibility.

Many institutions require all procurement activity to be processed through a single control point. Depending on staffing and the volume of transactions, this requirement can result in significant delays in the receipt of goods or services. As fiscal year-end approaches and departments attempt to spend the balances in their operating budgets, activity volumes rise and delays become longer. If staff and faculty recognize these patterns and plan accordingly, they can avoid the possibility of service interruptions or the loss of early payment discounts. To improve overall results and reduce costs at the same time, many institutions have moved to more automated and decentralized procurement systems.

State regulations often govern procurement procedures in public institutions. These regulations specify ceilings above which a bid or request for proposal process is required. Depending on the nature of the procurement, the institution might have to advertise bid requests for specified periods before selecting a vendor. And in many situations, the institution must accept the lowest bid from a qualified vendor.

Occasionally, regulations allow for single-source procurements. In these cases, when there is only one vendor qualified to provide the goods or services, the institution is allowed to contract directly with the vendor without using bid procedures. Some states require preliminary state review for the procurement of certain goods or services, including costly computer systems, certain personal service contracts, and real estate.

Although the regulatory environment affecting procurement generally impairs budget flexibility, there can be advantages. Public institutions, in particular, frequently benefit from the ability to use state procurement contracts to reduce the cost of goods or services.

In addition, most institutions belong to one or more buying cooperatives, such as E&I Cooperative Services—a group purchasing organization (GPO) serving higher education and K–12 schools. GPOs enable their members to benefit from volume discounts resulting from the combined purchasing power of higher education. They also gain access to standard contracts for many commodities. Both are significant benefits and help reduce the overall costs of procurement activities.

The use of credit cards in procurement, typically referred to as purchasing cards or p-cards, contributes to flexibility as well. The use of p-cards has streamlined procurement dramatically and significantly reduced the number of purchase orders processed throughout colleges and universities. With p-cards, designated individuals are authorized to use a credit card issued in the institution's name to purchase allowable commodities. The banks issuing the credit cards work with the institution to identify allowable commodities and the types of vendors that deal in those commodities. Employees are not authorized to use the cards with other vendors - and, in some cases, arrangements are made with vendors to ensure they do not accept the cards for institutional purchases.

Typical examples of allowable commodities include office supplies, scientific supplies, facilities supplies and repair parts, airlines, and hotels—but the range of allowable commodities is very extensive. Each card has an established limit to minimize the exposure to risk of inappropriate purchases. Department personnel are expected to reconcile the monthly statements with purchase receipts obtained from holders of p-cards. The accounting records are then updated to distribute the monthly charges to the appropriate accounts and expense categories.

Another innovation in the area of procurement is the establishment of relationships with selected vendors that allow institutional personnel to enter orders directly into the vendor's system. This facet of e-procurement allows the institution to streamline the procurement and payment processes and expedite the receipt of goods. Arrangements vary, but it's typical that they provide significantly reduced acquisition costs for many commodities because the vendor's transaction processing costs are much lower in these situations.

KEY POINTS

▶ Academic policies related to program direction, faculty allocations, faculty compensation, and use of part-time or temporary faculty heavily influence the approach to budgeting as well as the outcomes it produces.

▶ Administrative policies that affect the budget cover the gamut of support areas, including student services, facilities, information technology, and auxiliary enterprises.

▶ Independent institutions typically have more control over their policies and procedures than public institutions because the latter usually must adhere to the same guidelines established for state agencies.

CHAPTER 13: RESPONDING TO EXTRAORDINARY CIRCUMSTANCES

The more things change, the more they appear to remain the same. Along with the shifting perspectives about the value of higher education addressed in earlier chapters, the industry continues to be plagued by financial challenges that, in some cases, result in major institutional disruption. The third edition of this book was published as institutions were experiencing cutbacks triggered by the dot-com bubble burst at the turn of the millennium. The fourth edition followed another extraordinary circumstance—the Great Recession that began with the collapse of the U.S. subprime mortgage market in 2008 and continues to have long-lasting effects even as this edition is being written.

More recently, there is turmoil growing out of the 2016 presidential election. Higher education has not been a primary target for the Trump Administration and its new policies, but that does not mean that institutions have escaped impacts from its actions. A few of the more significant changes affecting institutions include:

- Visa challenges facing foreign students and faculty due to the travel ban affecting selected countries
- A variety of implications from the 2017 Tax Cuts and Jobs Act, including the potential for selected independent institutions to pay taxes on some endowment earnings, anticipated reduced philanthropy due to the doubling of the standard deduction, and changes to the unrelated business income rules
- Cost increases resulting from tariffs imposed on foreign-sourced goods

Colleges and universities are being forced to adapt to new financial challenges and the operational impacts from these and other dramatic policy changes. For some institutions, this represents another chapter in the ever-evolving environment in which higher education must operate. For others, however, changes of this magnitude have serious implications for the ongoing viability or even survival of institutions. Recent evidence suggests that the long-predicted closure and merger of institutions—especially smaller, poorly endowed independent institutions—finally has arrived.[215] Accurate data are hard to find, but there is evidence that the economic climate has led to more mergers and institutional closures than at any time since the Great Depression.

Long before the current distress, an institution would occasionally encounter unique problems that called for retrenchment. Such institutions typically would be guilty of a lack of emphasis on planning. As a result, a combination of factors would create a sustained period of financial distress with no clear solutions available. Or the institution might simply have failed to heed obvious warning signs. Sometimes, an unpredictable event prompted the retrenchment—such as a physical disaster that greatly exceeded the institution's insurance protection or the sudden closing of a local manufacturing facility, which led to a dramatic enrollment reduction.

In recent years, however, even higher education institutions employing best practices in the area of planning have had to retrench and adapt to what now is described as a new normal. Normal now means operating with reduced resources, coupled with increased demands for services—all under never-ending scrutiny by regulators and funders.

The broad gamut of financial distress ranges from serious—institutions that find it difficult to honor their debt service obligations—to those "on the brink" and facing imminent closure absent dramatic infusions of resources. There was a time when this group was limited to those with an ongoing structural deficit. That has changed, and it's fair to say that any institution with serious enrollment challenges that also is experiencing philanthropic shortfalls may be forced to consider merging or shuttering completely.

A structural deficit arises when annual operating expenses exceed annual operating revenues. An institution with substantial endowment resources can operate reasonably well in this condition by using nonoperating financial gains to offset operational deficits. The vast majority of institutions, however, will not survive for long if they continue to erode reserves by suffering ongoing operating deficits. Even modest enrollment shortfalls may be enough to drive such institutions out of the market.

WHAT EXACTLY IS RETRENCHMENT?

Retrenchment results from a financial crisis that, when serious enough, can threaten the institution's survival. It usually includes systematically (or, in some cases, haphazardly) eliminating major portions of an institution's programs and activities.

Because each financial crisis is unique, the elements of a retrenchment will vary from one institution to the next. Still, one action almost always accompanies retrenchment: personnel reductions. With such a large portion of institutional budgets committed to compensation, it is inconceivable that an institution can respond to a financial crisis without eliminating positions.

Though necessary for survival, personnel cutbacks have lasting negative effects on institutional culture. Any action that results in the elimination of someone's job has a devastating impact on a community—even when the position supported an activity that no longer added value for the college or university. When the cause is a financial crisis—especially one that should have been anticipated and avoided—the impact lasts for years.

Planning for circumstances that could result in retrenchment creates the opportunity to effect change that otherwise might be difficult to implement. As an example, the discussion of IBB in Chapter 9 includes a description of reallocation strategies. Some view reallocation as an exercise forced on an institution by external factors or organizations. In fact, it can better position an institution to respond to financial crises, possibly avoiding retrenchment in the process.

Reallocation allows an institution to systematically reduce the resources it devotes to some activities, thus freeing up resources that can be better deployed elsewhere. It is one mechanism for providing funds for initiatives that support new priorities. It has the added benefit of providing a cushion if an unexpected financial crisis arises. The institution may be able to avoid the more drastic responses that otherwise might be needed. In fact, if the reallocation enables the institution to weather the storm with only a minimal or zero loss of faculty and staff, short-term morale problems and a long-term negative cultural impact may be avoided.

PLANNING FOR RETRENCHMENT

Planning for retrenchment may be a misnomer. The more correct phrasing is planning to *avoid* retrenchment. In reality, prior to the Great Recession, few institutions had invested the effort in preparing for the possibility of significantly reduced resources. Admittedly, few could have anticipated the recession's magnitude. But even less pervasive cases of financial strife have caught institutions unprepared.

Just as institutions have developed disaster recovery and other emergency preparedness plans, they should develop plans to accommodate financial crises of varying proportions. In the wake of the 2008 recession, for example, several states imposed double-digit budget cuts on public colleges and universities. Some institutions could increase tuition rates to partially offset the reduction in public support, but others did not have this option because of state policies. The institutions best able to respond to the reduced resources were those with formalized contingency plans to deal with such a severe financial challenge.

It simply is not possible to plan effectively for every contingency—especially for something of cataclysmic proportions. Nevertheless, failing to prepare the institution in any way for financial difficulties increases the likelihood of having to operate in crisis mode—at least for the short term. A lack of preparation virtually guarantees that the time needed for considered judgment will not be available once the problem surfaces.

Generally, the less time an institution has to react to a fiscal emergency, the narrower the range of options available. Rather than carefully considering their options—which could include tapping into reserves or using a budget contingency, along with unallocated initiative funds—the institution typically responds by implementing travel bans, hiring freezes, and across-the-board budget cuts. None of these actions is strategic, and each demonstrates an unwillingness or inability to protect priority activities—assuming any have been identified.

Of course, the crisis may still necessitate actions affecting travel, discretionary spending, and the filling of vacant positions, but effective planning can have a mitigating effect. For instance, the planning process should already have identified activities that will be exempt from expense controls and established the criteria for making decisions about other exceptions to necessary controls. Sponsored research programs; recently undertaken academic initiatives; patient care operations; and safety activities, for instance, might represent priority areas and, therefore, should not be subject to cutbacks.

To minimize the negative effects of financial stress, planning must focus on both midrange and long-range activities and consequences. In the short term, institutions may achieve small savings by selectively reducing nonpersonnel costs, such as travel, equipment, and supplies. But some short-term actions, such as reducing purchases of library materials, deferring maintenance and renovations, or deferring the purchase of essential replacement equipment, might cause severe long-term programmatic damage if they continue beyond one cycle. Although deferring a roof replacement may seem appealing in the moment, the decision may prove unwise if the roof leaks and damages expensive laboratory equipment integral to ongoing sponsored programs.

With compensation absorbing so much of their budgets, institutions cannot make large-scale reductions without eliminating faculty and staff positions— or at least resorting to furloughs. If effective planning minimizes the impact of the financial problem, normal attrition might generate enough savings to meet the reduction target. However, normal attrition may create different problems because the vacated positions may be critical to operational effectiveness. Even so, this still is preferable to layoffs or reductions in force because of how these actions affect the community.

In planning their responses to fiscal crises, institutions must remain sensitive to legal constraints and external factors. Collective bargaining agreements, for example, may limit the available options. State governments have become more involved in personnel matters in public higher education. This involvement may extend from direct participation in the negotiation of faculty contracts to controlling the number of faculty and staff positions. Under some budget formulas, adjustments to instructional methodologies or staffing patterns may affect state appropriations. For instance, increased reliance on distance education affects student-faculty ratios and increases the need for academic support personnel, such as instructional technologists. Finally, special attention needs to be given to the resources associated with diversity programs, which sometimes represent state mandates.

A direct correlation exists between institutional size and the ability to reallocate resources and absorb deficits. Larger institutions tend to have more cushion than smaller ones simply because the magnitude of their operations creates opportunities for flexibility. The cushion may be spread throughout programs and support services spanning the full range of priorities. That's partly why large institutions frequently favor across-the-board cuts. The presumption is that serious, negative programmatic effects will be avoided because the impact on any single activity is nominal. Unfortunately, the reality may be quite different.

Some programs operate with little or no flexibility. Even a small cut in resources may cripple them. In other cases, even a larger cut may have no discernible impact. For this reason, the planning process must identify priorities—activities that will be protected—and either explicitly, or through omission, indicate the areas that will be sacrificed should cuts become necessary.

SPECIFIC STRATEGIES

The responses to financial hard times are as diverse as the universe of American higher education. Some cutback strategies, such as across-the-board cutting, are adopted solely because of their ease of implementation and the fact that everyone suffers together (albeit not fairly). Others reflect careful consideration of programmatic activities and prompt the institution to focus more on critical success factors.

When considering specific strategies, institutions should avoid arbitrarily cutting support areas. Understandably, an institution wants to preserve primary academic programs and activities as much as possible. On the other hand, effective delivery of primary programs requires adequate support. Even though it is much easier to eliminate staff support positions than faculty lines, this response may not be the most effective one to support the mission.

In the short term, for instance, it may be more appropriate to rely on savings generated through faculty vacancies than to eliminate support positions. Another alternative may be restructuring support operations to expand the range of units served by individual academic support personnel. Rather than each academic department having one support position, a single position might support all units housed within a given building. The most effective institutions balance the need to minimize the adverse impacts on primary programs against the need to ensure those programs operate effectively.

Seven Planning Principles

When planning how to address a financial crisis, employ these general principles suggested by Robert M. O'Neil* and revised in the wake of the Great Recession:

1. **Involve everyone in planning—especially in times of financial distress.** Boards, management, faculty, staff, and students—as well as alumni and donors—have a major stake in what happens on campus. They not only deserve to participate in meaningful deliberations and decisions but also can provide valuable insights about how resource distributions affect programs and support services.

2. **Provide participants with access to all available information.** The people responsible for planning should be sensitive to the implications of sharing information, especially when it pertains to personnel and programs. Establish confidentiality standards and emphasize the importance of adherence. Such standards facilitate access to the sensitive information needed to make informed judgments.

3. **Ensure planning does not ignore the institution's culture.** During times of financial distress, the institution may have to consider actions that run counter to its values, traditions, or operating style. Such actions, if deemed essential, should be undertaken only after extensive communication with constituencies and with acknowledgment that they represent a shift in the institution's evolution.

---

*The principles discussed in this section originally appeared in Robert M. O'Neil's article, "A President's Perspective," on pages 17–20 in *Academe* 69 (January–February 1983).

Seven Planning Principles

4. **Inform the governing board and—in a university system—central administrative staff of progress.** Educate the trustees or regents and central administration on how the financial crisis response is unfolding—the first step in building support for proposed actions. Similarly, communicate changes in programmatic directions to significant friends of the institution, including alumni, donors, and local supporters.

5. **Recognize the impact of the media—especially social media.** Thanks to technology, constituents have nearly real-time access to information about most activities taking place on a campus—including responses to financial challenges. Members of the media are especially interested in higher education because of its community impact—and because of the controversy that frequently surrounds the range of campus activities.

    Because information will likely be disseminated anyway, have a broad, consultative process when it comes to responding to financial challenges. Furthermore, proactively use various forms of technology and social media to distribute accurate information. This reduces the possibility of erroneous information being widely shared.

6. **Never ignore the state legislature (if a public institution).** Legislators who remain informed about planned actions tend to be more sensitive to institutional interests when setting state-level policy. Even in an environment in which the institution is granted significant autonomy, it is in the institution's best interests to remain closely connected with state government during financially challenging times.

7. **Avoid unintended consequences by projecting the long-term impact of retrenchment strategies before implementing them.** A simple but effective approach is to model the various strategies under multiple scenarios to determine the most likely outcomes. The administrative tools available make it possible—and easy—to predict the outcomes from various strategies with reasonable accuracy.

In addition to following these principles, institutions should seek out resources available from higher education associations. In times of significant financial distress, it's common for associations like NACUBO to offer toolkits, suggested strategies, and other resources to their members. In some cases, these resources are developed by the association staff and member volunteers while, in others, the resources come directly from member campuses and represent proven solution sets.

One final caution is in order. Too often, institutions immediately engage in cost shifting as a response to financial stress. Cost shifting refers to the practice of implementing a charge for goods or services that previously were funded centrally or as part of a service unit's budget. It may be appropriate to require units to begin paying for certain goods or services that they consume. In fact, this may be an effective mechanism for conserving scare resources. A problem is created, however, when units that must now pay for these goods or services do not receive any additional resources.

If the decision is made to begin charging units, it's best to first distribute a portion of the existing budget to the units that will be required to pay for the goods or services. Savings can be generated by not distributing the entire budget. If a good or service has been provided at no charge to the user, it's highly likely there has been some waste related to the item. By distributing a portion of the existing budget—say 70 percent—and capturing the balance as savings, the institution will achieve the objective of reducing expenses but without adversely affecting units that rely on those goods or services.

Institutional retrenchment strategies fall into one of two groups. They are either short term—spanning one to three years—or long term—beyond three years.

SHORT-TERM STRATEGIES

In the short term, institutions can respond to financial difficulties either by reducing expenses or by increasing revenues. Boosting revenues significantly in the short term usually is quite difficult. It takes time to identify and pursue new revenue sources. A robust economy might make it possible to improve short-term investment returns through enhanced cash management, but this scenario is unlikely with weak markets (and likely wouldn't produce material amounts of revenue anyway).

Because of the difficulty with identifying and quickly pursuing new revenue streams, attention usually focuses on reducing or deferring expenses. Unless institutions have been operating under severe conditions for an extended period, they usually can achieve modest savings by curtailing discretionary expenditures for supplies, travel, equipment, and minor maintenance.

Larger short-term savings can be achieved by carefully managing the number of faculty and staff. Faculty positions that become vacant may be left open, filled with lower-salaried faculty, or filled with temporary or part-time faculty. Similarly, leaving staff positions vacant or employing part-time or temporary personnel can result in savings. Fewer courses and larger sections can be scheduled while also offering fewer sections of some courses.

Without a plan focused on differential actions, short-term budget strategies invariably focus on across-the-board measures. Imposing the same burden on all units on short notice may seem more acceptable to the greatest number of people, but it fails to address the concern that priority areas could suffer serious damage.

Across-the-board actions result in high-priority activities being treated the same as those that may contribute little to no value to the institution. In addition, across-the-board philosophies carry the implicit assumption that all budgets are equally capable of responding to a modest cut. In fact, vast differences in budget adequacy may exist among programs. For some units or programs, an equal percentage cut may merely affect discretionary expenses, while for others, it could force the elimination of a staff position to meet the target.

Given the shortcomings of across-the-board cuts, it always should be preferable to apply cuts selectively rather than uniformly. Such cuts can be accomplished only with a clear understanding of priorities and the level of resources needed to maintain and deliver effective programs. Selective reductions, even in accordance with an established plan, will not be well received by all constituents—especially those experiencing the disproportionately higher cuts. Therefore, cutting budgets represents one of the most difficult tests for a campus administration. If the planning process is to have any credibility, however, it must guide the decisions.

Short-term strategies can generate quick savings. If the institution has not invested the effort to develop a plan, these savings can buy the time needed to undertake a more considered approach to cutting expenses. On the other hand, the amount realized through short-term strategies tends to be small compared to the overall budget. Significant reductions take considerably more effort.

In addition, short-term strategies can inflict long-term damage on programs as well as facilities. For instance, when significant scheduled maintenance is deferred, it can have a serious impact on operations. There's an accepted maxim in facilities management that poorly maintained facilities are more expensive to operate. Additionally, when forced to apply the maintenance, it's almost a certainty that costs will have risen.

Similarly, when temporary or part-time employees fill vacancies resulting from the retirement or departure of experienced faculty, the institution's character can change dramatically. Programs requiring extensive involvement of senior faculty may wither, and part-time or temporary faculty may not be interested in (or capable of) student advising and counseling.

Finally, relying on attrition to achieve salary savings may mean the programs being de-emphasized may not be the ones that experience vacancies. If the vacancies occur in priority areas, the institution will need to fill the vacancies and diminish the potential savings.

LONG-TERM STRATEGIES

Every institution should have infrastructural plans (see Chapter 7) that provide the context for establishing program priorities in core programmatic and essential support areas. These plans should establish and reinforce the institution's priorities and identify decision-making criteria. Without the principles embodied in the plans, an institution will find it difficult to alter its allocation of resources in an intelligent manner.

Institutions faced with the prospect of implementing major budget reductions, or with the need to force significant reallocations, must review their academic programs and support activities carefully. To achieve economies and maintain or strengthen the quality of the institution, program review must be an active process that, over time, examines all programs and activities—both primary and supporting.

Infrastructural plans provide the framework for examining the distribution of resources, while information garnered from program reviews describes how well the program array is executing the plans. A typical schedule results in a comprehensive review of each program on a five-year cycle. Programs should be reviewed with respect to their:

- Linkage to and support of the institution's mission
- Service load
- Uniqueness
- Enrollment demand (for academic programs)
- Service demand (for support activities)
- Overall effectiveness (for example, quality and productivity)
- Available resources and costs incurred

In the absence of planning, the need for significant resource reductions or forced reallocations requires aggressive program reviews. In general, passive program shrinkage or elimination—usually through faculty and staff attrition—is insufficient to meet reduction targets. This approach may offer the least contentious way to cope with program shrinkage from a political perspective, but it typically will not achieve the objective. Faculty and staff do not limit their resignations, transfers, and retirements to low-priority, mediocre-quality, or low-demand programs and support activities. Normal attrition generally will not free up sufficient resources quickly enough to avoid retrenchment.

Large budget adjustments require changes in staffing patterns. Thus, retrenchment ultimately must focus on personnel policies and procedures. One frequent response is to provide financial incentives for early retirement, voluntary separation, or unpaid leaves. As with most retrenchment strategies, the objective is to provide institutions with budget-reduction alternatives that help avoid forced terminations.

Ideally, the people opting to depart under such programs would be the least-needed or least-productive faculty and staff, but this rarely happens. In fact, the institution risks losing its most productive and valuable faculty and staff because of their marketability.

An additional concern is that the people remaining may not possess the requisite educational and research background to fulfill the commitments of those who have departed. Even faculty trained in the same discipline may not be adequately prepared to step in and teach another faculty member's courses—especially if they have not taught the content previously. A faculty member teaching in the accounting program may be well qualified to teach any accounting course, but there is no guarantee he or she has the ability to teach an auditing or tax course.

Moreover, unless used in conjunction with program review, these strategies do not identify the programs and support activities that are the preferred candidates for contraction or elimination. The only way to avoid significant problems with incentive programs is to design them carefully and establish criteria that minimize the risk of losing the most valuable faculty and staff. Even so, the institution must prepare for the possibility of losing them.

Long-term strategies for achieving salary savings fall into these categories:

Early retirement. Faculty and staff who meet specified age and service criteria are offered a lump-sum separation allowance for agreeing to retire or resign early. In addition to the lump-sum payment, the package typically includes benefits such as pension and health insurance.

Some public institutions are precluded from offering such programs unless they are consistent with programs available to all state employees. Still others must obtain special authorization to offer a program of any type. Another problem is the possibility that some excellent performers may choose to retire. To minimize this outcome, the program might set the severance compensation at the average salary for a particular age cohort. This criterion may discourage the best faculty from participating because they are more likely to earn well above the average salary.

Early retirement programs typically require significant front-end costs, such as a severance package and payouts in lieu of some benefits. It must be demonstrated that the program will ultimately save money and improve the overall financial picture. Nevertheless, an early retirement program may be a less expensive alternative than forced terminations that sometimes require one to two years of notice and frequently result in expensive legal challenges.

The current economic climate, the quality of life on campus, and the institution's general outlook play a significant role in a program's success. For instance, many programs offered in the wake of the Great Recession failed because of the depressed stock market at that time. Even with incentives, individual retirement portfolios had lost so much value that many feared they might not have sufficient retirement income. As a result, few were willing to participate in the programs.

Early retirement represents a big step, and employees appreciate having time to consider it carefully and consult with their advisors. Programs that require a commitment during a small window of opportunity may discourage participation. On occasion, institutions have offered programs in consecutive years with differing features and requirements. This technique usually is implemented when the financial condition continues to deteriorate or the retirement programs do not generate the level of participation needed to achieve reduction targets. Unfortunately, once this practice is utilized, it tends to encourage potential participants to wait for what they believe to be the best possible offer.

An additional concern with early retirement programs is that they may not work as effectively for staff as for faculty. By their nature and design, early retirement programs focused on faculty will be targeted to older faculty—typically those with the highest salary levels. To the extent that the programs are attractive, the faculty who depart will usually be replaced by more junior, lower-paid faculty. Even considering the extra costs incurred for the incentives, the institution will realize net savings fairly quickly. With staff, however, it has proven difficult in some cases to attract lower-cost talent. If the longer-serving senior staff take advantage of the program, it is possible that the individuals' salaries will not have kept up with compensation increases over time. When that's the case, the institution may find that it is not possible to attract affordable individuals to the positions. If this happens, the desired savings may not materialize.

Partial buyout. This approach enables faculty and staff to choose part-time appointments for a number of years up to an established maximum. During this period, they receive a prorated salary with full benefits. Participants commonly receive a full year of retirement credit for each year in the program.

Partial buyouts tend to appeal to senior faculty and staff because their salaries are larger and they are closer to retirement. For this reason, the program can generate substantial savings with relatively low participation.

Alternative approaches. Individual campuses have employed short furloughs, forcing staff to take unpaid time off. Others have implemented modest across-the-board pay reductions or introduced midcareer changes—a euphemism for retraining, a term sometimes found objectionable by faculty. With the latter arrangement, faculty or staff in programs targeted for reduction or elimination have the opportunity to transfer to other departments or positions to continue employment. In general, these strategies are difficult to implement unless existing policies already allow them. Otherwise, the opposition from faculty and staff can be overwhelming.

Another option involves liberalization of the existing guidelines used to determine retirement benefits. For instance, rather than develop a specific early retirement program, an institution can elect to provide full benefits at a lower retirement age or with fewer years of service. In a traditional early retirement program with unique features, individual negotiations may take place. With liberalized guidelines, everyone qualifying under the formula receives the amount of compensation and benefits available to anyone with the same combination of age and service.

Surviving Personnel Reductions

Personnel actions are a delicate subject in the best of times. When implemented as part of retrenchment, they take on an entirely different character. The following recommendations may prove useful if you become forced to take personnel actions to generate savings.

Analyze the possible strategies. If offering an early retirement program, for example, ensure the savings would outweigh the implementation costs by a margin sufficient to justify the effort and attendant disruption.

Avoid targeting specific individuals. Rather than focusing exclusively on faculty and staff assigned to a program deemed less essential, address the program itself. Singling out individuals may lead them to believe they were the victims of inappropriate discrimination.

Discrimination in and of itself is not illegal. It happens routinely and appropriately. For instance, assigning a larger reduction target to a low-demand program is a form of discrimination. On the other hand, discrimination against individuals based on age, gender, ethnicity, race, etc. clearly is illegal. Follow due process with any personnel reduction programs driven by retrenchment to ensure that employees do not feel they were coerced into making a decision and that those who choose to participate are not stigmatized.

Focus on more than the finances. Savings should not be the sole consideration when implementing new personnel policies. Consider also the impact on programmatic goals and objectives.

Take care to avoid actions that faculty may perceive as a threat to tenure, academic freedom, or academic due process. Both faculty and staff will find personnel reduction programs easier to accept if the risks associated with career transitions are minimal.

When developing personnel reduction initiatives, consult the constituent group members expected to participate in them. In addition, position and publicize the opportunities as providing benefits both for the individuals and the institution.

TERMINATION OF FACULTY

Sometimes, the magnitude of the reductions needed within a short time period makes termination unavoidable. The termination of faculty is particularly difficult because most institutions maintain a strong commitment to tenure. In addition, many American colleges and universities have policies that align with principles and guidelines established by the American Association of University Professors (AAUP).

These principles and guidelines cover academic freedom, tenure, financial exigency, and discontinuation of a program for reasons other than financial exigency. The AAUP guidelines, for example, oppose the dismissal of faculty or the termination of appointments before the end of specified terms, except when financial exigency occurs.

The guidelines are designed to prevent administrators from using financial exigency as a justification for capricious actions. They define financial exigency as, "A severe financial crisis that fundamentally compromises the academic integrity of the institution as a whole and that cannot be alleviated by less drastic means [than the termination of tenured faculty]." While helpful, this definition can be difficult to apply due to differing interpretations of what constitutes a severe financial crisis as well as disagreements about the availability and impact of less drastic means. Moreover, the AAUP's history of investigating campus actions and, in extreme cases, censuring institutions clearly indicate that there frequently is a strong difference of opinion about the appropriateness of institutional activities when responding to financial crises. It is, therefore, necessary to interpret the guidelines and adapt them to specific institutional settings whenever they are employed.

Views differ on whether enrollment fluctuations can be the impetus for exigency determinations. Some individuals argue that fluctuations are cyclical and should not serve as a basis for program discontinuation. Others contend that enrollment fluctuations constitute an appropriate aspect of educational policy and, therefore, should be considered.

Clearly, the quality of academic programs influences resource decisions. A program of mediocre quality with low enrollment, for example, might drain resources from higher-quality, more competitive programs. It might be necessary to respond to sagging institutional enrollments by shifting resources to make selected programs more attractive to potential students. Such action, though damaging to some programs, may be the only way to protect the financial viability of the institution as a whole.

The major issue in significant retrenchment efforts is how to handle personnel in all categories: tenured, nontenured, and staff. The AAUP guidelines address the elimination of entire academic programs. Absent financial exigency, the guidelines do not permit the termination of particular tenured faculty because of mere reduction in scope or reorganization of academic units. In a small institution with instruction as its primary mission, for example, enrollments might not justify a five-person, fully tenured philosophy department. If the institution wishes to reduce its commitment to philosophy, while also adhering to institutional policies compliant with AAUP guidelines, the only alternative may be to disband the entire program. Moreover, the institution would have to justify the elimination of the philosophy program on academic considerations other than enrollment.

This example helps explain why some institutions have modified the AAUP guidelines or abandoned them completely in favor of other approaches. Those institutions have more flexibility when dealing with low-demand or low-quality programs because they would have the option to reduce the number of faculty based on enrollment.

Rather than terminating tenured faculty members, an institution might allow the size of the program faculty and staff to shrink through natural attrition. This takes time though. Alternatively, faculty members can be reassigned or retrained to assume other duties or teach in related disciplines. When taking any such actions, institutions must be careful to honor commitments made to students currently enrolled in these programs.

It's noteworthy that in nearly all recent cases, accreditation actions taken by the regional accrediting agencies have included financial challenges as a factor. Financial challenges can include the inadequacy of resources as well as the lack of appropriate policies and procedures related to financial resources. Whether warning, probation, or loss of accreditation actions, finances play a disproportionate role to other factors that influence the accrediting bodies' actions. Given that regional accreditation is required for participation in federal financial aid programs, institutions placed on probation or warning due to financial issues would clearly be in financial exigency—whether declared by the institution or not.

Other institutions may not be in such peril but still face serious financial distress due to dramatic decreases in revenue from declining enrollment, tumultuous financial markets, reduced state appropriations, or other situations. If these colleges and universities have adopted the AAUP guidelines as written, they may struggle with how the guidelines apply as they respond to financial difficulties.

Any institution facing serious financial hardship must assess whether financial exigency—as defined in its own policies (whether adopted from AAUP guidelines or developed on their own)—actually exists. Because the phrase carries special meaning in the higher education community, great care must be exercised before it is invoked. In the past, some institutions have used the phrase prior to initiating actions that resulted in the termination of faculty because their policies required it.

Other institutions, recognizing that the phrase can trigger other serious consequences, have attempted to address financial crises without referring specifically to financial exigency. In doing so, they hoped to avoid problems with bond-rating agencies, bondholders, other creditors, and accreditation agencies. Unfortunately, failure to invoke the phrase does not guarantee that drastic measures can be avoided.

FOCUSING ON THE LONG TERM

STRATEGIC RESOURCE ALLOCATION (SRA)

Within the most effectively managed institutions, planning is a continuous activity because of the complexity of the academic enterprise and the need to act intentionally rather than haphazardly. The best planning processes are those that involve administrators, faculty, appropriate stakeholder groups, and—depending on culture—students. Even when things are going well, it usually is desirable to have some periodic process for evaluating the various activities that are consuming resources (i.e., people, money, space, technology, and equipment).

One option for responding to the need for structural change is periodic SRA, or prioritization, as described by Bob Dickeson.* At its core, SRA is undertaken to facilitate an orderly and systematic redistribution of resources away from underperforming academic programs and support functions toward those existing activities that will contribute to enhanced institutional effectiveness and long-term success.

Directed by senior leadership but relying on a broadly participative effort carried out by faculty, staff, and midlevel managers, a systematic process is undertaken to assess all activities that consume resources and compare them to other similar activities. Academic programs are evaluated by a task force comprised of faculty and academic department heads utilizing institutionally specific criteria to evaluate each program against all other academic programs. A parallel task force consisting of staff, midlevel managers, and faculty use different institution-specific criteria to evaluate all support functions within the institution. These assessments result in all programs and functions being classified into quintiles (i.e., five equal categories), with the goal of equal distribution based on the value of financial investments in the programs and functions. The recommended categories are:

I. **Enhance through additional resourcing** – Programs and functions whose contributions to institutional success would be enhanced with increased investment to the extent funds are available for reallocation

II. **Maintain with no change in resourcing** – Programs and functions that currently operate successfully and consume the appropriate amount of resources relative to the total amount of available resources

III. **Modify through reduced resourcing** – Programs and functions that will curtail some operations or reduce their quality due to a reduction of resources available to the programs and functions going forward

---

*The strategic resource allocation discussion is influenced significantly by the book: Prioritizing Academic Programs and Services by Robert C. Dickeson (San Francisco, CA: Jossey-Bass, 2010).

IV. Transform – Programs and functions deemed essential to the institution's character or operations but that are underperforming in comparison with programs and functions in categories I through III. Such programs and functions must be reengineered or reenvisioned due to their inability to perform at levels that meet current needs. Programs and functions in this category may receive additional resourcing or may be transformed in such a way that previous resource levels can be reduced.

V. Phase out or merge – Programs and functions no longer deemed essential to the institution's character or operations that underperform compared to programs and functions in categories I through III. Programs and functions in this category will be subjected to an additional thorough examination to determine whether and how best to carry out the recommendation for a phaseout or merger.

It should be noted that, except in very rare situations, it is inconceivable that 20 percent of an institution's investments could be curtailed without adversely affecting the institution's operations and its ability to carry out its mission. In particular, care must be taken that disproportionately large cuts in support areas do not prevent the institution from adequately delivering the academic programs that will remain following implementation of recommendations coming out of the process.

The use of quintiles, as described above, is recommended because of the difficulty to carry out the classification without forced distribution. Realistically, except in dire situations, the maximum amount that can be reduced in a reasonable time period is in the range of 10 to 12 percent. It should be noted that the savings using this approach will not be available immediately. Instead, given the obligations to students currently registered in programs slated for phaseout—as well as contractual and other obligations to current staff and faculty—it may take up to four years to fully realize the savings from SRA.

Once completed, the classification of programs is reviewed by senior leadership. In addition to the work of the task forces, they will receive the benefit of input from individuals and stakeholder groups throughout the institution who will want the opportunity to weigh in on the recommendations. Ultimately, senior leadership will make the decisions about which recommendations to accept and implement—and in what sequence. The end product of the effort (i.e., management's intentions) should be communicated to the board. In most instances, the board will be required to formally endorse or approve the plan. Implementation begins following board action.

Although significant coverage is given to SRA—the author's preferred approach, there are other models that can help establish the prioritization of activities with resulting resource redistribution. Some campuses have employed the Balanced Scorecard approach. In carrying out the process, institutions view activities from four perspectives and develop key performance indicators, targets, and actions relative to each one of them. The perspectives include financial, customer (or stakeholder), internal business process, and learning and growth.[216]

Another approach, the Resource Allocation Map,[217] relies on four dimensions to help align organizational resources with strategic priorities. The dimensions are the mission/strategic plan, financial performance, internal competencies, and market trends. While both SRA and the Balanced Scorecard are holistic systems that can be used to evaluate and prioritize all operations, the Resource Allocation Map is focused primarily on academic programs and activities.

Another option for tackling in-depth academic program analysis is available from Gray Associates, Inc. In addition to examining the current complement of programs, it has the expertise (and robust database) to assist institutions with the identification of potential new programs that would lead to improved financial performance. Its integrated program analysis tool examines four dimensions referred to as MAMM:

- ▶ Mission
- ▶ Academic standards
- ▶ Markets for programs
- ▶ Money

The resulting information is used to provide a program scorecard incorporating numerous data points for each program offered by a college or university.

Gray has a proven track record of helping institutions examine their programs in a detailed manner that allows them to identify those that have stopped contributing to institutional success. Acting on this information, institutions can free up resources to pursue new programming that will better serve the institution's current students and attract new ones.

PROGRAM REVIEW

In the absence of a comprehensive approach, such as the one suggested by Dickeson, there is a need for some type of in-depth program review. A typical process would usually include the following elements:

▶ Confirmation of the continuing relevance of the mission statement

▶ Review and modification (if necessary) of campus-wide or system-wide policies, procedures, and statements of priorities

▶ Examination and updating (if necessary) of personnel policies

▶ Establishment of guiding principles specifically applicable to program review

▶ Establishment of policies and procedures, including criteria, for the review of existing and proposed programs and activities

Fiscal conditions ultimately are the force behind retrenchment and any significant exceptional reallocation effort. Nevertheless, finances often are overshadowed by genuine concern for personnel policies and procedures—especially those related to faculty and staff welfare and legal rights—and the potential impact from program reviews.

PROGRAM REDUCTION

Program reduction has obvious political costs and a devastating impact on morale. These costs must be compared with the net savings and other benefits, such as the ability to respond to enrollment pressures and hire quality faculty. Institutions sensitive to the well-being of those affected by program elimination will incur costs for early retirement, buyouts, outplacement services, or retraining.

If faculty and staff must be terminated, the institution will be responsible for severance payments. Invariably, some faculty and staff will contest their dismissals through the courts, so legal defense represents another cost to factor into the equation. The net savings from program reduction will be a function of the specific strategies employed. To the extent that the institution elects to assign faculty and staff to positions elsewhere within the institution, savings may be reduced as compared with outright or phased terminations.

Program reduction or elimination may be a consequence of enrollment decline. These decisions will result in a loss of tuition and fee revenue and, for public institutions, possibly reduced operating appropriations. Public institutions may not be authorized to reinvest savings gained through retrenchment in other programs and activities. Instead, these institutions must return savings to the state. Finally, programs that enjoy significant external financial support may require considerable institutional support to continue. Reducing or eliminating such programs may not generate any net savings.

Other effects of retrenchment and reallocation may be more subtle and difficult to quantify. Faculty teaching in a department being downsized may find they no longer have the job satisfaction they desire. They may elect to seek employment elsewhere, potentially impairing the ability to sustain the program at the expected levels. For example, if an institution reduces the scope of a program from the doctoral to the master's level, faculty whose primary interest is doctoral training and research may not be satisfied teaching at the undergraduate and master's levels.

Taking actions that affect programs that enjoy significant support from donors may result in reduced support. Thus, it may be desirable to include external support as a criterion to consider during program reviews. This is a risky action to take because it can lead to individuals who are not part of the institution having significant influence over operational matters. The question must be asked whether the external financial support is sufficiently large to allow this to happen.

Similar to the situation involving donors, certain programs may have strong political connections. If a prominent political figure serves on a program advisory board, or the program participates in projects with important community organizations, the intangible costs of contracting or eliminating the program may outweigh the financial benefits. In terms of diminished public support, the institution as a whole bears the cost of reducing or eliminating such a program.

Retrenchment may disrupt shared governance, unless faculty are meaningfully involved in establishing the policies that guide the retrenchment steps. Even when review criteria and related policies and procedures have been established, governance groups may struggle to specify the programs or activities to reduce or eliminate. Morale problems will assuredly arise as specific plans become known, and until they are announced, the rumor mill will be fully consumed with guessing what might happen.

Faculty who have served the institution for a long time may suddenly feel unwanted. If faculty terminations are decided on the basis of seniority, as is frequently the case, conflict may develop between junior and senior faculty. Retrenchment also may lead faculty and staff to pursue collective bargaining as a way to gain greater influence over the process. Adverse publicity about program reductions may exacerbate declining enrollment. Finally, situations leading to retrenchment may highlight the deficiencies within the current administration. Although the steps taken may be positive in the long run, the short-term effects can create havoc.

The economics of retrenchment require long-term plans for all programs and activities, with responsible parties held accountable for meeting plan objectives. In the academic arena, enrollments may have to be restricted to maintain the desired level of service with the available resources. Enrollment can be controlled for high-demand programs by establishing special admission requirements or implementing variable-rate tuition pricing. Long-range enrollment targets can be established for all academic programs so that planners can better gauge resource needs. Programs that fail to achieve the targets will experience consequences, which might include financial penalties (for example, reduced resources in future periods) or personnel actions (for example, demotions or dismissal).

The development of long-term enrollment targets also supports the establishment of projected staffing patterns. Institutions can project the impact of enrollment levels on decisions about the promotion, tenure, turnover, and hiring of new faculty with the objective of making future decisions in a proactive way.

Plans for program reduction also should anticipate changes in programs and activities. If an academic program is to be phased out, for example, arrangements must be made to accommodate its current students. Tenured faculty in the program being eliminated may need to be placed elsewhere within the institution. The elimination of a degree program may affect other programs that depend on it for courses or for students. Finally, the impact of retrenchment on diversity objectives must be considered both in terms of staffing and enrollment.

KEY POINTS

▶ Retrenchment is more than belt-tightening—it is a dramatic contraction of activities and operations, usually resulting in the elimination of positions.

▶ In extreme situations, retrenchment will be accompanied by a declaration of financial exigency—a statement to the internal and external communities that the institution's long-term viability will be in question if extreme actions are not taken. Beyond just eliminating positions, exigency typically entails the elimination of entire programs with the eliminated costs used to help close the budget gap.

▶ Financial exigency is likely to result in action by an institution's regional accreditor. Failure to respond appropriately could cause the institution to lose accreditation and, as a result, cease participation in federal financial aid programs.

▶ Strategic resource allocation (or similar comprehensive evaluation processes) can help prevent retrenchment or, at the least, deal with it effectively. Such processes evaluate all activities in a manner that supports the establishment of priorities and directs resources toward those priorities. Ultimately, the goal is to redirect resources away from underperforming programs and activities toward those that contribute more to institutional success.

CHAPTER 14: CLOSING THOUGHTS

One of the alarming things that was discovered during the process of writing this edition is that budgeting in American colleges and universities has not gotten any easier during the nearly 15 years since the third edition was written. Yes, there now are sophisticated tools, apps, and modeling resources that make the mechanics less troublesome. And many central office personnel better understand the nuances and relationships among and between various revenues and expenses. Advanced analytics are being employed across the industry, helping us become more skilled at integrating the various types of planning with each other and then aligning them with resource allocation and assessment processes.

Despite all of this enhanced capability, developing a budget that meets the needs of today's incredibly complex organizations is a challenging endeavor that leaves large numbers of individuals frustrated. Even when they are afforded the opportunity to be direct participants, stakeholders still do not understand why there are not more resources to support the activities they care most about. This is not because the stakeholders are not trying or are unable to comprehend the flow of resources. In fact, it's because there are insufficient resources to carry out the important work undertaken by our colleges and universities.

It's understood that higher education no longer is perceived as being a universal good that benefits society, but the truth is that it holds the key to the future well-being of society. The education provided and the discoveries that have surfaced have dramatically improved the quality of life for people around the world. We live longer, experience better health throughout our lives, and take advantage of opportunities that were unthinkable by past generations. Much of this occurs because of what happens every day on college campuses throughout the country.

Could higher education be conducted more effectively, more affordably, with greater access, etc.? Of course, it could—and thousands of colleges and universities are committed to doing so. I've said many times, no college or university plans to get worse. Every institution seeks to improve on its past successes and continues to push for new ones every day. Budgeting never will be easy because we will never be satisfied with what is being accomplished. Even if we are doing all of the right things, we will never be content with the levels of quality we're able to achieve. We always will want to do more. In spite of the frustrations, no one has devised a better approach to carrying out the mission than regularly examining what we do, understanding the resources required to do it, and then honestly evaluating what was accomplished. For that reason, we must continue to rely on planning, budgeting, and assessment to drive institutional success.

A budget tells a story about an institution—especially if comparative information for the prior year is available. It highlights the institution's priorities because, presumably, more resources are devoted to these areas.

The budget also leaves clues about the specific model used by the institution. If all budgets in the new year reflect the same relative change from the previous year's amounts, for example, one can conclude that the institution relies on incremental budgeting rather than RCB or PBB.

Budgeting is part of the larger topic of resource allocation, which also encompasses planning and assessment. Through the planning process, an institution decides what activities to undertake and, by omission, what activities not to pursue.

Strategic planning—the highest level of planning—usually covers a five-year period. At the other end of the spectrum is operational planning, which focuses on one fiscal year (or, possibly, two fiscal years). The strategic plan guides operational planning by providing direction for the day-to-day activities conducted throughout the year.

Because strategic plans are limited to a handful of priority areas, infrastructural plans are also developed to address the institution's core programmatic areas (academics, student engagement) and essential support areas (facilities, information technology), usually for a three- to four-year period. Collectively, the different levels of planning should be integrated with one another and aligned with both budgeting and assessment. That alignment puts the institution in the best position to successfully carry out its mission while moving closer to its aspirational vision.

Through the assessment process, an institution evaluates the results of its activities to determine whether changes in approach are needed. Assessment—an action-based endeavor—must have decision-making as its main purpose.

The results of assessments may cause an institution to alter its plans or its resource allocation—or to intentionally keep things moving as they are. Assessments may demonstrate that the original plans were too ambitious and, therefore, expectations must be lowered. Instead of accommodating x number of participants in an advising activity, only 85 percent of x can be accommodated because of the time needed for students to demonstrate mastery of the relevant concepts. Alternatively, the institution might decide to add resources (for example, an additional advisor) to give students more individual attention, thereby allowing them to complete the process as originally planned.

The examples used throughout the book focus primarily on reducing expectations against plans or adding resources to meet target outcomes, although this does not have to be the case. On occasion, plans prove too conservative or resources too generous. Assessment processes should uncover either situation and lead to appropriate actions—in other words, decisions.

Here are some thoughts to keep in mind when participating in any part of the resource allocation process.

Compare the budget narrative with the budget numbers. The narrative report that accompanies a budget reveals whether the institution puts its money where its mouth is. If the narrative articulates priority areas that the quantitative tables and schedules do not reflect, it raises the issue of whether the narrative reflects reality. True institutional priorities are demonstrated through the allocation of resources, not through rhetoric.

Consider the institution's character. Planning and resource allocation approaches vary from campus to campus. What works at an older institution, with decades of established culture, probably won't work at a relatively young campus still in the development phase.

Public institutions operate differently from independent institutions, and wide variations occur even within independent institutions. Enrollment-dependent religiously affiliated institutions, for example, may approach resource allocation with different values than wealthy independent institutions.

Foster internal transparency. When constituents have access to factual information, they become much less likely to fill the information void with rumors and misinformation that chip away at the institution's stability. Transparency builds trust among all levels of participants in the resource allocation process. If an open, transparent process is inconsistent with the current campus culture, the institution must acknowledge this reality and enlist the community's support in making a change.

Acknowledge external realities. While higher education has always been subjected to extensive regulation and mandates, the situation is worsening. Both public and independent institutions are regularly besieged by excessive regulation and demands for accountability. All of these measures contribute to increased operating costs, thereby reducing amounts available for programmatic purposes.

As a result of competition from other social sectors and concerns regarding tuition prices, legislators, media representatives, and the general public routinely raise questions about the value of higher education. Fortunately, ample data exist to demonstrate that investments in higher education have a significant financial return, to say nothing of the lifelong value of being an educated person.

The number of for-profit institutions has dropped significantly in recent years, yet those that remain continue to compete directly with two- and four-year traditional institutions for students, faculty, and resources. Using distance offerings, rented facilities operated to meet local demand, or a combination of the two, these for-profit institutions operate in a business-like manner with a clear bottom line—increased profits. That focus makes them a credible participant in the marketplace.

Traditional higher education suffers from a lack of clarity about the bottom line because so many disciplines and functional areas are critically important within an institution. If the institution has a medical school with a patient- care mission, some would argue that the most important institutional activity is treating patients. Many working within a community college may believe meeting the workforce needs of the community represents the top priority. For others, the most important activity taking place is intercollegiate athletics because of the brand recognition, private support, and student experiences it brings. Notice that nothing has been said about educating students! In reality, traditional higher education has multiple bottom lines, which makes institutions vulnerable to competitors with the single focus of financial gain for investors.

Globalization represents another external factor that influences budgets. U.S.-based institutions have opened campuses throughout the world to extend their brand, export quality educational approaches to underserved regions, or simply gain access to new revenue streams. At the same time, U.S. institutions continue to attract record numbers of international students to their domestic campuses. Offsetting the importation of international students is an increase in American students studying abroad. Accommodating these various global experiences carries a cost—both in terms of dollars for out-of-pocket expenses and the more intangible impact on institutional systems and processes.

Focus on all institutional resources. This includes both those that are unrestricted and those that are restricted. Yes, it's significantly harder to precisely project the amount of gift support that an institution will receive or the level of success it will enjoy when pursuing sponsored programs' support. Nevertheless, to the extent that an institution's overall success depends on restricted resources—and it nearly always does—those resources must be subjected to the same levels of oversight as those that are easier to predict and manage. All-funds budgeting should be the norm for the entire industry.

Consider demographics. Tuition revenues depend upon students, so the population shifts occurring within the United States will affect all institutions, particularly enrollment-dependent ones.

Institutions located in the Northeast, Midwest, and the West—the regions losing students—run the risk of coming up short in the competition to fill seats. Remember, reduced enrollments do not necessarily translate into eliminated costs. On the other side of the equation, institutions located in the South—where student numbers are growing—may experience demand that exceeds available resources.

Favor flexibility. To manage the day-to-day bumps in the road that occur throughout the year while maintaining financial equilibrium, institutions must adopt policies and procedures that contribute to budgetary flexibility.

A key aspect of flexibility is anticipating and preparing for the unexpected. This can be accomplished through contingency funds built into the expense budget to accommodate revenue shortfalls, expense overruns, or unanticipated opportunities. A good rule of thumb is to devote 3 percent of the expense budget to a contingency fund. Barring catastrophic occurrences, this should provide sufficient flexibility for the institution to make it through the year without dipping into reserves.

Of course, if conditions deteriorate markedly, protecting reserves may not be possible. This certainly will be the case if planning efforts prove ineffective or external forces create negative conditions that exceed the institution's financial capabilities. Relatively few institutions plan for catastrophes and, therefore, most experiencing them will be forced to take extreme measures if the financial situation becomes dire. Retrenchment may mean eliminating or contracting programs, which typically results in the termination of faculty and staff. As a last resort, the institution will declare financial exigency, which usually leads to large-scale program contraction.

Adopt an accountability mechanism rather than controlling policies and procedures. At the end of the day, control practices are about preventing mistakes. Nearly every law, policy, regulation, directive, procedure, edict, etc. came about because of something having gone wrong in the past. The goal of controls is to prevent it from happening again and, as a result, massive amounts of inefficiency are introduced into the system. Although it's more true for public institutions, independent institutions are not immune to these issues.

Rather than emphasize control, instill a culture based on trust with accountability. Inform the community of what is expected and train it, resource it, and support it with the expectation that the vast majority of individuals will perform properly. And when they do, they should be rewarded in whatever ways are most rational for the subject. Use assessment mechanisms—reasonable checks and balances—to identify the rare instances when things are not carried out properly. When they surface, provide additional training, support, or resources. If it turns out that a few bad actors are unwilling or unable to perform acceptably, have appropriate sanctions available to prevent further damage from occurring. In summary, do not design systems and processes to catch or prevent the small amount of problems that might arise. Instead, design them to support the multitudes of individuals who strive to succeed and perform appropriately each day.

Become actively involved. Anyone interested in participating in an institution's planning and resource allocation processes should make that interest known. If the campus climate does not prove receptive to this participation, work through the organizational structure—for example, by informing a supervisor or department head about a desire to serve on a resource allocation committee or task force. Established forums on campus—such as the faculty senate and administrative council—offer another avenue for voicing interest. If you always adopt an institutional (versus self-interested) perspective, you should be welcomed into the process.

KEY POINTS

▶ A budget tells a story about an institution and its priorities. When accompanied by a narrative expanding on the numbers, it becomes a detailed story about what matters most.

▶ If the financial information in the budget is supplemented with comparable information for the previous year, it is easy to identify the institution's priorities. It also becomes evident if the narrative is at odds with how the institution actually allocates resources.

▶ The most effective budgeting processes are those that are aligned with planning and assessment processes. They consider all resources and provide for significant levels of transparency, openness, and participation.

APPENDIX A: BUDGETING AND ACCOUNTING CONSIDERATIONS

One need not be an accountant to understand budgets and budgeting. Although knowledge of accounting may aid the understanding of relationships between various budget elements, budgets are not subject to accounting rules.

Nevertheless, some accounting issues affect higher education budgeting. An understanding of the issues summarized below will benefit participants in the resource allocation process and help them interpret the institution's audited financial statements.

NONCASH EXPENSES

Budgets usually focus on cash, while accounting considers cash activity as well as accruals. Accruals include revenues that have been earned but not collected in cash (receivables) and expenses that have been incurred but not yet paid for (payables).

Noncash expenses represent a different type of accrual. Unlike normal payments and payables, a noncash expense is a cost of doing business that must be recognized without a corresponding disbursement of cash. The most common example is depreciation.

Depreciation is the accounting mechanism used to spread the cost of capital assets, such as buildings and equipment, over the periods equating to their expected useful lives. Without this convention, funds expended to acquire high-cost assets would be charged entirely to the current year— automatically generating a financial loss and ignoring the reality that the assets will still be in use in the future. Therefore, the amounts invested to construct or acquire capital assets are recorded as assets rather than expenses.

The useful life for such assets is estimated, and the recorded value of the asset is divided by this number, thus generating the amount representing the annual charge for using or consuming a portion of the asset. This amount represents the expense (depreciation) attributable to each period during which the asset will provide service to the organization.

In recent years, depreciation (or amortization) has been applied to major investments in computer software such as ERPs. Treating these costly investments as expenses attributable to one fiscal year would dramatically distort the expense totals for that year. Just as with buildings, these systems are expected to provide service for many years, so the investment is capitalized and amortized over the expected useful life. As the system updates increase the system's functionality or extend its useful life, the costs to install these enhancements are added to the unamortized cost of the system. This is the same process used with building renovations.

A key consideration related to depreciation (and amortization) is whether an attempt is made to generate revenues sufficient to offset the expense. In other words, are tuition and other revenue sources managed to cover all expenses or only cash expenses? Without generating revenues sufficient to cover both cash expenses and depreciation, the institution would operate at a financial loss or deficit. That is, expenses would exceed revenues.

FUNDING DEPRECIATION

An institution that funds depreciation (or amortization) sets aside resources equal to the amount of depreciation expense recognized during that period. The funds, held in a reserve and invested, provide resources to replace the asset when its useful life has expired. Although it's possible that the investment return will not keep pace with the annual cost increases related to a replacement asset, this is a much better situation than would occur if no reserve existed.

Funding depreciation draws mixed reviews. Some accounting professionals believe it necessary to recognize the expense of using facilities and to establish reserves to provide for their replacement. Under current accounting practices, depreciation addresses only the original cost of a facility—or the estimated market value in the case of donated assets. This amount obviously falls far below what might be needed to replace the facility in 30 years. Nevertheless, recognizing depreciation and reserving the value of the expense each year generates funds that can be invested. The funds may grow enough to cover most, if not all, of the replacement cost.

Other accounting professionals argue that the institution won't likely need to generate the funds for replacing obsolete or aging facilities. They suggest that donors—or, in the case of public institutions, the government—will provide the necessary funds. However, the states hit hardest by the Great Recession still are recovering and unable to provide the resources needed to fund higher education at reasonable levels, let alone fund capital asset replacement. Likewise, as facilities age or become obsolete, donors might not be willing or able to provide the resources for maintaining the built environment required by colleges and universities.

It can be helpful to compare annual depreciation expense to amounts being invested in facilities. If an institution does not invest at least as much as the annual depreciation charge, it will experience a problem over time. Essentially, the built environment will become outdated. This easily calculated metric will indicate whether the institution is appropriately investing in its facilities.

FINANCIAL AID

Some forms of financial aid represent true inflows of resources to the institution. Others merely pass through the institution's accounts en route to the students. Under accounting rules, revenues must be counted only once. If a form of financial aid is treated as revenue by the institution when it is received (for example, a gift for scholarships), the tuition for the student receiving the scholarship is reduced by the amount of the gift applied as a scholarship. The net result is that both the gift and the balance of tuition actually paid by the student are recognized as revenues.

Despite the accounting requirements, it is important to consider tuition and financial aid as separate categories in the budget—even though they likely will be addressed at the same time because of their strong connections to one another. From a management perspective, tuition and financial aid are closely linked. Therefore, it is important to focus attention on the aggregate rather than the net amounts.

ACCOUNTING STANDARDS

Public and independent institutions follow different rules for financial reporting purposes. Independent institutions must comply with rules established by the FASB, while public institutions are subject to rules promulgated by the GASB. Although the basic rules are similar, subtle differences make it difficult to compare financial reports prepared by public and independent institutions.

For instance, independent institutions have a more narrow definition of restrictions: Only donors can restrict resources. At public institutions, any external entity, including donors, governments, laws, and even contracts, can establish restrictions. This inconsistency leads to differing accounting treatment. Public institutions treat resources derived from sponsored programs as restricted, while independent institutions consider these funds unrestricted. In addition, unrestricted net assets at independent institutions include the net investment in plant (the carrying value of facilities minus accumulated depreciation and plant debt). At public institutions, the net investment in plant is presented in a separate net asset category—net investment in capital assets.

Other differences center on how to record certain revenues or expenses. Pell Grants offer one example of this type of difference. These are federal grants for financial aid. Public institutions include Pell Grants as nonoperating grant revenues. Independent institutions do not count Pell Grants as revenue at all. Instead, they treat these grants as pass-through funds with no effect on revenues, expenses, or net assets.

Even though such differences have little impact on budgeting practices, their potential impact should be considered if one attempts to compare budgets for otherwise similar institutions.

RECONCILING BUDGET REPORTING
WITH ACCOUNTING REPORTING

Any discussion of finances on campuses is bifurcated. When discussing external financial reporting, for instance, the emphasis is on accrual-basis reporting compliant with established GAAP. When discussing internal financial reporting, the focus tends to be on cash-basis budgets (cash in and cash out). This carries over to how institutions share financial information with boards—the bodies that approve the budget and periodically review updates on the status of revenues and expenses as compared with the budget.

The final step in the budget process for a given period should be determining how well the budget predicted the revenues and expenses that would arise as the institution carried out its many day-to-day activities. In reality, however, the final budget is not shared with the board. Instead, the board sees a set of audited financial statements—a GAAP-compliant, accrual-basis series of reports that tell the story of the revenues and expenses that materialized during the year.

Two audited statements focus on the financial operations during the period. The first is the activities statement, prepared on the accrual basis of accounting. Independent institutions refer to this report as the statement of activities, while public institutions call it the statement of revenues, expenses, and changes in net position. It is difficult to compare cash-based budget reports to accrual-based activities statements. In addition to the differences caused by the basis of accounting, the formats tend to be very dissimilar.

The other audited statement provides a solution to this problem. It is referred to as the statement of cash flows by both independent and public institutions. As the name implies, this report focuses on cash rather than accruals. For this reason, it's the ideal statement to use for budgetary comparisons following the end of the fiscal year.

Relatively few institutions use the statement of cash flows in any meaningful way. Instead, they present the accrual-basis activities statement and expect the board to accept it as evidence of how well the budget worked to guide the institution's operations. But measurement and format differences make this an apples-to-oranges comparison.

Other institutions recognize that the board is better served if the statement of cash flows is reconciled to the final budget for the year. Because the final budget is in the same format that board members have seen throughout the year, they will readily understand it. This enables management to explain the variances between the original approved budget, any authorized revisions, and the final official audited financial statements for the year—a critical step in the board satisfying its fiduciary responsibilities.

REPORTING FORMATS

Standard reporting formats for independent institutions do not require the presentation of an "operating measure"—the subtotal in a financial statement indicating whether the operating activities generated a net surplus or deficit. Many independent institutions provide an operating measure, but others elect merely to show the increase or decrease in net assets. Accounting standards require institutions presenting an operating measure to explain the measure in the notes to the financial statements if the details of what is included or excluded are not clear, as presented on the statement of activities. Beginning in fiscal year 2018–19, independent institutions will be required to provide additional information about board actions that affect the use of resources and the operating measure either on the statement of activities or in the notes.[218]

The failure to present an operating measure, though allowable, masks some aspects of the institution's performance. The change in net assets addresses the issue of whether the institution is better off at the end of the year than at the beginning, but it doesn't demonstrate whether operating revenues are adequate to finance operating expenses. By their nature, nonoperating revenues are less predictable and may be less sustainable. Relying on them to offset structural deficits is a risky proposition.

Public institutions face a different problem. The prescribed reporting format requires them to present an operating measure but, from a management perspective, the measure is meaningless. Because they are precluded from treating certain revenue categories as operating revenues—even categories that support operations—public institutions are all but guaranteed to report an operating loss (deficit).

The three revenue categories that support operations—but must be reported as nonoperating—are nonendowment gifts, governmental operating appropriations, and investment income. The appropriations, in particular, represent a substantial resource used to underwrite operating expenses. Excluding this from the determination of the operating measure makes the statement of revenues, expenses, and changes in net position grossly misleading. Because of this situation, the vast majority of public institutions supplement their audited financial statements with analysis demonstrating whether they generated an operating surplus or deficit.

It is noteworthy that, as this edition is being written, the GASB has issued a document indicating that a change is under consideration. As part of its standards-setting process, the GASB is soliciting feedback on a proposal to allow organizations like public colleges and universities to present a measure that takes into consideration two of the three revenue categories. Along with nonoperating grants (e.g., Pell Grants), both appropriations for operations and nonendowment gifts would be classified as noncapital subsidies and included in the determination of "operating income or loss and noncapital subsidies." If this becomes a standard, many public institutions would report a surplus via this measure in most years. It must be recognized, however, that this is a proposal and may go through major changes before it would be issued as a final standard.[219]

KEY POINTS

▶ Budgets are not subject to accounting rules in the same way that audited financial statements are. Budgets usually focus on cash, while audited financial statements must be prepared using accrual accounting principles.

▶ Most financial aid is received by the institution and counted as one type of revenue (gifts, endowment income, or governmental grants). If applied against amounts owed by the student for tuition, housing, dining, etc., the financial aid reduces the appropriate revenue that is recognized.

▶ The accounting rules for public institutions differ from those applicable to independent institutions. Different measurement principles may lead to misleading conclusions when comparing financial information for public colleges and universities with that of their independent counterparts.

APPENDIX B: INSIGHTS FOR CANADIAN READERS

This book focuses on North American English-speaking higher education, with particular emphasis on education in the United States. Still, the majority of the content is just as relevant to Canadian higher education as it is to U.S. higher education. This appendix serves as a guide for Canadian readers who may wish to skip sections that are particularly U.S.-centric without a parallel in Canada. It is organized to match the chapter sequence in the main body of the book. The information below follows that structure and highlights differences between U.S. and Canadian higher education and suggests sections that may not be relevant to Canada. Students of higher education, however, may want to read those sections to gain a deeper understanding of the U.S. higher education environment.

Although their higher education systems are strikingly similar in many ways—including most operational characteristics—they vary dramatically in size. Currently, there are 237 colleges and universities operating in Canada[220], while as of 2016, there were 3,321 public and independent institutions operating in the United States.[221] For fiscal year 2014–15, Canadian enrollment was 2.1 million students[222] and U.S. enrollment in public and independent institutions was 18.6 million students.[223] The average enrollment of 8,700 per Canadian institution is more than 50 percent larger than the 5,600 average enrollment at U.S. institutions.

Expenses reported by Canadian institutions for fiscal year 2015-16 were CAN$34.6 billion,[224] equivalent to US$26.6 billion at the average exchange rate for the period.[225] Expenses for U.S. public and independent institutions totaled US$543.4 billion during the same period. On the revenue side, Canadian institutions generated revenues of CAN$34.8 billion,[226] equivalent to US$26.6 billion using the same exchange rate. The revenues for U.S. public and independent institutions totaled US$547 billion during the same period.

The preface serves as an introduction to the book and explains its structure and approach. It describes the book's sections and serves as a high-level road map for what's to follow. Chapter 1 begins the dive into budgeting and explains why it is worthwhile, the roles a budget can play, and the types of budgets typically encountered. The chapter also establishes the premise that budgeting is the second major step—after planning—in the effort to achieve institutional effectiveness. Everything in these sections would be equally applicable to Canadian readers.

Chapter 2, addressing the political and regulatory environment, is where things start to diverge between the United States and Canada. Canadian readers will understand that they also are subject to political and regulatory forces. The main difference is the impact and source of those forces. The U.S. political environment has created instability for higher education institutions due to uncertainty about policies, especially since the national election in 2016. Historically, the situation has been more stable and predictable in Canada. It should be noted, however, that the provincial government of Ontario triggered significant unrest and concern when it unilaterally imposed a 10 percent rollback of tuition without advance warning.[227]

There are several significant differences between the organization and structure of higher education in Canada and the United States. First and foremost, the overwhelming majority of students in Canada are attending public colleges, polytechnics, and universities. Moreover, these institutions were established through provincial or territorial legislation. There are a relatively small number of independent institutions, many of which are religiously affiliated. Overall, as mentioned above, both the number of higher education institutions operating in Canada and the number of students they serve are much smaller than in the United States.

Canada does not have a comparable organization to the U.S. Department of Education. This department is part of the executive branch of the U.S. federal government and exerts significant influence on every U.S. college and university. Also influencing U.S. colleges and universities are the 50 states, four territories, and the District of Columbia. Each of these entities has a distinct approach to higher education, causing public institutions to operate differently across the United States. Canadian institutions, though not influenced by a large federal agency focused on higher education, must pay attention to one of 10 provinces or three territories. Each of these entities influences how higher education is conducted in the respective province or territory.

As mentioned above, there are parallels for Canadian and U.S. institutions in that they both must pay attention to federal laws applicable to all organizations operating in their respective country. They also are subject to various laws, regulations, policies, etc. promulgated by their respective state, provincial, or territorial governments. However, there is one major difference in Canada. For the most part, U.S. federal laws trump state or local laws. If the federal government has established laws governing conduct in a specific area, contradictory state or local laws will not be enforceable. The same is not true in Canada. The application of Canadian federal laws is subject to interpretation by the provinces and territories. The U.S. laws listed in Chapter 2 address many issues covered by similar Canadian laws; what's different is the influence that provincial regulations have on the way the laws are applied. Readers should understand that the principles discussed in Chapter 2 have relevance in Canada, but the specific laws and regulations—along with the politics—are markedly different.

It's also worth mentioning the Canadian approach to underserved populations. One of the more significant factors affecting Canada's approach to underserved populations is the Truth and Reconciliation Commission of Canada.[228] The commission was active from 2008 to 2015, and its calls to action continue to influence Canadian higher education to this day. As described earlier, the United States has a fragmented approach that results in traditional colleges and universities, HBCUs, HSIs, and TCUs all seeking to address the needs of various underserved or marginalized populations. Additionally, the United States has special federal funding programs targeted to each of these groups—either directly or through colleges and universities.

Similar to the United States—where the bulk of the effort occurs in specific parts of the country, primarily the South and West—Canada's efforts are focused primarily (though not exclusively) in Western Canada. Approximately 35 colleges, polytechnics, and universities have been established in Canada to serve indigenous peoples—some as far east as Ontario. The majority of these institutions receive special funding from their respective province or territory. Beyond these institutions are the traditional Canadian colleges and universities that seek to attract indigenous populations and, therefore, have undertaken special programming focused on their needs and interests.

Although there is some targeted governmental financial support in the Western provinces, for the most part, these programs are financed from institutional resources.

The focus in Chapter 3 shifts from politics and rules to the economic factors influencing higher education. Once again, there are some differences but not so many as to make the chapter irrelevant to Canadian readers. In fact, most of the economic forces operating in the United States are similar to those in Canada. Issues related to sustainability, technology, the built environment, competition, labor, shifts in provincial/territorial funding, etc. are just as significant in Canada as in the United States.

Moreover, some topics that are addressed in the chapter have even more significance in Canada. For instance, while unions are a factor in the United States, they are much more prevalent across Canadian higher education, where approximately 80 percent of university faculty are covered by collective-bargaining agreements.[229] Similarly, because of the dependence on provincial/territorial funding, this is of greater concern to Canadian institutions. This is not to say it's not relevant in the United States, but U.S. institutions have more diverse revenue streams than their Canadian counterparts.

Other topics have somewhat less relevance in Canada than in the United States. Examples include shifts in federal funding (due to greater reliance on provincial/territorial funding), philanthropy, and demographic changes. Because Canada does not have a parallel to the U.S. Department of Education, the primary federal impact that Canadian institutions would feel relates to research funding—discussed below. However, the federal government plays a role in student aid both generally and, more specifically, for First Nations people. Philanthropy is changing in Canada, with most institutions now focusing on fundraising, but it is not as well rooted in Canadian culture as it is in the United States.

The portions of Chapter 4 that examine the relative reliance on types of revenue for the public, independent, and for-profit sectors probably will not have much relevance for those interested solely in Canadian higher education. However, the discussion of the various revenue sources will be valuable because, with a few notable exceptions, the operational factors do not change when one crosses the border between Canada and the United States. Terminology is different in some cases such as with Canada's ancillary operations versus the United States' auxiliary enterprises as terms describing the self-supporting activities serving students, faculty, staff, and—to a lesser extent—the general public. Apart from federal appropriations, nonfederal research funding, and the revenue implications of NCAA Division I athletics, the categories of revenue received by Canadian institutions mirror those of U.S. institutions. Scale is a differentiating factor though—particularly with respect to federal funding of research.

While the United States has multiple major federal entities supporting sponsored research such as HHS, NSF, DOD, etc., Canada relies on only three major federal funding agencies. The total support from U.S. federal agencies in fiscal year 2015-16 was US$34.5 billion.[230] The comparable amount for Canada was CAN$3.0 billion.[231] The support was provided primarily by three different agencies. The agencies included the Canadian Institutes of Health Research (CIHR), the National Science and Engineering Research Council (NSERC), and the Social Sciences and Humanities Research Council (SSHRC). The CIHR's portfolio is equivalent to that of the United States' NIH, while the NSERC's focus is similar to the United States' NSF. The SSHRC does not have a single counterpart in the United States, as its portfolio would align with multiple federal agencies sponsoring research in the social sciences and humanities.

Apart from the scale and structure differences between research in the United States and Canada, there are two significant operational differences. As suggested earlier, faculty in the United States routinely use federal sponsored programs' funding to cover some or all of their salaries, freeing up institutional resources for other purposes. This is not possible with resources provided by the CIHR, NSERC, or SSHRC. Additionally, although the three Canadian research agencies provide some support to cover institutional overhead related to research, the amounts are significantly lower than the costs actually incurred by the institutions. This is true in the United States as well, but the gap is considerably larger in Canada, requiring a greater relative investment by institutions to support research.

Much of Chapter 5 will be relevant to those focused on Canadian higher education. The critical processes of attracting, retaining, and serving students operate very similarly whether in Canada or the United States. A major difference, however, is financial aid. In fact, nearly all discussion of financial aid will have little to no relevance to those focused on Canadian higher education. Although many Canadian students finance their education through loans, including government loans, the mechanisms and programs are quite different. Similarly, there are some grant programs benefiting students—either from the province/territory, the institution's resources, or its endowment—but these are not nearly as significant as they are in the United States. Another difference relates to tuition setting. Despite some limited exceptions, the vast majority of Canadian institutions are subject to provincial/territorial control when it comes to setting tuition rates. Some of the practices prevalent in the United States—for instance, differential pricing and tuition discounting—occur in Canada but not to the levels experienced in the United States. Ignoring these few exceptions, the remainder of the chapter is directly relevant for Canadian higher education.

Chapter 6 parallels Chapter 4 in that the discussion of the relative levels of expenses probably has no relevance for Canadian higher education. However, with the exception of student financial aid and independent operations, Canadian institutions incur expenses in the same programmatic categories as in the United States. Because Canadian financial statements tend to present expenses by natural classification, without corresponding matrices to indicate the respective share of programmatic expenses, the programmatic discussion would be relevant only for understanding the nature of the categories.

The remaining chapters in the book all are relevant to those interested in Canadian higher education—some more than others. Though there are a few isolated differences, the guidance provided in these chapters would be directly transportable to north of the border. For instance, the recommended structure for and types of planning addressed in Chapter 7 are just as relevant for Canadian institutions as they are for U.S. institutions. In fact, the only significant difference is that some Canadian institutions favor longer strategic plans than the five-year plans more prevalent in the United States.

Another difference that shows up in Chapter 7 is accreditation. The U.S. system of higher education relies heavily on the regional accreditors that provide the stamp of approval authorizing U.S. institutions to participate in federal financial aid programs. Due to the lack of a similar federal financial aid system, Canadian institutions are not subjected to an equivalent comprehensive accreditation process. The remaining content of Chapter 7 is directly applicable to Canadian higher education.

Chapter 8 focuses on the budget process and, just as for public institutions in the United States, provincial/territorial requirements weigh heavily. In the same way that it's impractical to discuss all the variations seen across the United States, it doesn't make sense to try to describe the disparate practices among the 13 provinces and territories. Suffice it to say that there are a number of process differences dictated by the respective governments.

Also addressed in this chapter is the role of various stakeholder groups. One of the unique features about Canadian higher education institutions is that nearly all of them are established through legislation. Moreover, it's almost universal that specific stakeholder groups (e.g., boards, faculty, students) are invested with shared governance authority. This can play a significant role in the process for developing and gaining approval of a budget. Just as public institutions in the United States must comply with state requirements, Canadian institutions must adhere to the relevant provincial/territorial requirements when developing their budgets. The basic approach presented in Chapter 8 can be amended to incorporate these requirements.

Finally, with respect to Chapter 8, the impact of institutional character is highlighted throughout the chapter. Most importantly, there is discussion about a change in character. This can come from various factors, and one that is particularly relevant to colleges in Canada is movement toward either university or polytechnic status. Unlike the United States, where there may be no meaningful distinction between the missions of a large complex college and a smaller, comprehensive university, the distinctions among institutions in Canada are more well-defined.

Canadian colleges are akin to community and technical colleges in the United States and tend to focus on two- or three-year diploma and certificate programs in both academic and vocational fields. Polytechnics share characteristics of both Canadian colleges and universities with their focus on skills-intensive and technology-based programs typically leading to a bachelor's degree. Unlike colleges and universities in Canada, few polytechnics include that term in their names. Instead, most identify as colleges. Canadian universities parallel universities in the United States. They run the gamut from research-intensive universities (e.g., the U-15 Group of Canadian Research Universities similar to the Association of American Universities) to universities similar to the New American Colleges and Universities, along with everything in between.

There are no substantive variations between Canadian and U.S. institutions relevant to Chapter 9, which focuses on the various budget models seen in U.S. higher education. Canadian institutions are just as prone to rely on hybrid budget models incorporating elements of the previously discussed comprehensive and special-purpose budget models. Similarly, the various steps outlined for operating and capital budgeting in Chapter 10 would work equally well in Canada as in the United States. The key trigger for deviations from the cycles presented would be the provincial/territorial requirements and their impact on the budget calendars.

Chapter 11 is another chapter that has general applicability for both U.S. and Canadian institutions. The one exception is the discussion of UPMIFA. These uniform laws are unique to the United States, and there do not appear to be equivalent laws in Canada, although various provincial/territorial laws may exist to guide the management and spending of endowments. For the most part, Chapter 12, addressing the impact of institutional policies on budgeting, is equally applicable to Canadian and U.S. institutions. A few of the topics—e.g., overhead recovery on research grants, financial aid—are relevant but do not represent as big an issue. Other issues are of significant importance in Canada. Topics of particular interest to Canadian institutions are the academic policies that could be the subject of negotiation during collective bargaining. Such issues could include reliance on part-time and temporary faculty, utilization of graduate assistantships, sabbaticals, and many more.

Chapter 13 may be the chapter of least relevance to Canadian institutions—for one reason. With most institutions being publicly supported and operating under authority granted by a provincial or territorial government, it's highly unlikely that the government would sit idly by as an institution descended into serious financial distress. Yes, it's possible that a Canadian institution could experience financial difficulties due to labor strife, poor management, shifting demographics, general economic turmoil, or provincial action such as that described above in Ontario. But the majority of them have sufficient enrollment that they likely would be able to contract operations to avoid serious disruption due to resource insufficiency. Nevertheless, readers are encouraged to read the sections devoted to SRA, the Balanced Scorecard, program review, etc. Each of these models can help an institution ensure that its offerings remain vibrant and responsive to student interests while also demonstrating that the administrative and support investments are serving the needs of the institution.

The final chapter, Chapter 14, presents the closing thoughts and reinforces the most important points presented throughout the book. It has equal relevance for those interested in U.S. and Canadian higher education. Appendix A is focused on GAAP for U.S. organizations but may be of interest to those primarily focused on Canadian higher education as well. With the exception of the coverage of financial aid and its impact on reporting tuition revenues, most of the appendix's content has relevance to Canadian institutions.

KEY POINTS

▶ The book's focus is North American English-speaking higher education with a primary emphasis on U.S. higher education.

▶ The majority of the text is relevant to both the United States and Canada; however, some chapters are less relevant to those readers primarily interested in Canadian higher education.

▶ Information has been provided to highlight the relevant differences between U.S. and Canadian higher education.

GLOSSARY

Accrual. An accounting measurement method that ignores whether cash has been received or paid. Revenues are recognized and recorded when earned. Expenses are recognized and recorded when incurred and measurable.

All-funds budgeting. A budgeting model that encompasses all resources, including those that may be subject to restrictions (such as gifts or endowment income).

Amortization. The allocation of the cost of intangible assets to multiple periods. The intangible asset's cost is divided by the number of periods the asset is expected to provide benefit. The resulting amount is treated as an expense during each period.

Appropriation. Allocation of funds from a governmental entity to an institution for operating or capital purposes.

Auxiliary enterprises. Self-supporting campus-based activities that provide services to students, faculty, and staff. Examples include dining operations, residence halls, and bookstores.

Base-budget funds. The portion of an operating budget that covers ongoing recurring activities. Also called continuing budget. Contrast with *one-time budget funds*.

Bottom up. A budgeting philosophy that involves decentralized decision-making, starting at the most basic unit level.

Budget cycle. The series of scheduled events that must occur to develop a budget and complete the activities supported by the budget.

Built environment. The collection of buildings, roads, sidewalks, infrastructure, etc. representing the long-lived physical assets of an organization.

Capital assets. Physical resources with a cost (or fair market value, if donated) exceeding an established dollar threshold that are expected to provide service for more than a single year. Unless the resources are expected to maintain or increase their value over time, the cost of the assets is allocated to the benefiting periods through amortization or depreciation. Examples include land, buildings, equipment, and leasehold improvements.

Capital budgeting. The process used to identify and monitor resources and investments related to large-dollar projects undertaken either to acquire, construct, or improve capital assets such as buildings.

Capitalization. The process of recording expenditures for long-term resources as assets rather than as expenses. Expenses are recognized as costs of a particular period, while capital assets' costs are recognized over time through amortization or depreciation.

Carryforward. The ability to use unspent budget resources from one fiscal period in a subsequent fiscal period. Also called carryover.

Charge-back. A process by which campus service units charge other campus units for services they receive. Examples include physical plant and information technology.

Commonfund Higher Education Price Index (HEPI). An inflation index maintained by the Commonfund Institute that tracks higher education cost drivers. Contrast with *Higher Education Cost Adjustment*.

Cost center. An organizational unit that incurs expenses but does not generate revenues. Contrast with *revenue center*.

Cost shifting. The practice of forcing units to pay for goods or services, which were previously funded centrally, without providing the resources needed to pay for the goods or services.

Debt service. The combined principal and interest amounts paid annually to bondholders.

Deferred maintenance. The cumulative value of scheduled or routine maintenance and repairs for the built environment that an organization chooses not to undertake when originally scheduled or needed (frequently due to financial constraints).

Depreciation. The allocation of the cost of tangible assets to multiple periods. The tangible asset's cost (or fair value if donated) is divided by the number of periods the asset is expected to provide benefit. The resulting amount is treated as an expense during each period.

Designated funds. Unrestricted resources that the governing board or management has reserved for specific purposes. Contrast with *restricted funds*.

Direct costs. Costs that can be identified with a particular project or activity.

Endowment. A gift carrying a stipulation that the principal be invested in perpetuity, with the investment income generated by the gift being available for program support or other purposes. Income from restricted endowments supports specific programs identified by the donor, while income from unrestricted endowments may be used for any institutional purpose. True endowments are gifts of principal that may never be expended. Term endowments require that the principal be maintained and invested until a specified time passes or a specific event occurs. Quasi-endowments are resources set aside by an institution's governing board and combined with true and term endowments for investment purposes, with only the investment income available for use. Unlike true or term endowment principal, the principal of quasi-endowments can be expended at the governing board's discretion.

Endowment income. Revenue earned by investing endowment principal, typically in stocks, bonds, and other investments. The revenue consists of dividends, interest, rents, royalties, unrealized appreciation, and realized gains from the sale of stocks, bonds, or other investments. Typically, only a portion of the earned income is made available for spending in a given fiscal year.

Facilities and administrative (F&A) costs. The portion of a sponsored program award that reimburses the institution for support costs incurred for the project. Also called indirect costs or overhead.

Financial exigency. A severe financial crisis that fundamentally compromises the academic integrity of the institution as a whole and that cannot be alleviated by less drastic means. (Source: American Association of University Professors Policy Documents and Reports, "The Role of the Faculty in Conditions of Financial Exigency.")

Fiscal year. A 12-month period representing one operating cycle.

Fixed costs. Costs incurred irrespective of volume. Contrast with *variable costs* and *semi-variable costs*.

Formula budgeting. A budget strategy that relies on quantitative measures to distribute resources. Typical measures include student full-time equivalents, employee full-time equivalents, and assignable square feet.

Full-time equivalent (FTE). A method for converting the number of part-time individuals (e.g., students or faculty) into a standard equating to full-time status. For example, 30 students each taking six credit hours would equal 12 FTE students if the standard for full-time status is 15 credit hours. Contrast with *head count*.

Functional classification. A method of categorizing expenses based on their purpose rather than the nature of the expense. Examples include instruction, research, and academic support.

Furlough. Unpaid time off from work that employees are required to take as a cost-saving measure. Furloughs are usually of short duration (e.g., several days or a week).

Generally accepted accounting principles (GAAP). The standards that must be adhered to when preparing financial statements that will be subject to an independent audit.

Head count. The total number of full- and part-time individuals in a given category (e.g., students or faculty). Contrast with *full-time equivalent*.

Higher Education Cost Adjustment (HECA). An inflation index maintained by the State Higher Education Executive Officers that tracks higher education cost drivers. Contrast with the *Commonfund Higher Education Price Index*.

Hybrid budgeting. A budget strategy that blends elements of various discrete budget strategies (e.g., responsibility center, zero-based) to allocate an institution's resources.

Incremental/decremental budgeting. A budget strategy that focuses on percentage adjustments to the existing base budget rather than on specific priorities.

Indirect costs. Costs incurred for multiple purposes and, therefore, cannot be linked to a particular project or activity.

Infrastructural plans. Long-term (three- to four-year) plans that guide the institution's operational activities. Such plans focus on core programmatic activities (e.g., academics, student engagement) or essential campus-wide support activities (e.g., facilities, information technology).

Infrastructure. The foundational assets and resources needed to operate a college or university. Some assets are tangible (e.g., roadways, steam tunnels, computer system cables), while others are intangible (e.g., systems, policies, procedures).

Initiative-based budgeting (IBB). A budget strategy that focuses on distributing resources to support specific priorities established during the planning process. Typically, such resources are not part of the base budget.

Lapsed salary. The portion of salary recaptured centrally when departments choose not to fill a vacant position or hire a replacement at a lower salary. Also called salary savings.

Line-item budgeting. A type of budgetary control under which resources are distributed in detailed categories such as salaries, travel, and contractual services, with a requirement that funds be spent within those categories unless authorization is obtained.

Master plan. A depiction of the planned physical development of a campus, usually identifying existing boundaries and facilities as well as planned additions. Also called campus master plan.

Merit aid. Financial aid awarded to a student based on criteria other than demonstrated financial need. Frequently, merit aid is based on accomplishments in the classroom or on special skills or talents. Contrast with *need-based aid*.

Natural classification. A method of categorizing expenses by the type of expense rather than the purpose for which the expense is incurred. Examples include salaries, benefits, supplies, and travel.

Need-based aid. Financial aid awarded to a student solely on the basis of demonstrated financial need, as determined using an established methodology. Need can be met either with federal student aid programs or with institutional funds. Contrast with *merit aid*.

One-time budget funds. The portion of an operating budget that covers nonrecurring activities. Contrast with *base-budget funds*.

Operating budget. The quantitative manifestation of an organization's (or one of its subunits') planned revenues, expenses, and contributions or withdrawals from reserves during a fiscal period (usually one year). Operating budgets typically are supported by narrative documents identifying priorities and, in some cases, performance standards related to the various activities and programs to be supported by the budget.

Outsourcing. Contracting with a third party to provide required on-campus services. Fairly common for bookstores and dining operations, outsourcing can extend to a wide range of services such as housekeeping, arena management, and various aspects of technology.

Overload. The additional workload of a faculty member in excess of the requirements for his or her normal full-time academic appointment. Also refers to the additional compensation provided for the additional effort.

Performance-based budgeting (PBB). A budget strategy that relies on the establishment of specific institutional performance objectives to justify a portion of base-budget resources or incremental resources.

Reallocation. A process through which managers of programs and activities identify a portion of existing resources to return to central administration for redistribution in accordance with established priorities.

Reserves. Funds set aside as savings in accordance with organizational plans. Reserves frequently are designated for specific purposes, such as facilities maintenance and renewal, quasi-endowment, or a rainy-day fund.

Responsibility center budgeting (RCB). A budget strategy that treats individual units and programs as revenue centers or cost centers. Revenue centers are allowed to control the revenues they generate and are responsible for financing both their direct and indirect expenses. Cost centers are supported by centrally owned revenues, resources generated through charge-backs to benefiting units, assessments on the revenues generated by revenue centers, or by centrally administered allocations.

Restricted funds. Resources provided by external sources that must be retained and invested or expended in accordance with stipulations established by the provider. Under existing accounting rules, only donors can establish restrictions for independent institutions, while any external party (such as a donor, a creditor, or another government) can create restrictions for public institutions. Contrast with *designated funds* and *unrestricted funds*.

Retrenchment. Actions undertaken in response to serious financial difficulties; frequently includes elimination or reduction of programs and activities.

Revenue center. An organizational unit with the ability to generate revenues by direct action. Contrast with *cost center*.

Semi-variable costs. A refinement of variable costs that combines features of fixed and variable costs. They remain fixed within ranges but are affected by changes in volume. Contrast with *fixed costs* and *variable costs*.

Shared governance. The practice at many colleges and universities through which institutional governance is provided collaboratively by the governing board, management, and faculty (and, in some instances, students). The level of involvement for each stakeholder group varies depending on the issue. The practice typically involves collaboration but not always decision-making. Faculty, for instance, may have primary responsibility for most facets of curriculum, but the board may still have final authority over which programs will be offered.

Shared services. The practice of establishing decentralized support operations to serve multiple units or specific geographical areas of a campus with the objective of gaining efficiencies and reducing administrative costs.

The term also can refer to the practice of multiple institutions relying on a specific support service and sharing the costs for the service. In addition to the objectives for internal shared services, shared services across institutional boundaries can reduce costs through economies of scale.

Spending rate. The portion of resources related to each endowment fund that is made available for spending in a given fiscal year. Usually expressed as a percentage, the amount typically includes both current investment yield (e.g., dividends and interest) as well as a portion of accumulated appreciation and realized gains. Also called payout rate.

Sponsored program. An agreement between an institution and an external entity (such as a federal agency, corporation, or foundation) under which the former undertakes an activity with financial support from the latter. The agreement specifies what will be accomplished and identifies the amounts and types of costs that will be reimbursed.

Strategic resource allocation. A comprehensive process through which investments in academic programs and support functions are classified, using holistic criteria, into categories relating to future resource deployment.

Structural deficit. The amount by which operating expenses exceed operating revenues.

Top down. A budgeting philosophy that involves highly centralized decision-making, with most direction filtering down through the organizational hierarchy from central administrative offices.

Tuition dependency. Excessive reliance on tuition and required fees to finance operations, especially when the tuition generated is not from a diverse population of students. An institution is tuition dependent if 85 percent or more of its revenue come from enrollment-related revenues such as tuition, required fees, state appropriation (when linked to enrollment), etc.

Tuition discounting. The practice of using institutional resources to award financial aid, thereby lowering the cost of attendance for selected students. Although the aid can address demonstrated financial need, it frequently is awarded on a merit basis.

Underwater endowments. Endowments with a current market value that is lower than the original value of the gift(s) that established the endowment.

Unrestricted funds. Institutional resources that can be used for any purpose consistent with and supportive of the overall purpose of the organization. Contrast with *designated funds* and *restricted funds.*

Variable costs. Costs that vary directly with increases or decreases in volume. Contrast with *fixed costs* and *semi-variable costs.*

Zero-based budgeting (ZBB). A budget strategy that requires programs and activities to rationalize their use of resources based on accomplishments.

ANNOTATED BIBLIOGRAPHY

Banta, Trudy W., and Catherine A. Palomba. *Assessment Essentials: Planning, Implementing, and Improving Assessment in Higher Education.* 2nd ed. San Francisco: Jossey-Bass, 2015.

> This is the second edition of the authoritative treatise on higher education outcomes assessment. Written by two of higher education's leading authorities on assessment, the volume provides a road map to the establishment of an effective assessment environment and related processes. As suggested in the title, it covers the essentials from defining assessment and engaging participation by faculty and students to developing direct measures. This is supplemented with indirect assessment and the examination of other areas such as student affairs and other central operations.

Barr, Margaret J., and George S. McClellan. *Budgets and Financial Management in Higher Education.* 2nd ed. San Francisco: Jossey-Bass, 2018.

> This is the second edition of a book focusing on budgeting from the perspective of a budget manager in a support unit. In addition to very solid information directed at individuals who are new to the responsibilities of a budget manager, the book includes an excellent discussion of budget-related issues relevant to auxiliary enterprises and capital budgets. Running throughout the book is a case to illustrate many points relevant to budgeting.

Chabotar, Kent John. *Strategic Finance: Planning and Budgeting for Boards, Chief Executives, and Finance Officers.* Washington: Association of Governing Boards of Universities and Colleges, 2006.

> This book is written as a high-level guide to the critical tasks of planning and budgeting. It offers insights about strategic plans, what they should include, and how they can be developed. It highlights the importance of supporting a strategic plan with a financial plan and then linking both to the annual budgeting process. The book is full of useful charts and tables to illustrate the key concepts and also includes a case to illustrate the application of the concepts.

Curry, John R., Andrew L. Laws, and Jon C. Strauss. *Responsibility Center Management: A Guide to Balancing Academic Entrepreneurship with Fiscal Responsibility*. Washington: NACUBO, 2013.

> This book is a primer on responsibility center management (RCM) and addresses its key principles, benefits, and operational considerations, along with an assessment of how RCM operates today as compared with the authors' previous writings covering the 25-year period ending in 2002. Of significant value in this volume are nine case studies.

Dickeson, Robert C. *Prioritizing Academic Programs and Services: Reallocating Resources to Achieve Strategic Balance*. San Francisco: Jossey-Bass, 2010.

> This is the "bible" of prioritization, providing the road map for conducting the prioritization process on campus. It describes the process from start to finish (i.e., implementation) and offers suggested criteria for prioritizing both academic and administrative programs and activities. The appendices are particularly rich with examples and additional resources.

Dickmeyer, Nathan. *Budgets and Budgeting for College and University Department Chairs: How to Maximize Department Resources*. Briarcliff Manor: Chelmsford Press, 2013.

> This book is directed at academic department heads, particularly those who are new to the role and seek to understand how to succeed in obtaining increased resources. Focused primarily on academics, it explains departmental, grant, project, and capital budgets in the context of the university budget and its financial statements. The book includes two appendices—one focused on budgeting systems and the other on financial statements.

Middaugh, Michael F. *Planning and Assessment in Higher Education: Demonstrating Institutional Effectiveness*. San Francisco: Jossey-Bass, 2010.

> The reference to planning in this title is off target because the book really does not address planning. Nevertheless, it does an excellent job of explaining assessment and institutional effectiveness in terms easily understood by those not working in institutional research. In particular,

Middaugh provides wonderful information about communicating the results of assessment so as not to overwhelm the audience.

Sanaghan, Patrick. *Collaborative Strategic Planning in Higher Education.* Washington: NACUBO, 2009.

This is a "how to" publication for those interested in conducting or participating in engaged, collaborative strategic planning. It offers insights about creating opportunities for effective group interaction and describes a five-phase process for developing a strategic plan that actually can be implemented. Although the book is focused on *strategic* planning, the approaches and activities can be applied to nearly any type of planning—whether infrastructural or operational. This is a true user's guide for effective planning.

Sevier, Robert A., Ronald P. Mahurin, and Becky L. Morehouse. *Vision-Centric Strategic Planning for Colleges and Universities: A Thoughtful Guide to Strategy Formation and Execution.* Hiawatha: Strategy Publishing, 2015.

This is a "how to" publication focused on strategic planning. It presents a model that is vision-centric, market driven, and highly inclusive. It replaces the traditional strengths, weaknesses, opportunities, and threats (SWOTs) with barriers, opportunities, and competitive advantages. Numerous resources are included such as a planning retreat design, assessment questions, and planning worksheets.

Snyder, Thomas D., Cristobal de Brey, and Sally A. Dillow. *Digest of Education Statistics 2016* (NCES 2017-094). Washington: National Center for Education Statistics, Institute of Education Sciences, U.S. Department of Education, 2018.

This is the definitive source for data about higher education. Chapter 3, focused on postsecondary education, contains nearly 250 pages of narrative, tables, and charts addressing a wide range of higher education issues such as enrollment, staffing, degrees, finances, and financial aid.

Strauss, Jon C., and John R. Curry. *Responsibility Center Management: Lessons from 25 Years of Decentralized Management.* Washington: NACUBO, 2002.

This short publication provides a useful overview of the key issues related to RCM. It discusses both planning and budgeting in an RCM environment. Additionally, it provides guidelines for developing and implementing resource-allocation processes based on RCM principles. Finally, and potentially most valuable, it tackles the criticisms of RCM and offers responses to each of them.

Tahey, Phil, Ron Salluzzo, Fred Prager, Lou Mezzina, and Chris Cowen. *Strategic Financial Analysis for Higher Education.* 7th ed. San Francisco: Prager, Sealy & Co., LLC, KPMG LLP, and Attain LLC, 2010.

This publication continues the series begun in 1982 by Peat, Marwick, Mitchell & Co., the predecessor firm of KPMG. It examines ratio analysis for higher education, including the Composite Financial Index, as well as other strategic financial analysis tools focused on resource allocation. The seventh edition expands the analysis of strategic financial risks and offers an extensive discussion of liquidity, including the suggestion of a ratio for measuring liquidity risk.

Tahey, Phil, Ron Salluzzo, et al. *Update to the 7th Edition of Strategic Financial Analysis for Higher Education.* San Francisco: Prager, Sealy & Co., LLC, KPMG LLP, and Attain LLC, 2016.

This publication continues the series begun in 1982 by Peat, Marwick, Mitchell & Co., the predecessor firm of KPMG. The focus of this update is correcting misconceptions that have arisen since publication of the seventh edition and also addressing questions about the impact of newly released accounting standards.

Whalen, Edward L. *Responsibility Center Budgeting: An Approach to Decentralized Management for Institutions of Higher Education.* Bloomington: Indiana University Press, 1991.

This book provides an in-depth examination of Indiana University's (IU's) approach to developing and implementing a system of responsibility center budgeting (RCB). It provides the details of the decision-making process, the lessons learned, and offers insights that can be applied at other institutions pursuing RCB. IU may have the most complex cost-allocation model in higher education, and the book includes an appendix containing a detailed explanation of its development. Additional value is provided by John Curry's afterword addressing the University of Southern California's experience with RCB.

ABOUT THE AUTHOR

Larry Goldstein is president of Campus Strategies, LLC—a management consulting firm providing services to colleges and universities as well as organizations serving higher education. He previously served as NACUBO's senior vice president and treasurer and as the University of Louisville's chief financial officer. His campus experience covered 20 years in financial administration and also included positions with The University of Chicago, the School of the Art Institute of Chicago, and the University of Virginia.

Goldstein, a certified public accountant, earned a bachelor of accountancy degree from Walsh College and a master of science degree from the University of Virginia. He is a recipient of NACUBO's Daniel D. Robinson Award in recognition of his contributions to higher education accounting and financial reporting.

Goldstein lives in Crimora, Virginia (in the Blue Ridge Mountains), with his wife, Sue, two Labrador retrievers—Abby and Lindy—and Marcus the cat. When he's not working or spending time with his family, he usually can be found riding his Harley-Davidson Heritage Softail Classic.

NOTES

1   Adam Harris, "Outlook for Higher Ed in 2018 Is Bleak, Ratings Agency Says." *The Chronicle of Higher Education*, January 23, 2018, accessed October 14, 2018, https://www.chronicle.com/article/Outlook-for-Higher-Ed-in-2018/242319.

2   Cailin Crowe, "Moody's Gives Higher Ed a Negative Outlook, Again." *The Chronicle of Higher Education,* December 4, 2018, accessed December 6, 2018, https://www.chronicle.com/article/Moody-s-Gives-Higher-Ed-a/245258.

3   Pew Research Center, Anna Brown, *Most Americans say higher ed is heading in wrong direction, but partisans disagree why* (Washington, DC: Pew Research Center, 2018).

4   Ibid.

5   The College Board, *Trends in College Pricing 2018* (New York, NY: The College Board, 2018).

6   Ibid.

7   Ibid.

8   U.S. Department of Labor, Bureau of Labor Statistics, "Consumer Price Index for All Urban Consumers (CPI-U)," accessed October 10, 2108, https://www.bls.gov/news.release/cpi.nr0.htm.

9   Commonfund Institute, *Commonfund Higher Education Price Index 2017 Update* (Wilton, CT: Commonfund Institute, 2017).

10 State Higher Education Executive Officers, *The Higher Education Cost Adjustment: A Proposed Tool for Assessing Inflation in Higher Education Costs* (Boulder, CO: State Higher Education Executive Officers, 2017).

11 Congressional Budget Office, *The Budget and Economic Outlook 2018 to 2028,* Tab 1. Revenues, Outlays, Deficits, Surpluses, and Debt Held by the Public Since 1968 (Washington, DC: Congressional Budget Office, 2018).

12   Bureau of the Public Debt, *Monthly Statement of the Public Debt of the United States December 31, 2010* (Washington, DC: Bureau of the Public Debt, 2011).

13   Congressional Budget Office, *The Budget and Economic Outlook 2018 to 2028,* Tab 1. Revenues, Outlays, Deficits, Surpluses, and Debt Held by the Public Since 1968, op cit.

14   Bureau of the Public Debt, *Monthly Statement of the Public Debt of the United States December 31, 2017* (Washington, DC: Bureau of the Public Debt, 2018).

15   National Center for Education Statistics, "Table 334.10. Total expenditures of public degree-granting postsecondary institutions, by purpose and level of institution: 2009-10 through 2015-16," accessed February 11, 2019, https://nces.ed.gov/programs/digest/d17/tables/dt17_334.10.asp?current=yes.

16   National Center for Education Statistics, "Table 334.30. Total expenditures of private nonprofit degree-granting postsecondary institutions, by purpose and level of institution: Selected years, 1999-2000 through 2015-16," accessed February 11, 2019, https://nces.ed.gov/programs/digest/d17/tables/dt17_334.30.asp?current=yes.

17   National Center for Education Statistics, "Table 334.50. Total expenditures of private for-profit degree-granting postsecondary institutions, by purpose and level of institution: Selected years, 1999-2000 through 2015-16," accessed February 11, 2019, https://nces.ed.gov/programs/digest/d17/tables/dt17_334.30.asp?current=yes.

18   The World Bank, "GDP (current US$) – World Bank national accounts data, and OECD national accounts data files," accessed February 11, 2019, https://data.worldbank.org/indicator/NY.GDP.MKTP.CD?locations=US.

19   National Center for Education Statistics, "Table 303.25. Total fall enrollment in degree-granting postsecondary institutions, by control and level of institution: 1970 through 2015," *Digest of Education Statistics 2016* (Washington, DC: National Center for Education Statistics, 2018).

20   National Center for Education Statistics, "Table 317.10. Degree-granting postsecondary institutions, by control and level of institution: Selected years, 1949-50 through 2015-16," *Digest of Education Statistics 2016* (Washington, DC: National Center for Education Statistics, 2011).

21   The Association for the Advancement of Sustainability in Higher Education, *2016 Annual Report* (Philadelphia, PA: 2017).

22   The American Association for the Advancement of Sustainability in Higher Education, "About STARS," STARS, accessed September 25, 2018, https://stars.aashe.org/pages/about/stars-overview.html.

23   National Center for Education Statistics, "Table 314.30. Employees in degree-granting postsecondary institutions, by employment status, sex, control and type of institution, and primary occupation: Fall 2015," *Digest of Education Statistics 2016* (Washington, DC: National Center for Education Statistics, 2018).

24   Ibid.

25   Ibid.

26   Ibid.

27   "2018 Top 10 IT Issues," EDUCAUSE, accessed September 12, 2018, https://www.educause.edu/research-and-publications/research/top-10-it-issues-technologies-and-trends/2018.

28   "Top 10 IT Issues: 2000-2017," EDUCAUSE, accessed September 12, 2018, https://library.educause.edu/~/media/interactive-content/2017-it-issues-trends/index.html.

29 Babson Survey Research Group, I. Elaine Allen, and Jeff Seaman, *Digital Learning Compass: Distance Education Enrollment Report 2017* (Babson Park, MA: Babson Survey Research Group, e-Literate, and WCET, 2017).

30 Ibid.

31 Ibid.

32 Ibid.

33 National Center for Education Statistics, "Table 303.10. Total fall enrollment in degree-granting postsecondary institutions, by attendance status, sex of student, and control of institution: Selected years, 1947 through 2026," *Digest of Education Statistics 2016* (Washington, DC: National Center for Education Statistics, 2018).

34 National Center for Education Statistics, "Table 303.25," *Digest of Education Statistics 2016*, op cit.

35 Ibid.

36 Ibid.

37 Ibid.

38 Western Interstate Commission for Higher Education, *Knocking at the College Door* (Boulder, CO: Western Interstate Commission for Higher Education, 2016, revised 2017).

39 Ibid

40 Ibid.

41 Ibid.

42 Ibid.

43 Ibid.

44 Ibid.

45 Ibid.

46 Ibid.

47 National Center for Education Statistics, "Table 401.10. Federal support and estimated federal tax expenditures for education, by category: Selected fiscal years, 1965 through 2017," accessed March 11, 2019, https://nces.ed.gov/programs/digest/d17/tables/dt17_401.10.asp.

48 Ibid.

49 Ibid.

50 Council for Advancement and Support of Education, *Voluntary Support of Education* (Washington, DC: Council for Advancement and Support of Education, 2019).

51 Ibid.

52 Ibid.

53 Ibid.

54 Ibid.

55 Ibid.

56 National Center for Education Statistics, "Table 317.10," *Digest of Education Statistics 2016*, op. cit.

57 Ibid.

58 Ibid.

59 Ibid.

60 Ibid.

61 National Center for Education Statistics, "Table 303.25," *Digest of Education Statistics 2016*, op. cit.

62 Ibid

63 "Open Doors 2018 'Fast Facts,'" Institute of International Education, accessed November 7, 2018, https://www.iie.org/Research-and-Insights/Open-Doors/Fact-Sheets-and-Infographics/Fast-Facts.

64 Ibid.

65 Ibid.

66 Ibid.

67 Ibid.

68 Ibid.

69 Ibid.

70 Ibid.

71 Ibid.

72 National Center for Education Statistics, "Table 333.10. Revenues of public degree-granting postsecondary institutions, by source of revenue and level of institution: Selected years, 2007-08 through 2015-16," accessed February 11, 2019, https://nces.ed.gov/programs/digest/d17/tables/dt17_333.10.asp?current=yes.

73 Ibid.

74 Ibid.

75 Ibid.

76 Ibid.

77 Ibid.

78 Ibid.

79 Ibid.

80 Ibid.

81 Ibid.

82 Ibid.

83 Ibid.

84 Ibid.

85 Ibid.

86 Ibid.

87 Ibid.

88 Ibid.

89 Ibid.

90 Ibid.

91 Ibid.

92 Ibid.

93 Ibid.

94 Ibid.

95 Ibid.

96 Ibid.

97 Ibid.

98 Ibid.

99 NACUBO & TIAA, *2018 NACUBO-TIAA Study of Endowments* (Washington, DC: NACUBO & TIAA, 2019).

100 Ibid.

101 Ibid.

102 Ibid.

103 Ibid.

104 Ibid.

105 National Center for Education Statistics, "Table 333.10," op. cit.

106 Ibid.

107 Ibid.

108 Ibid.

109 Ibid.

110 Ibid.

111 Ibid.

112 Ibid.

113 Ibid.

114 Ibid.

115 National Center for Education Statistics, "Table 333.40. Total revenue of private nonprofit degree-granting postsecondary institutions, by source of funds and level of institution: Selected years, 1999-2000 through 2015-16," accessed February 11, 2019, https://nces.ed.gov/programs/digest/d17/tables/dt17_333.40.asp?current=yes.

116 Ibid.

117 Ibid.

118 Ibid.

119 Ibid.

120 Ibid.

121 Ibid.

122 Ibid.

123 Ibid.

124 Ibid.

125 Ibid.

126 Ibid.

127 Ibid.

128 Ibid.

129 Ibid.

130 Ibid.

131 Ibid.

132 National Center for Education Statistics, "Table 333.55. Total revenue of private for-profit degree-granting postsecondary institutions, by source of funds and level of institution: Selected years, 1999-2000 through 2015-16," accessed February 11, 2019, https://nces.ed.gov/programs/digest/d17/tables/dt17_333.55.asp?current=yes.

133 Ibid.

134 Ibid.

135 Ibid.

136 Ibid.

137 Ibid.

138 Ibid.

139 Ibid.

140 Ibid.

141 Ibid.

142 Ibid.

143 Ibid.

144 Ibid.

145 Ibid.

146 Ibid.

147 Western Interstate Commission for Higher Education, *Knocking at the College Door,* op. cit.

148 Ibid.

149 National Center for Education Statistics, "Table 331.10. Percentage of undergraduates receiving aid, by type and source of aid and selected student characteristics: 2011-12," *Digest of Education Statistics 2016* (Washington, DC: National Center for Education Statistics, 2018).

150 Ibid.

151 "Education Department Budget History Table: FY 1980—FY 2019 President's Budget," U.S. Department of Education, accessed November 2, 2018, https://www2.ed.gov/about/overview/budget/history/index.html.

152 "Federal Pell Grant— How much money can I get?" Federal Student Aid, accessed November 2, 2018, https://studentaid.ed.gov/sa/types/grants-scholarships/pell#how-much-money.

153 "A Federal Supplemental Educational Opportunity Grant (FSEOG)—How much money can I get?" Federal Student Aid, accessed November 2, 2018, https://studentaid.ed.gov/sa/types/grants-scholarships/fseog#how-much-money.

154 U.S. Department of Education, "Education Department Budget History Table: FY 1980—FY 2019 President's Budget," op. cit.

155 Ibid.

156 Ibid.

157 Ibid.

158 State Higher Education Executive Officers, *State Higher Education Finance FY 2017* (Boulder, CO: State Higher Education Executive Officers, 2018).

159 National Center for Education Statistics, "Table 334.10," op. cit.

160 Ibid.

161 Ibid.

162 Ibid.

163 Ibid.

164 Ibid.

165 Ibid.

166 Ibid.

167 Ibid.

168 Ibid.

169 Ibid.

170 Ibid.

171 Ibid.

172 Ibid.

173 Ibid.

174 Ibid.

175 Ibid.

176 Ibid.

177 Ibid.

178 National Center for Education Statistics, "Table 334.30," *Digest of Education Statistics 2016*, op. cit.

179 Ibid.

180 Ibid.

181 Ibid.

182 Ibid.

183 Ibid.

184 Ibid.

185 Ibid.

186 Ibid.

187 Ibid.

188 Ibid.

189 Ibid.

190 Ibid.

191 Ibid.

192 Ibid.

193 Ibid.

194 Ibid.

195 Ibid.

196 Ibid.

197 Ibid.

198 National Center for Education Statistics, "Table 334.50," op. cit.

199 Ibid.

200 Ibid.

201 Ibid.

202 Ibid.

203 Ibid.

204 Ibid.

205 Ibid.

206 Ibid.

207 Ibid.

208 "The Delaware Cost Study: The National Study of Instructional Costs & Productivity," University of Delaware, accessed October 25, 2018, https://ire.udel.edu/cost/.

209 National Community College Benchmark Project, accessed October 25, 2018, https://www.nccbp.org/.

210 Attain, LLC, Ron Salluzzo, and Phil Tahey, *Current State of Financial Health for Private Masters and BACC Institutions* (McLean, VA: Attain, LLC, 2018).

211 National Center for Education Statistics, "Table 317.10," *Digest of Education Statistics 2016*, op. cit.

212 American Council on Education, *American College President Study* (Washington, DC: American Council on Education, 2017).

213 Inside Higher Ed, *The 2011 Inside Higher Ed Survey of College & University Business Officers* (Washington, DC: Inside Higher Ed, 2011).

214 National Center for Education Statistics, "Table 315.10. Number of faculty in degree-granting postsecondary institutions, by employment status, sex, control, and level of institution: Selected years, fall 1970 through fall 2015," *Digest of Education Statistics 2016* (Washington, DC: National Center for Education Statistics, 2018).

215 Rick Seltzer, "Days of Reckoning." *Inside Higher Ed*. November 3, 2017, accessed September 13, 2018, https://www.insidehighered.com/news/2017/11/13/spate-recent-college-closures-has-some-seeing-long-predicted-consolidation-taking.

216 President and Fellows of Harvard College, Robert S. Kaplan and David P. Norton, *The Balanced Scorecard* (Cambridge, MA: President and Fellows of Harvard College, 1996).

217 Prager, Sealy & Co., LLC, KPMG LLP, and Attain, LLC, Phil Tahey, Ron Salluzzo, Fred Prager, Lou Mezzina, and Chris Cowen, *Strategic Financial Analysis for Higher Education* (Washington, DC: Prager, Sealy & Co., LLC, KPMG LLP, and Attain, LLC, Phil Tahey, Ron Salluzzo, Fred Prager, Lou Mezzina, and Chris Cowen, 2010).

218 Financial Accounting Foundation, "Financial Accounting Standards Board Accounting Standards Update 2016-14, Not-for-Profit Entities (Topic 958): Presentation of Financial Statements of Not-for-Profit Entities" (Norwalk, CT: Financial Accounting Foundation, 2016).

219 Financial Accounting Foundation, "Preliminary Views of the Governmental Accounting Standards Board on Major Issues Related to Financial Reporting Model Improvements, Project No. 3-25" (Norwalk, CT: Financial Accounting Foundation, 2018).

220 The Greenest Workforce, "A Complete List of Canadian Universities and Colleges," accessed December 12, 2018, http://thegreenestworkforce.ca/index.php/en/schools/.

221 National Center for Education Statistics, "Table 317.10," *Digest of Education Statistics 2016*, op. cit.

222 Statistics Canada, "Table 37-10-0018-01. Postsecondary enrolments, by registration status, institution type, status of student in Canada and sex," accessed December 12, 2018, https://www150.statcan.gc.ca/t1/tbl1/en/tv.action?pid=3710001801.

223 National Center for Education Statistics, "Table 303.25," *Digest of Education Statistics 2016*, op. cit.

224 Statistics Canada, "Table 37-10-0027-01. Expenditures of universities and degree-granting colleges (x 1,000)," accessed December 12, 2018, https://www150.statcan.gc.ca/t1/tbl1/en/tv.action?pid=3710002701.

225 OFX, "Yearly Average Rates," accessed December 12, 2018, https://www.ofx.com/en-us/forex-news/historical-exchange-rates/yearly-average-rates/.

226 Statistics Canada, "Table 37-10-0026-01. Revenues of universities and degree-granting colleges (x 1,000)," accessed December 12, 2018, https://www150.statcan.gc.ca/t1/tbl1/en/tv.action?pid=3710002601.

227 Ontario Newsroom, "Government for the People to Lower Student Tuition Burden by 10 per cent," accessed February 10, 2019, https://news.ontario.ca/maesd/en/2019/01/government-for-the-people-to-lower-student-tuition-burden-by-10-per-cent.html.

228 Truth and Reconciliation Commission of Canada, accessed December 12, 2018, http://www.trc.ca/.

229 Laura Hubbard, "A Few Differences Among Friends." *University Manager*, Summer 2016.

230 National Center for Education Statistics, "Table 401.10," *Digest of Education Statistics 2016*, op. cit.

231 Statistics Canada, "Table 358-162. Spending on research and development in the higher education sector, 2015," accessed December 13, 2018, https://www150.statcan.gc.ca/n1/daily-quotidien/171116/dq171116d-eng.pdf.

INDEX

Note: *f* indicates a figure, and *t* indicates a table.

A

Academic affairs in enrollment management, 105, 108

Academic computing, 54

Academic performance, 108, 109

Academics
  programmatic infrastructural plan in, 164–165
  sustainability issues in, 43

Academic support
  budgeting and, 286–288
  expenses for
    drop-off in, 144
    for for-profit institutions, 140
    at independent institutions, 136
    in public education institutions, 131

Accountability
  adopting mechanism for, 340–341
  enhanced, 178

Accounting, 298–300
  accrual, 2, 343, 346–347
  cash, 2, 347
  reconciling budget reporting with reporting, 346–348
  rules for higher education institutions, 127
  standards for, 346

Accreditation, 149–150
  losing, 150

Accrual accounting, 2, 343, 347, 361

Activities statement, 347

Activity-based budgeting, 205

Adaptive Insights, 231

Ad hoc budget advisory committee, 187

Admissions
  in enrollment management, 105, 106
  "need-blind" practices n, 117
  standards for, 111–112

Advanced placement courses, 56–57

Aggregate nonsalary expense pool, 178

Agriculture, U.S. Department of, funding from, 74

Alignment, ongoing assessment in, 162

All-funds budgeting, 292, 361

Allotment process, distribution of appropriated resources in, 36

American Association of University Professors, 323–324
  guidelines of, 325

Americans with Disabilities Act (ADA) (1990), 29

Amortization, 344, 361

Anaplan, 231

Ancillary costs, 52

Ancillary planning, issues in, 155–167

Animals, research on, 27

APPA
  Key Facilities Metrics survey and, 44
  Leadership in Educational Facilities, 43

Appropriation, 361

Appropriations bill language, 34

Assets
  capital, 361–362
  net, 157

Association for the Advancement of Sustainability in Higher Education (AASHE), 43
  organization of sustainability issues and, 43–44
  STARS program of, 43, 44

Athletics
  as an auxiliary enterprise, 127
  intercollegiate, 131
  NCAA Division I, 69, 76, 133, 167
  variable infrastructural plans in, 167

Audit standards and mandated management practices, 29–30

India, export of students to the United States, 60

Indirect costs, 365

Inflation, 21

Inflows, 12

Information as resource, 1

Information technology
    budgeting and, 289–290
    in support infrastructural plans, 166–167

Infrastructural planning, 8, 148–149, 153–154, 317–319

Infrastructural plans, 365

Infrastructure, 365

Initiative-based budgeting (IBB), 210–213, 309, 365

Initiatives, reallocation to fund new, 212

Institutional advancement, in support infrastructural plans, 166

Institutional character in budget process, 170–176

Institutional closures, tracking of, 19

Institutional effectiveness committee (IEC), 161

Institutional policy impacts, on budgeting, 271–305
    academic side in, 273–287
    enterprise risk management in, 271–272
    operational policies and practices in, 298–304
    revenue policies in, 293–298
    support side in, 287–293

Institutional resources, 339

Institutional support, expenses for
    drop-off in, 144
    for for-profit institutions, 140
    at independent institutions, 137
    at public education institutions, 131–132

Instruction, 3
    expenses for
        for for-profit institutions, 139
        at independent institutions, 136
        at public education institutions, 130

Intercollegiate athletics, 131

Internal banking arrangements, popularity of, 13

International education, 60–61
    partnering in, 61

International students, importation of, 339

Investment income, 348

Investment return
    reporting of, 86
    as revenue source, 93–94, 97
    as source of revenue, 82–86

IPEDS (Integrated Postsecondary Education Data System), 71
    data on public institutions, 71, 73, 77

K

Kaufman Hall, 153, 231

Key Facilities Metrics survey, 44

L

Labor
    in the economic environment, 48–50
    labor relations and, 27

Labor relations, 27

Land-grant institutions, 78

Lapsed salary, 365

Lawrence Livermore National Laboratory (LLNL), 77

Leadership attention as resource, 1

Leadership in Energy Efficiency and Design (LEED program), 42

Learning resources, programmatic infrastructural plan in, 165

Liberalization of guidelines, 321

Libraries, in attracting and retaining students, 106

Lifetime Learning Credits Programs, 62

Line-item budgeting, 299, 365